# A City Mismanaged

**Also by Leo F. Goodstadt**

*China's Search for Plenty: The Economics of Mao Tse-tung*

*Poverty in the Midst of Affluence: How Hong Kong Mismanaged Its Prosperity*

*Profits, Politics and Panics: Hong Kong's Banks and the Making of a Miracle Economy, 1935–1985*

*Reluctant Regulators: How the West Created and How China Survived the Global Financial Crisis*

*Uneasy Partners: The Conflict Between Public Interest and Private Profit in Hong Kong*

# A City Mismanaged

## Hong Kong's Struggle for Survival

Leo F. Goodstadt

Hong Kong University Press
The University of Hong Kong
Pokfulam Road
Hong Kong
https://hkupress.hku.hk

ISBN 978-988-8455-98-0 (*Hardback*)
ISBN 978-988-8528-49-3 (*Paperback*)

British Library Cataloguing-in-Publication Data
A catalogue record for this book is available from the British Library.

10 9 8 7 6 5 4 3 2

Printed and bound in Hong Kong

# Contents

# Preface

In 2013, I wrote a book entitled *Poverty in the Midst of Affluence: How Hong Kong Mismanaged its Prosperity*, which made grim reading. Little did I realise that another crisis was overtaking Hong Kong which would get completely out of control. A potential catastrophe was threatening the million households in the private property sector where buildings were deteriorating at an increasing rate. Dilapidation of Hong Kong housing began with a lack of maintenance and professional management. Multi-storey housing estates with hundreds and often thousands of flats need regulation just as much as banks, share markets, and medical services—to quote only a few of the services essential to the community's well-being which are policed to protect the public. But the government steadfastly opposed accepting a similar responsibility for private housing, no matter how shocking the latest evidence of the dangers to health as well as safety highlighted by the media. There was also a financial loss involved. Many families in the private sector had struggled with mortgages to become owner-occupiers over the years. Increasing numbers of them had to face the prospect of losing most of their investment because the premises become less and less fit for human habitation with each decade and thus unattractive to potential buyers.

This state of affairs seems incredible when compared with the quality of the rest of Hong Kong's performance. Despite mounting tensions over political reform and the rise of radical protest movements, Hong Kong ranked as one of the safest and most successful societies in the world. Its economy had faced severe challenges from 1997 onwards. Twenty years later, the economy had expanded by 80 per cent in terms of real GDP. Labour productivity was growing faster for much of this period than in Singapore, the United States and other advanced economies. Nevertheless, in this century, Hong Kong could not guarantee its families that they would have access to a most basic amenity: safe and affordable homes.

Why did the looming threats to private housing not arouse the community's indignation? Despite Hong Kong's extraordinary record of success in the face of political, financial and social challenges of every kind, survival is never taken for granted. For the average family, what had come to matter most was political risk and Hong Kong's ability to survive 1997. By 2012, anxieties had intensified about Hong Kong's way of life and what changes 2047 might bring. Thus, the preservation of 'Hong Kong values' became an overwhelming concern. Shortfalls and scandals affecting housing and social services were given a much lower priority

For me, watching this phenomenon was personally very painful. I had arrived at the University of Hong Kong as a Commonwealth Scholar in 1962 to research housing problems, and I continued this project as a lecturer there. The overall housing scene seemed dreadful, with large squatter colonies which the colonial administration was making as uncomfortable as possible to deter refugees. The existing stock of private housing was made up mostly of decrepit slum tenements. But in that era, there was a promise of progress. Colonial officials had been compelled by public demand to embark on public housing schemes and to better regulate the growing number of new, multi-storey blocks of homes.

These programmes gathered momentum in the decades that followed so that Hong Kong's housing crisis seemed to have been finally overcome by 2000. In reality, the private sector was about to be hit by a dreadful blight made inevitable principally by the refusal of Chief Executives and their political appointees to intervene in the private housing sector. The damage done by the owners' defective management and maintenance was aggravated by a growing shortage in the relevant government departments of the personnel, facilities and funding needed to implement existing legislation and to develop the new legal and technical solutions required. By 2016, government statements on these issues bordered on open despair of being able to find workable solutions.

An additional complication has been the decline in the public's confidence in the government's commitment to preserving Hong Kong values. This trend has created a new barrier to overcoming this century's housing crisis. It is imperative to rapidly increase the supply of public housing in order to provide new homes for most of the families who should be removed from dangerously dilapidated private buildings. It is equally urgent to increase the private supply to a level at which it matches demand. To achieve these goals requires creating new building sites and renovating existing estates. The public has proved extremely reluctant to cooperate with government proposals for projects to do so because among Hong Kong's values is a growing insistence on preserving the environment, national parks and public amenities. The community has become highly mistrustful of the government on these issues, and there are considerable protests against government housing projects and site creation.

Housing has become the most serious example of government mismanagement, but tragically, almost identical problems can be found across the whole of government. Virtually every branch of government is having to provide services below standard and often without regard for relevant legislation. Almost everywhere throughout the administration, quality of performance has been damaged by lack of staff and inadequate funding.

Thus, the housing crisis has to be set in a wider context to see the full dimensions of maladministration. The areas of mismanagement chosen in this book as case studies for this purpose include the way in which post-secondary students have been denied access to university and have been exploited by providers of paper qualifications which were almost useless to their careers. And the government stood idly by. Another set of case studies investigates the direct threats to the public through poor policing of public health, transport hazards and building safety. Included here is a review of the reluctance of the Independent Commission Against Corruption (ICAC) to get involved.

The book begins and ends with the Mainland, on which future survival depends. The first chapter introduces the most striking example of improper administrative performance: the Basic Law and how Chief Executives and their teams have enforced it selectively over the years. The Mainland drafters intended Hong Kong to maintain the existing standards of social and related services after 1997 and to introduce further improvements. These provisions have been ignored. Chief Executives did not listen to the adverse comments made by former Premier Wen Jiabao on the extent to which the public's social rights were being denied. The book ends with a review of the grossly mismanaged relationship with the Mainland. The evidence shows that Hong Kong's leaders persistently misunderstood the barriers to economic cooperation erected by the Mainland's administrative systems at local levels, and they overestimated the welcome to be expected by the average Hong Kong investor and entrepreneur. Here again, advice from the Premier was not heeded.

The book throws light on why there was a common pattern of weak government over the last 20 twenty years. Chief Executives lacked confidence in Hong Kong and its resilience. They were too remote from the community to recognise its outstanding qualities. They looked on Hong Kong's past successes as some sort of historical accident. They repeatedly warned the people of Hong Kong that they were inferior to their Mainland counterparts who would soon overtake them. Chief Executives expressed little cause for confidence in Hong Kong's survival except in a dependent's role. None of which did anything to convince the general public that their leaders would struggle to protect Hong Kong interests.

The negative attitude of Chief Executives was in direct conflict with the message from the nation's leaders. In this century, all three Premiers have emphasised Hong Kong's indispensable contribution to the nation's development. It seemed highly significant that, at the celebrations for the twentieth anniversary of reunification, President Xi Jinping highlighted the outstanding success of Hong Kong people and the nation's confidence in their ability. 'When our country does well', he said, 'Hong Kong will do even better'.

This book's focus is on incompetent leadership and what has gone wrong. 'Our duty is to hold ourselves responsible to the people', Mao Zedong declared. 'Every word, every act and every policy must conform to the people's interests, and if mistakes occur, they must be corrected', he continued. Fortunately, despite controversy over democratisation, increasing accountability and open government have been features of Hong Kong in the last twenty years. These qualities are what have maintained public cooperation with the political leaders and trust in the civil service. Without these features of the Hong Kong political system, this book could not have been written.

Personally, I find it impossible to be pessimistic about Hong Kong's prospects. It is so well-equipped for survival because of the political maturity and social discipline of its people. I have more than half a century's daily experience of Hong Kong's resilience in the face of the most menacing political and economic conditions. I have never once felt that I or my family and friends were in danger in this community, for which I am for ever grateful to the people of Hong Kong.

## Acknowledgements

I am indebted to the Hong Kong Institute for the Humanities and Social Sciences at the University of Hong Kong which has provided me with generous use of its facilities. The Institute is the ideal environment in which to do research, which enabled me to complete this volume between October 2014 and June 2017. I owe a great deal to the Director, Professor Angela Leung Ki Che. She has provided the perfect environment for my research, and I am most grateful to her for her unfailing encouragement and for her personal interest and many kindnesses. I must also thank the Institute's staff for looking after me so patiently.

In the course of writing this book, I was fortunate enough to be selected for a substantial award from the WYNG Foundation Ltd, for which I am very grateful. I deeply appreciate the commitment which the Foundation has shown to the needy and the vulnerable in Hong Kong and to the pursuit of good governance. I am proud to have been associated with it.

My research on the historical development of Hong Kong's housing programmes and its social services would have been impossible without the assistance in past years of the Government Records Service. The professionalism and efficiency of Mr Bernard Hui Sung-tak and his colleagues in the Public Records Office enabled me to create a collection of archival material which has facilitated my work over many years.

I am, as always, indebted to Trinity College, University of Dublin. I am especially grateful to Professor Lorna Carson, Director of the Trinity Centre for Asian Studies, for many kindnesses and shared enthusiasms. Colleagues at the School of Business Studies, in particular my friend, Professor Gerard McHugh, continue to support me with interest and encouragement, as well as access to Trinity's facilities, throughout my stay in Ireland.

It is a special pleasure to express my sincere thanks to Dr Susie Han Jia, of Hong Kong University Press. She has been an excellent editor: very efficient as well as encouraging, highly professional and always patient and pleasant.

None of the institutions or individuals referred to in these acknowledgements has any responsibility for any part of the contents of this book or the views which it expresses.

Hong Kong has been made all the more pleasant for me in the twenty-first century by the kindness and hospitality which my friends and former colleagues at the Central Policy Unit so generously offer me. Among those I can acknowledge here with gratitude are Barry Cheung, Helen Cheng, T. L. Tsim, Dr Rikkie Yeung, Professor Cecilia Chan and their families who take such good care of me.

Hong Kong
January 2018

# Introduction

This book is about survival. Not the survival of the million or so individuals officially classified as 'poor'. Nor the 600,000 officially estimated to suffer from disabilities.[1] It does not discuss Hong Kong's political survival and related issues of constitutional reform, although this source of uncertainty is of the greatest concern to the community and dominates the political agenda. The threats to survival which the chapters that follow will investigate are those fundamental to the well-being of the community at large.

Why is it, for instance, that middle-class individuals who built up the savings needed to buy a decent flat, usually with a mortgage, cannot take it for granted that these premises will remain a safe and comfortable home to be inherited by the next generation? Since 2009, the evidence has mounted that thousands of private sector buildings are already unsafe and rundown, and more are likely to become so in the future.[2]

How is it that parents who are willing to pay the full costs of further education for their children who have done well enough in their secondary school examinations to meet university entrance requirements but are refused a place can be grossly misled by government-sponsored alternatives? Large numbers of these students have been encouraged to enrol in commercially-run associate degree, diploma and other post-secondary courses. Yet, there have been repeated warnings since 2008 about the inferior quality of most of these qualifications, which may not lead to better careers or higher earnings.[3]

Why is it that the safety of the general public could be ignored when human lives were known to be at risk but the authorities did not intervene to prevent serious tragedies?

A common factor in all these cases, it will be shown, was the mistaken policies and defective administration on the part of Chief Executives and many of their ministers. In particular, their financial policies have led to the steady erosion of the civil service's capacity to deliver the quality and quantity of services essential for the proper management of a city as advanced as Hong Kong.

There is another category of threat which affects the entire community. The Basic Law provides the guarantee of survival for Hong Kong, economically and socially. This legal protection has been undermined, the book will show, because Chief Executives and their ministers have chosen to implement the Basic Law selectively. Also endangering Hong Kong's future survival has been the government's gross mismanagement of business relations with the Mainland, Hong Kong's largest commercial 'client'.

## The Hong Kong ethos

In every chapter, it will quickly become clear that Hong Kong's current well-being and future survival have been endangered as a result of deliberate decisions made by Chief Executives and the gross policy mistakes which they were extremely reluctant to reverse. The results of their flawed policies and defective leadership have been endured by the public on a very painful scale in many key areas of life and work.

Governing Hong Kong should not have been difficult, however. Its people were ideal citizens who, between 1997 and 2017, took in their stride a series of unexpected and potentially disastrous threats: the 1997–1998 Asian financial crisis and the 2007–2009 global financial crisis; the atypical pneumonia (SARS) epidemic of 2003; the dismantling from 2007 of the Hong Kong–financed manufacturing complex in Guangdong province employing 10 million workers; and the increasing public discontent over political issues and mass public protests from 2012.

Despite these setbacks, Hong Kong's businesses flourished, particularly the international financial centre. Between 2000 and 2015, the Mainland received some US$700 billion in foreign direct investment (FDI) from Hong Kong, almost half the nation's total inflow. At the same time, Hong Kong was playing a major role in China's drive to internationalise its currency. Hong Kong was 'the global hub for RMB trade settlement, financing and asset management [with] the world's largest offshore RMB liquidity pool'. It handled 75 per cent of the nation's offshore RMB transactions worldwide.[4]

Work ethic was a crucial feature of Hong Kong's outstanding performance. Between 2000 and 2010, wages were stagnant, educational and medical fees were rising and the housing situation deteriorated. Nevertheless, the performance of the average employee continued to improve despite the lack of monetary incentives. During this period, labour productivity in Hong Kong rose by 3.4 per cent a year, faster than in Singapore (2.4 per cent), the United States (1.4 per cent) and Germany (0.8 per cent).[5]

Business profitability increased handsomely, as tax revenues showed. The contribution of profits tax to total government revenue rose from 20 per cent to 25 per cent between 1997 and 2017. Gross Domestic Product (GDP) in real terms rose by more than 80 per cent. The government had ample finances. Its reserves in 2017 totalled $936 billion, almost double the 1997 figure, and were sufficient to cover total spending by the government for a full two years.[6]

Those responsible for governing Hong Kong consistently failed to match the standards of excellence taken for granted in every other sphere of Hong Kong life. This Introduction first presents profiles of Chief Executives and what went wrong under their leadership. It then proceeds to outline the individual chapters which demonstrate the damage caused by the incompetence and the misguided convictions of those in power.

## The collapse of good government

On 1 July 1997, Tung Chee Hwa began his term as Hong Kong's first Chief Executive full of confidence about what lay ahead. His optimism was justified, he explained, because of Hong Kong's remarkable achievements.

> Hong Kong is at present the freest and the most vibrant economy in the world. Free enterprise and free trade; prudent financial management and low taxation; the rule of law, an executive-led government and an efficient civil service have been a part of our tradition.

There were challenges, he frankly admitted, which must not be ignored: inflation, an ageing population, a housing shortage and employment issues. But he conveyed a strong conviction that Hong Kong would find the solutions.[7]

By the time the fourth Chief Executive, Carrie Lam Cheng Yuet-ngor, took office in 2017, Hong Kong appeared to have changed beyond all recognition. And very much for the worse. Gone was Tung's pride in Hong Kong's achievements and the confidence that the government would overcome the challenges it faced. In her first public speech after her appointment, Carrie Lam highlighted serious mismanagement: government performance was unsatisfactory and policy-makers were out of touch with public aspirations. A 'new style of governance' was needed, she declared, and 'policies that would respond more pertinently to the aspirations of the people'.[8] This frank admission struck the right note.

In her election manifesto, Carrie Lam had described the reforms she would introduce to tackle mismanagement. The 'new style of governance' would include 'objective research and hard evidence to review existing policies'. Professionalism, it seemed, was to replace misinformed generalisations and unwarranted assumptions at the policymaking level. Management would surely improve. Unfortunately, she herself was in breach of her pledge to rely on 'hard evidence'. The manifesto claimed that Hong Kong faced a long-term crisis.

> Our strengths and advantages in many aspects have recently been challenged as a result of both political issues here in Hong Kong and the economic situation overseas. Hong Kong has also been experiencing social conflict and economic slowdown during the past few years, causing many people to become concerned and even discouraged.[9]

These comments were grossly inaccurate. 'Hard evidence', to stick to her own phrase, demonstrated that Hong Kong's social stability had improved remarkably in 'the past few years'. The crime rate had dropped by 29 per cent between 2007 and 2016. Labour relations had improved, and the total number of working days lost through industrial disputes had fallen from 8,027 in 2007 to 169 in 2016, an extraordinarily low level by international standards.[10] As for the economy, it was hard to understand why the fourth Chief Executive believed that it was performing so badly when GDP had increased by 46 per cent between 2007 and 2016. Apparently, she had not bothered to listen to the 2017 Budget Speech in which the Financial Secretary presented a very positive picture of the state of economic affairs.

> Hong Kong is one of the most advanced economies in the world, despite the relatively small scale of our economy. Our GDP per capita has now reached US$44,000, overtaking Japan and many advanced economies in Europe.[11]

For a person with ten years' experience as a minister, five of them as Chief Secretary, the flawed picture of Hong Kong's challenges which Carrie Lam had presented to the public was alarming. But there was nothing unusual about this incident. Her confusion over key indicators of Hong Kong's continuing success was a symptom of the inferior performance which Hong Kong has had to put up with from all its Chief Executives and the average minister. The chapters that follow are filled with evidence of similar misconceptions at the very top of government.

Mismanagement began with the Chief Executives, who poured out a flood of comments and commitments designed to direct policymaking and to win popular credibility but were remote from the realities of life in Hong Kong and its economic and social needs. The first three Chief Executives suffered from a level of incompetence which they could not conceal. In the case of Tung Chee Hwa and Donald Tsang Yam-kuen, they eventually made public self-criticisms summarising their own disastrous shortcomings, and Leung Chun-ying stated he was unable to face a second term in office. The Chief Executives' shortcomings were aggravated by the introduction of a 'ministerial' system in 2002, with political appointees whose qualifications for high office were generally unimpressive.

## No place for a businessman

Tung's lack of political talent had been obvious from the start. He was a wealthy businessman and had much the same social attitudes and political views as the rest of Hong Kong's business leaders. In particular, he shared their conviction that the public sector is inherently inferior in management and performance to business enterprises. In 1998, he confessed to feeling confused. 'As a businessman one has to be very bottom-line oriented,' he said, 'So I go into this office [of Chief Executive] very bottom-line oriented. And I felt that if I deliver the bottom-line, never mind what happens in-between'. It took him a year, he said, to realise that 'in the political life this does not work'—that 'what happens in-between' matters to the community.[12]

By 2003, China's leaders could tolerate his shortcomings no longer. Tung Chee Hwa was a failure. He lacked the necessary skills. He was just 'an entrepreneur' with no political experience, State Councillor Tang Jiaxuan commented that year. Tung had done his best in a job for which he was unsuited.[13] Tang's verdict was all the more damaging because he was a former Foreign Minister with ample experience of the Western-style administration which Hong Kong followed.

Eventually, Tung's credibility evaporated to a point at which he felt compelled to make a last, desperate move to remain in office. He went before the Legislative Council in 2005 and confessed that 'shortcomings and inadequacies have undermined the credibility of our policymaking capability and our ability to govern'.

> In formulating policies, we fell short of "thinking what people think" and "addressing people's pressing needs". Second, we were not sufficiently mindful of the impact of some policies on the community's capacity to bear and the potentially controversial nature of these policies. We introduced too many reform measures too hastily, putting heavy burdens on our people. We also lacked a sense of crisis, political sensitivity as well as the necessary experience and capability to cope with political and economic changes. We were indecisive when dealing with emergencies.[14]

This self-criticism was an accurate summary of his unfitness for office, and within six months he was gone. He resigned on health grounds.

His public account of his own deficiencies helped to explain the previous seven years of cruel and unjustified austerity, falling earnings, worsening housing conditions and rising medical and educational charges suffered by Hong Kong's families. This suffering was being inflicted by his personal choice, he had openly admitted in 2000.

> It would have been easier for all of us, in the short run, to ease back into another bubble economy. Instead we have embarked on another [way] that will perhaps take longer, involve more hard work, and certainly more learning; one that perhaps imparts more pain in the short term as well, but is ultimately healthier.[15]

But his policy did not prove 'ultimately healthier'. Business confidence slumped, and with it private sector investment. Its full recovery did not begin until 2006 and remained below the 1997 level until 2012. As for the average family, few escaped serious financial losses. As he himself admitted in 2004, his determination to minimise public spending had created a deflation which he described as the worst in world history since the 1920s. 'Almost 90 per cent of our working families' suffered 'job losses and reduced income', he said, and 'personal wealth' shrank following 'a drop in property prices of 70 per cent'.[16]

But Tung's departure did not lead to a retreat from his misguided formulas for governing Hong Kong. On the contrary, he left a legacy of misrule which was to survive in the form of toxic policies which have since blighted virtually every area of public administration.

## Local boy does not make good

When Tung Chee Hwa stepped down on grounds of ill health in 2005, Hong Kong felt a genuine sense of relief. It seemed inconceivable that under his successor, Donald Tsang Yam-kuen, the quality of life for the average family could deteriorate still further than it had done under Tung. It seemed equally improbable that Tsang would be as remote from the ordinary men and women of Hong Kong and as unfeeling about their well-being as Tung had been (more from ignorance than deliberate design, to be fair to him).

Tsang had started off low down the social ladder. He had risen to the top of the civil service with no social advantages, no business connections and minimal educational qualifications. But he stood out, thanks to an ability to acquire very fast the technical expertise to deal with serious political and economic challenges—from management of a complex scheme to reduce political panic after the June 4 tragedy in 1989 and then a transfer to overall responsibility for foreign trade policies and negotiations.[17] With this background, and after a final apprenticeship as Treasury overlord, he had excellent qualifications for appointment as Financial Secretary in 1995. And when Anson Chan Fang On-sang suddenly resigned on a matter of principle from the post of Chief

Secretary in 2001, Tsang offered the best prospect of replacing her and maintaining civil service morale after the Chief Executive introduced a ministerial system which he had been contemplating for a year.[18]

But Tsang was not the typical civil servant who could be expected to be politically neutral, wary of business leaders' motives and anxious to defend the public interest. Tsang was openly committed to the promotion of business interests and was convinced that they must come first, not just for the policy-makers and but for the entire civil service. This had been made clear in 1996 when he declared in his first Budget Speech: 'I believe the whole of the Government has a duty to provide a business-friendly environment'. What this would mean in practice was set out in an Addendum to the Speech. His goal, this document had revealed, was to increase the business world's priority in government policymaking: 'Civil servants should not see their role merely as regulators but more as supporters and partners for business.'[19] Tsang maintained this mindset throughout the rest of his career.

Tsang's definition of the correct relationship between the government and the business world was to have damaging consequences for good governance. In the years to come, the government would face a growing tide of serious scandals in almost every sector: from unsafe drinking water to marine disaster, from dangerous housing to airport mismanagement. Not surprisingly, because the civil service was being steadily deprived of the leadership, motivation and the resources to enforce business-related laws and regulations and contractual obligations. A particularly shameless example was the public announcement of a policy to minimise prosecutions of employers who defied the labour laws.[20] At the same time, government departments and agencies providing social services and housing were denigrated by Chief Executives and their ministers. Thus, the civil service as a whole had every reason to believe that their first duty was to facilitate business even at the expense of the general public.

When Tsang first became Chief Executive in 2005, he was well aware of problems crying out for attention. He listed them: 'employment difficulties for workers with low academic qualifications and skills; declining real pay levels in certain jobs; the polarisation of the middle class; a widening income gap; an ageing population'.[21] But he did not set out measures to solve them. His response to widespread public dismay about the widening gap between rich and poor in Hong Kong, for example, was an insistence that there was no solution. Income inequality was among the 'inevitable phenomena' of a capitalist economy, he declared.[22]

Policy-makers no longer had to conceal their personal interests. Tsang had explained in 2001 that in dismantling the public housing programmes he had made sure it would take years to resurrect them.[23] His aim, he admitted frankly, was to end potential competition from the public sector which might reduce the value of privately owned property, including his own.[24]

By 2011, the public had the impression that those in high office could make what modifications they liked to their properties, regardless of the law. The Ombudsman felt forced to investigate. 'Since 2011, a number of local celebrities (including senior Government officials and Members of the Executive Council and the Legislative Council) had become the subjects of extensive media coverage for suspected unauthorised building works in their properties', he commented. The Ombudsman's investigation found no clear evidence of favouritism for celebrities. Indeed, the Buildings Department had tried to give priority to investigations of this privileged group in order to allay public suspicions. Nevertheless, he felt obliged to state in his report that favouritism could not be ruled out completely. This possibility was increased by the restriction on the Buildings Department's ability to respond to suspected breaches of the law because of a shortage of staff, his report pointed out.[25] Lack of staff, funding and other essential resources were a universal threat to good governance, several chapters of this book will show.

Tsang realised in 2008 that he was in serious danger. His credibility had fallen catastrophically, as he openly admitted.

> People have doubts about certain issues: Have the core values of the [Hong Kong Special Administrative Region] Government changed? Is the Government trustworthy? Is the Government fair and impartial? Is it less capable than before? Does the Government still adhere to the principle of meritocracy? Does it take into account public opinion in formulating policies?[26]

In practice, he did nothing to recover the public's trust. Instead, he devoted increasing time and attention to business leaders, he subsequently confessed to the Legislative Council, because he felt he needed their insight and advice.[27]

As Tsang's credibility continued to ebb, he made yet another public speech on political leadership, setting out the qualities necessary for success as Chief Executive of Hong Kong. He listed the essential criteria in the following sequence.

- '[First] you need the highest moral and ethical standards'.
- 'Next comes passion . . . for the people of Hong Kong . . . to understand their aspirations and changing moods'.
- 'In the broader context, passion for our country, or patriotism, is just as important for a leader of Hong Kong . . . The Chief Executive must always remember that he is responsible to the Central Government'.
- 'Leadership indeed requires vision . . . that is relevant to the people, relevant to the time, and possible to achieve'.

Not until the very the end of his presentation did he mention any concrete problems to be solved. He then dealt with 'important issues that are of concern to the community' in a mere eight words: 'housing, bridging the wealth gap and elderly services'.[28]

In 2012, he followed Tung Che Hwa's example when faced with a total loss of credibility. Tsang made a pitiful self-criticism before the Legislative Council. But even this humiliation won him no sympathy. He tried to convince the public that his failings had been unintentional. 'My 45 years of experience in public service . . . has created "blind spots" that make me overlook the fact that as times change, public expectations have also changed', he pleaded, 'and people have turned more demanding towards public officers'.[29]

In fact, these standards had not changed over the years. Zero tolerance of questionable behaviour by senior officials had become the norm after the 1974 revelations about corrupt senior police officers, which had led to the establishment of the Independent Commission Against Corruption (ICAC). Tsang failed to see that this standard would apply to him. Just as he had failed to see that allegations of unauthorised alterations to his own private property would scandalise the community.[30]

Tsang had to pay a ruinous price for his misconceptions about the privileges of those in power. A criminal investigation was launched in 2012, but he was not brought to trial until 2017, a delay which was inexcusable in a society as dedicated to the rule of law as Hong Kong. He suffered considerable distress because of the financial and emotional strain of this protracted waiting, together with the total destruction of his private life by the media's unrelenting surveillance of his daily activities and contacts. Nevertheless, his court trials were an important illustration of Hong Kong's core values. No one, not even the highest ranking and best connected, can evade criminal investigation and prosecution.

## Doomed from the start

The third Chief Executive, Leung Chun-ying, was to face immediate and unrelenting criticism on taking office for his inability to win public trust, no matter what his policy proposals might be. The community seemed to sense that he did not share Hong Kong's core values. He took a very detached, almost academic approach to issues which most of the community regarded as matters of survival.[31]

He had always been very open about his belief that a survival culture was unnecessary. In 1994, for example, he had adopted a rather patronising line towards Hong Kong people and their anxieties about the future. He narrated how he had searched 'the main text' of the 1984 Sino-British Joint Declaration, which he described as belonging to 'a fossilized date-sealed environment', for specific pledges of 'no change'.

He found only seven such guarantees in 'twelve short paragraphs'. He also listed the community's worries, which concerned, he said, 'rather mundane issues—passports, currency (and its international convertibility), the education system'. For most families, these involved their personal survival. Leung was unimpressed. Although he was secretary-general of the Hong Kong Basic Law Consultative Committee, he did not regard the Basic Law as providing much comfort to those apprehensive about the future. He warned that Hong Kong should not hope to rely on 'these historic deeds', 'these "no change" statements that have been written into the Joint Declaration and the Basic Law'. They offered no such guarantees, on his analysis.[32] His message was that regardless of the priorities of Hong Kong people and the letter of the Basic Law, the Special Administrative Region government's freedom to adjust to new political and economic realities would not be limited.

When it came to economic survival, Leung's views were to prove similarly misinformed. He was convinced that economic integration would give Hong Kong access to a national market on the Mainland which was fully competitive and operating in much the same way as any modern economy. This view was hopelessly wrong. He appeared totally unaware of the struggle that had been waged since the 1990s by the Central People's Government to raise business standards and remove the barriers to commercial and financial progress imposed by local administrations determined to protect local businesses. The Mainland did not offer the ideal business environment described by Leung, and Hong Kong was not the vulnerable economy which he depicted.[33]

Leung came into office in 2012 with what he regarded as a unique advantage. He believed that he had the credentials and connections that would ensure a much closer relationship with senior Mainland officials than his predecessors. In the colonial era, he had played a major public role in promoting China's policies for Hong Kong, and he seemed to have won considerable respect in Beijing.[34] His appointment to Hong Kong's Executive Council in 1997 and his promotion to Convenor of that body seemed to confirm that he was highly trusted by the nation's leaders who have to approve all such appointments.

Leung himself certainly thought so. He boasted in 2013 of 'strong government-to-government contacts' with both the central authorities and provincial administrations to whom he had been given preferential access. He announced that he would jettison what he called 'this unspoken tradition' that had previously prevented Hong Kong's Chief Executives from making more than two visits a year to Beijing. He would be seen much more frequently in the Chinese capital.[35] Furthermore, he was confident that by adopting a new negotiating strategy, what he called 'internal diplomacy', he would win concessions from the Mainland officials who previously had attached little importance to Hong Kong.[36]

Leung had badly miscalculated, however. He soon discovered that state leaders saw no reason to give him any greater access than his predecessors. It was made very clear that the agenda for his visits, as well as their frequency, would be controlled by Beijing.[37] He was unable to drop in for a chat with the policy-makers in Beijing whenever he felt the need. But worse was to follow. After a meeting with Leung, the Director of the Hong Kong and Macao Affairs Office, Wang Guangya, allowed himself to be quoted by the media as saying that when making future duty visits to the President and Premier, the Chief Executive should identify his shortcomings instead of reciting his achievements. This advice was interpreted as an indication of reservations at the top about the quality of Leung's performance.[38]

The political embarrassments continued. In 2015, Leung's formal ranking within the state hierarchy was 'redefined' during his 'duty visit' to the capital. The seating for a public photo session with President Xi Jinping was carefully arranged to demonstrate that Leung no longer enjoyed the same status as in the past. In a political environment as sensitive to protocol and precedence as China, his 'demotion' could not have been more clearly highlighted. Leung himself appeared to be taken by surprise, and his own explanation of this event to the media was a cryptic claim that it 'reflects the constitutional relationship between Hong Kong and the Central Authorities'.[39] To be fair to him, he soldiered on manfully in an unsuccessful quest for Hong Kong to have fair access to Mainland markets.

It was Leung's inability to establish any credibility with the community that made his position impossible. He paid the price for this failure in the stubborn opposition and hostile protests that blocked so many of his policy initiatives. Very often, his proposals were flawed. But crucial reforms were also held up because of his personal unpopularity with legislators, pressure groups, the media and the general public. Unfortunately, he intensified public hostility by openly expressing his serious mistrust of a large proportion of the population. In a 2014 newspaper interview, he said that the political system must insulate Chief Executives from alleged electoral pressures to create a welfare state and must ensure that business-friendly policies prevailed. To achieve this goal, no one should qualify for full political rights, he said, whose monthly earnings were $14,000 or below—a category to which half the labour force belonged.[40]

Leung seemed to have forgotten the totally different image which he had tried to project when he first began his campaign to become the third Chief Executive. In a 2009 speech, he had declared himself to be on the side of the most vulnerable groups in the community and expressed outrage at increasing mismanagement within the government. 'Development in Hong Kong has slowed down in the past twelve years compared with what the colonial government achieved before the handover', he was reported to have said, 'The government should care for the needs of low-income families and speed up economic growth'. He rejected the cost-cutting imposed by Tung and Tsang.

> We are not short of funds. We are not short of ideas or capabilities, he said, when asked how the government could improve things. What we have been lacking in the past 10 to 15 years was speed.[41]

This frank critique of the record of Tung and Tsang left him vulnerable to criticism. He had held on to his senior position of Convenor of Executive Council under both his predecessors as Chief Executives instead of resigning in protest, and so he could not avoid sharing responsibility for the serious mismanagement under the rule of Tung and Tsang. Thus, he had come into office with limited credibility.

But it was his performance which let him down most. He claimed, as just quoted, that lack of 'speed' had crippled his predecessors. But his own 'speed' proved worse than theirs in solving the community's most urgent problems. Furthermore, before his appointment, he had said that there was no shortage of money. But once in office, he allowed his Financial Secretary to predict financial catastrophe unless spending on social services was reduced immediately. This inconsistency showed little respect for the public's intelligence, for which there was a heavy price to pay.

Unlike Tung Chee Hwa and Donald Tsang, Leung did not make a self-criticism in an effort to retrieve his reputation. Instead, in the dying days of his term in office, he issued what amounted to a self-indictment of his own performance although it was intended as a proud roster of his achievements. This *Report on the Work of the Fourth-Term Government of the Hong Kong Special Administrative Region June 2017* was intended 'to summarise the progress and achievements of our work', he explained, but it provided compelling evidence of what had gone wrong for him. Leung had made numerous policy pledges since 2012 but relatively few long-term policy commitments in terms of staff or funding. As a result, the document was dominated by details of 'consultations', 'pilot' programmes and 'trial' measures. There were also signs of a desperate search to find as many positive items to list as possible, even when they were of limited interest to the public. The presentation of the work report itself was confusing, which made its contents difficult to use. The document was not the product of well-run government or competent political leadership.

Of special interest to this book is the work report's section on housing. This had been among Leung's highest priorities on taking office but became one of his most embarrassing failures. His work report reveals why no other outcome should have been expected. His Housing Minister was also in charge of the transport sector. The work report devoted three times the wordage to transport than it allocated to Hong Kong's housing crisis. This imbalance accurately reflected the superior political and financial priority given by Leung's administration to transport issues.

The work report paid little attention to inadequate building management and maintenance, which were major threats to homes in the private sector. Measures to tackle this challenge were not listed under 'housing' but buried in the 'Culture, Leisure, Municipal Services and Administration' section.[42] Leung also included among his achievements 'The Handbook on Tree Management'. Published in 2016, this booklet was intended 'to further raise the awareness of responsibility on tree management among private property owners and property management companies'.[43] At that date, the government was still grappling with the introduction of a modern system of property management. To include the care of trees in built-up Hong Kong was an additional complication which could not be justified as a contribution to safer homes. This was not good administration.

By the end of Leung's first term, his remaining credibility was in tatters. He found it impossible to continue as Chief Executive, he stated, because of the strain inflicted on his family. He had proved even more vulnerable to the pressures of high office than Tung Chee Hwa.

## A Hong Kong success story

Carrie Lam Cheng Yuet-ngor's rise to power as Hong Kong's fourth Chief Executive was a typical Hong Kong success story and very different to her three predecessors. Her career before her appointment as Chief Executive had been remarkable. Yet she had retained the special qualities of women of her age group who had made the best of their educational opportunities. They balanced work and family and took service to the community seriously on a voluntary basis or, in her case, as a profession. And their careers flourished. Thus, her special political advantage was that she came into office with more personal credibility with the public than the first three Chief Executives.

She herself described her background as under-privileged. The first sentence in her election manifesto declared: 'I come from a grassroot family and did my homework on a bunk bed when I was a student'.[44] But in that era, a bright young woman would not be deprived of a decent education because of unaffordable fees. That barrier was only erected in the current century. She went to an excellent school for her primary and secondary education and won a place in Hong Kong's premier university. There she started out as a social work student but switched to a less confining syllabus after one year. She also enjoyed considerable personal freedom at university. She said that as an undergraduate, she became 'an activist fighting for social compassion and justice' after undertaking 'social service voluntary work in her secondary school days'.[45]

Carrie Lam entered the Civil Service as a member of the élite Administrative Service and was selected to attend a course at world-renowned Cambridge University in England. She returned to Hong Kong and became a government high-flyer. She was helped in discarding her youthful enthusiasm for public protests in defence of 'social compassion and justice' by a long but very successful spell with the Treasury. Here, she reached the conclusion that the costs of social services to government were potentially toxic. Hong Kong's public finances were always insecure, she came to believe, so that cost-cutting must be an absolute priority. She also became convinced that fiscal stability would only be assured if government departments adopted the private sector model.[46]

When she was transferred to the Social Welfare Department as its Director in 2000, she set about reforming its management and funding. 'Every dollar spent on welfare is at the expense of other policy areas', she declared, creating the impression that her Department's services merited only a low priority in Hong Kong's annual budget. Her remedy for a shortfall in funding for the Department's programmes was to seek partners in the business world. 'Private sector participation', she claimed, 'through its enterprise and efficiency, can come up with more economical solutions to deliver a public service'. Ignored was the very different motivation of the caring professions and the profit-driven business executive.[47] When she was made the senior official at the Housing, Planning and Lands Bureau, she left behind in the field of social services a powerful legacy which shaped their policies for years to come. But at a serious cost to those in need in terms of quality and availability of these services.

Carrie Lam continued to emulate the business sector after she accepted a political appointment as one of Donald Tsang's ministers in 2007. Among her most important duties was to tackle a mounting crisis in the private housing sector. Here, lack of maintenance and inadequate management were causing increasing numbers of flats to become threats to both public health and safety. She proved successful in minimising the government's role in tackling the crisis by linking emergency maintenance measures to job creation.[48]

Her firm belief in the importance of minimal intervention by the government remained unshaken even after the collapse in 2010 of a dilapidated building causing deaths. This accident could have been prevented if sufficient government staff had been available and safety regulations enforced. Nevertheless, as the minister in charge of building safety, Carrie Lam commented 'that, at the end of the day, the responsibility to maintain buildings rests with the owners'.[49] That disclaimer of government responsibility left the public at risk in a dangerous environment over which they had no control.

## Rights denied

An extraordinary feature of Hong Kong is the way that its constitution, the Basic Law, and its application have become more a matter of financial considerations than legal principles. The government has come to take it for granted that it can refuse the rights of Hong Kong people clearly defined by the Basic Law on no stronger grounds than the advice of economists. Chapter 1 traces the origins of this paradoxical situation, which is in direct conflict with the rule of law, normally regarded as essential to Hong Kong's survival.

The analysis reveals how the Basic Law drafters had intended to safeguard the individual's social as well as civic rights. Yet, as soon as the Law came into force in 1997, business leaders, politicians and academics began a highly successful campaign which made Financial Secretaries' budget forecasts the crucial criterion as to which Articles of the Basic Law should be applied and which ignored. The assumption that its financial Articles must be paramount went hand in hand with a doctrinaire belief that the private sector would always outperform public services in efficiency, ensuring lower costs for the benefit of the taxpayer. Thus, a parallel campaign was mounted to discredit government spending on social services, with a sustained effort to convince the community that these programmes were both unaffordable and a waste of resources— 'just like pouring sand into the sea to reclaim land', to quote Donald Tsang.[50]

As a result, the general public was led to believe that social rights, such as those set out in the Basic Law, were irrelevant to the quality of life of the community at large. This was not the case, and the disregard by successive Chief Executives of these rights meant that the community as a whole was no longer assured of access to decent housing and the good standards of health services and education which the Basic Law had envisaged and which was also required under Hong Kong's own legislation. Chapter 1 makes clear that the Law's drafters did not intend to exempt the government from a duty to provide high-quality administration and to maintain and, where necessary, to improve existing social and related services.

Most astonishing of all, there seemed to be a genuine unawareness among government and business leaders that their policy priorities were in direct violation of the Basic Law. Throughout this book, failure to comply with the Basic Law will be shown to be a major cause of the rise of mismanagement.

## From public service to ministerial mismanagement

By 2002, Tung had taken into his owns hands total control over government. The Chief Executive's decisions were to be implemented by political appointees: 'ministers' and their deputies. Chapter 2 investigates how the introduction of this 'Principal Officials Accountability System' (POAS) was warmly welcomed by senior civil servant and applauded by most commentators and why its results have proved very disappointing.

From the start, there was a powerful reason to doubt POAS' likely contribution to good government. It was always obvious that novice political appointees would find it extremely difficult to provide a higher quality of administration than civil servants had in the past. This discouraging prospect had been made clear in the most explicit terms.

> Despite the popular game of bashing the civil service, practiced daily by our media and politicians, our top civil servants still maintain a comfortable lead in opinion polls over most politicians in the legislature. And despite the poor rating for the Government as a whole since the Asian financial crisis and the ensuing recession, a neat 32 per cent of the public still perceived this administration as being responsive to the will of the people, compared to the worldwide average of 10 per cent and a corresponding rating of 14 per cent in the UK and just 5 per cent in the US, according to the results of the same Gallup poll.[51]

This stark statement was made by Lam Woon-kwong, an official who had broken ranks with the contrary views of his more optimistic civil service colleagues in 2000. He was Secretary for the Civil Service, which might suggest special pleading and even nostalgia for the colonial past. Lam, however, was above suspicion. He had a long record of total commitment to the Central People's Government and enjoyed a close personal rapport with Tung. His warning was well-founded but ignored.

The ministerial system was crippled from the outset and never recovered. The pool of political and administrative talent outside the civil service was extremely small. Inexperienced and inexpert ministers were appointed. Over time, fewer and fewer persons of any standing were willing to accept ministerial appointments, which brought little public prestige and considerable personal frustration. Political appointees' credentials were often poorly presented to the public. In 2017, for example, a senior member of Carrie Lam's ministerial team was asked by the media what the two new political appointees in his bureau would contribute. He had 'a very good team of civil servants' helping him, he said. But as for the political team, he was unable to cite its specific functions. He voiced the vague hope that it 'can enrich our strength and we can take things forward in a more effective manner', whatever that might mean in practice.[52]

Standards of public services deteriorated. Laws and regulations were no longer vigorously enforced. The quality of life declined for the population as a whole, contrary to the intentions of the Basic Law. The slide into mismanagement was aggravated by an earlier decision by Tung Chee Hwa to impose an immediate cut in the funding for all government departments and agencies, to drastically reduce their manpower and to make government bureaux and departments adopt business practices. This Enhanced Productivity Programme (EPP) was launched in 1998 and implemented ruthlessly. The Programme has exerted a destructive influence on public administration ever since. For the next two decades, the civil service was expected to provide new and improved services regardless of the inadequate resources made available. Time after time, this book will show, a continuing shortage of funds and staff meant that the government's basic duties were neglected, including enforcement of the law.

There seemed little hope that this situation would change in the next decade. On assuming office as the fourth Chief Executive, Carrie Lam acknowledged that a continually increasing workload was severely straining all ranks of the civil service. However, her solution ignored reality: to 'ask the Heads of Departments to reduce the demand for manpower'. She also saw a remedy in 'leveraging technologies'. Unfortunately, the overall standard of IT and related equipment in government departments was grossly inadequate, both in quality and supply, as several chapters will report. She promised a future 3 per cent increase in the overall civil service. But the additional staff were to be hired solely 'to ease the work pressure on civil servants' who were carrying out her 'new policies and initiatives'.[53] This measure would do nothing to relieve the existing strain on the civil service.

Chapter 2 includes a case study of how financial stringency led to the dismantling of the Social Welfare Department's programmes. This hindered the major provider of basic services needed by the community as a whole even though they were specifically guaranteed by the Basic Law. The case study also provides a review of how government standards of administration deteriorated. Before the Enhanced Productivity Programme was introduced, the Department had developed a highly efficient partnership with the welfare charities—the voluntary agencies now known as 'non-governmental organisations' (NGOs). This relationship had grown up in the colonial era to counter government hostility to 'welfare'. Medical, educational and social professionals had developed an informal alliance with the social workers in the Department to establish facilities, train staff and organise the funding for a modern system of social services. This chapter will show how this partnership was dismantled and how care for clients disappeared from the government's welfare agenda.

## Unfit for human habitation

The most damning evidence of mismanagement is the long-standing failure to provide safe and affordable homes for the people of a city as prosperous and sophisticated as Hong Kong. Chapter 3 traces how this crisis seriously threatened the well-being of the million families living in private sector housing. Many of those who had prudently saved money, taken out mortgages and bought their own homes saw a precious family asset diminished or destroyed on an increasingly rapid scale over the last two decades. The damage was done by the mismanagement and the neglected maintenance of buildings whose life span was not designed to be as long as that of the owner-occupiers themselves. Furthermore, a desperate shortage of affordable housing in the private sector led to illegal subdivision of buildings to create additional premises to rent out. Overall, the private sector's buildings stock came to include an increasing proportion of premises which were unsafe and unhealthy and whose owners could not afford to pay for their renovation. In 2013, 10 per cent of the total stock of private residential buildings (containing 1.6 million flats) was classified as uninhabitable. Another 30 per cent was dilapidating seriously.[54]

There is no mystery about the principal causes of this disaster: the refusal of those in power to supply the staff needed to enforce effectively existing legal and regulatory systems to ensure health and safety. The government also postponed as long as possible new legislation to modernise the standards of management and maintenance in Hong Kong's multi-storey and high-density housing complexes. This attitude was in marked contrast to other sectors where the public was not left so unprotected. Stock markets, banking institutions, medical and legal services, food suppliers, for example, were closely regulated.

## The rise of 'invisible' slums

The plight of the average family was aggravated by the overall housing policies adopted by Chief Executives. Chapter 4 investigates the mistaken decisions made by the first two Chief Executives about how to manage Hong Kong's housing supply. They were convinced that the private sector would provide the solution for Hong Kong's housing needs far more effectively than the government itself. So, the Housing Authority's programmes were shrunk. Its land bank was sold off. Hong Kong was left at the mercy of a market long dominated by a handful of developers, with the result that competition was minimal.[55] They cut supply, leaving prices to soar and looked forward to the profits. This situation could not continue indefinitely. The need grew desperate for increased production of both public and private housing. A larger supply for the public sector was essential in order to offer rehousing to those who had to be cleared from dilapidated and dangerous private buildings. The private sector had to expand its supply in order to provide affordable homes for those who could pay fair and competitive purchase prices or rents.

## Nowhere to build

These targets were not to be achieved very quickly. By 2016, the government's building programmes faced paralysis because of acute difficulties in finding enough construction sites. Chapter 5 traces why such a situation had occurred when the government itself owned extensive areas of undeveloped land.[56] It traces how successive administrations failed to police these land holdings and allowed rural land to be used for unlawful building purposes. The public funding to correct this past negligence was not forthcoming. In addition, the shrinking credibility of Chief Executives and their ministers made it virtually impossible for them to win the public support needed to revive the level of building activity of the previous century. The crisis became so frustrating for Leung Chun-ying that he was reported to have been on the verge of tears when faced with the media demanding to know what solution he could offer in 2016. He announced his decision not to stand for a second term shortly afterwards.

Carrie Lam's Election Manifesto had given considerable attention to the shortage of building sites. Nevertheless, the practical solution she put forward as Chief Executive seemed uninspired although she had spent five years as the minister dealing with land and related problems. She established a 30-member task force, chaired by a former banker, with three ministers, five senior civil servants and a collection of political and business figures and academics. The primary goal of the task force was to persuade a suspicious public to cooperate with future government proposals to create more building land. It was possible that the community might be reassured by the calibre of task force members.[57] But what was really needed was a minister capable of mobilising public support for a land programme which the people of Hong Kong would accept as the essential foundation for overcoming the mounting housing crisis.

## Students at the market's mercy

The breakdown of responsible administration created a longer-term threat to survival through failing to maintain the educational standards which a post-industrial economy like Hong Kong must have in order to maintain its competitiveness. The most serious example of how this had happened was provided by the post-secondary education sector, which is examined in Chapter 6.

Higher education has been constantly invoked by Chief Executives as the key to Hong Kong's future success. Yet, throughout the last two decades, access to universities has been tightly restricted by a 1989 ceiling imposed on the admission of undergraduates and which continued to be enforced in this century. As a result, every year, a substantial number of students who qualified for university places had to be rejected. Chief Executives and their Education Ministers expected them to turn to commercial institutions which offered self-financed associate degrees and diplomas.

The results thoroughly discredited the private sector model as a source of high-standard education programmes. The qualifications they offered had little credibility academically, in the market place or with the parents who invested very heavily in them. The lack of quality control was the target for severe criticism from independent investigations. Yet, the government did as little as possible to ensure that students and their parents got value for money.

## Lives at risk

Chapter 7 shows that there is virtually no limit to the maladministration that has come to be tolerated. To illustrate how even threats to public safety have been ignored in the pursuit of minimum public spending, this chapter provides four case studies.

Management of the outbreak of atypical pneumonia (SARS) in 2003 was a disgrace to Hong Kong and its previously outstanding reputation for control of infectious diseases. SARS provided convincing evidence of the flaws in the ministerial system. Official post-epidemic enquiries revealed the managerial incompetence of the Chief Executive and the failure of his political appointees to understand how health services and disease control are subject to legal regulation. The outcome was chaotic. There was also a longer-term impact on the quality of medical services. The government declined to provide adequate additional funding to combat the SARS epidemic. The Hospital Authority, whose finances had already been squeezed since 2000, had to cover the costs from existing resources, with adverse consequences for future patients.

A ferry disaster in 2011 with loss of life will be shown to have been largely due to inadequate Marine Department staffing. However, the most alarming outcome of the tragedy was the open admission by the Transport Minister that although the independent inquiry's recommendations for improving marine safety had been accepted, the Department would not be given the resources to implement them.

The casualties caused by the collapse of an entire block of a dilapidated building in 2010 led to public outrage. Its dangerous state had been known for years. The government bureau and departments concerned defended themselves convincingly: their staff were over-worked to a degree which had made the comprehensive enforcement of safety regulations impossible. A programme was quickly introduced to increase the staff available to inspect buildings at risk and to help owners improve their management. These measures were strictly temporary, and they were presented by the ministers involved as justified principally as an initiative to increase employment opportunities. No long-term solution was launched, and the risks to the public continued.

The final case study examines the reluctance of the ICAC to tackle malpractices in the management and maintenance of residential build-ings. Although these had been the largest source of public complaints from the private sector for many years, the ICAC struggled for over a decade to avoid intervening. As a result, law enforcement in this sector was under greater threat than it should have been, with serious implica-tions for health, safety and the preservation of the value of the owners' property.

## Limited Mainland markets

Chief Executives have given the Special Administrative Region's relationship with the Mainland the highest priority, and Chapter 8 is devoted to this issue. It avoids discussion of political matters because these involve complex constitutional issues which will be decided at the national, not the Hong Kong level. Instead, it looks at the business rela-tionship, which is described by Hong Kong leaders as the foundation for Hong Kong's prosperous future. Without integration into the national economy, they repeatedly warn, Hong Kong would no longer be able to survive in increasingly hostile global markets. Furthermore, they claim, Mainland cities will overtake Hong Kong and ruin it with their superior technology.

Unfortunately, the Chief Executives' management of this relation-ship was disastrous. They displayed alarming ignorance of the Mainland economy and its limitations. They showed little understanding of how the central and local governments operate and, in particular, the extent of local protectionism. In 2003, a 'Closer Economic Partnership Arrangement' (CEPA) with the Central People's Government was signed. This 'free trade agreement' was supposed to give Hong Kong businesses a 'passport' to operate freely throughout the national economy. Premier Wen Jiabao warned Hong Kong not to be over-optimistic,[58] rightly so because there was no free market on the Mainland. Instead, local gov-ernments maintained 'administrative monopolies, forced deals, and market blockades' in defiance of the Central People's Government.[59] This disregard of the national policy was still untamed ten years later.[60] And CEPA's implementation remained incomplete.

Chief Executives believed that when it came to business, they knew best. Despite strong Mainland reservations, the second Chief Executive decided to seek to have Hong Kong included in the national five-year economic plans. Mainland officials, including the Premier, warned that inclusion of Hong Kong in national plans did not conform with the Basic Law's requirement that it should retain its capitalist economy. Furthermore, the Hong Kong government lacked the infrastructure required for state planning. It had no control over the private sector nor direct influence over the flow of investment funds. These limitations were ignored, and business sectors were selected for inclusion in the national plans without prior research. They proved wholly unsuitable in practice. It was also significant that Donald Tsang's desire to participate in state plans was motivated in part by a relatively minor issue: public criticism of the price of meat and the monopolistic practices of the Mainland supplier.

Chapter 8 concludes with an account of how Chief Executives failed to protect the extensive investments made by Hong Kong manufacturers in Guangdong since 1978 and which had turned the province into a model for the rest of the nation. By 2007, Hong Kong firms employed 10 million workers in the province, producing almost exclusively for world markets. This industrial base was shrunk rapidly thereafter, not by market forces but because of changes in state development policies.

Donald Tsang found himself unable to protect Hong Kong firms. He was outranked by his provincial counterpart and was reduced to openly pleading for concessions for at least the small and medium enterprises. Hong Kong businesses were able to delay their demise for some years through sheer efficiency. In the end, however, they closed down in large numbers. The losses to the Hong Kong investors and entrepreneurs who had responded to Deng Xiaoping's appeal in 1978 to lead China's modernisation drive were substantial.

## The politics of pessimism

Throughout this book, the reluctance to view Hong Kong's prospects more optimistically is shown to have had a defining role in shaping government policies in the last two decades. This outlook in part reflected the political and administrative inexperience of Chief Executives and most of their ministers. But it was also a matter of 'ideology'. They, in common with the business and professional élite, were convinced that financial disaster constantly threatened Hong Kong because of potential demands for more public spending from a discontented community, while economic disaster was only a matter of time as Mainland cities modernised. They underestimated the resilience of the Hong Kong survival culture that had been forged in the last century and which continued to operate in this one.

Although Chief Executives, their ministers and business leaders have taken a consistently negative view of its prospects, Hong Kong's economy is not a problem when it comes to survival. Its past financial and commercial performance has been outstanding, and the future is no less promising, as President Xi Jinping acknowledged in 2017. 'When our country does well, Hong Kong will do even better', he said, before going on to spell out the reasons for this optimism.

> We should have confidence in Hong Kong. Hong Kong is blessed with many favorable conditions and unique strengths for development . . . With its internationally recognized legal, accounting and regulatory systems, a full-fledged service sector, clean and efficient government and business-friendly environment, Hong Kong has the full confidence of outside investors.[61]

This book offers powerful evidence for rejecting claims that contemporary Hong Kong cannot afford to finance a public service of adequate size to meet the needs of this sophisticated post-industrial society or to meet the welfare and social service requirements as laid down by the Basic Law.

In 2017, the most senior national official in charge of Hong Kong affairs, Zhang Dejiang, issued a reminder of the four essential qualifications that Chief Executives must possess. His list included the requirement that they should be 'capable of exercising governance, and [are] supported by the Hong Kong people'.[62] The first three Chief Executives did not meet these conditions. The first two openly admitted their failure, while the third felt compelled to put his family's well-being first and did not seek to remain in office.

The public has grown increasingly resentful over the years at the government's poor performance. On the evidence produced in this book, higher standards of selection for Chief Executives and their teams would reverse the growing dissatisfaction with the government which, since 2010, has been increasingly translated into victories in Legislative Council elections for protest groups and public cynicism about government programmes. There would also be an increase in the community's appreciation of the Basic Law's merits, thus allaying the misgivings of the nation's leaders.

In this complex environment, objectivity of analysis and discussion is both crucial and challenging. Fortunately, there is an important and reassuring feature of modern Hong Kong. When serious incidents of misgovernment and maladministration occur, it is virtually impossible to conceal them in this open society. What goes wrong is made available to the public almost immediately through an astonishing flow of information, week after week. This ranges from enquiries by the Legislative Council, its Committees and Panels to judicial and similar reviews by the courts and investigations by the Director of Audit and the Ombudsman.

As a result, the quotations and the data that reveal mismanagement and its consequences which are analysed in this book are based, almost exclusively, on the statements of Chief Executives and their ministers, the information supplied by officials to the public and the results of official investigations and inquiries. It is on these official sources that the book's grim findings are founded. What is uncovered is generally so frank and self-incriminating as to challenge belief. Hence, the source of each fact and assertion is given in full. There is one exception. In the case of basic statistics which are published routinely in regular official series, the reader can assume that they are taken from the monthly or the annual *Digests of Statistics*.[63]

It is to Hong Kong's credit that the public is still able to demand a very high degree of accountability from which Chief Executives, ministers and other political appointees are not exempt. This independent monitoring is especially important in ensuring the integrity of the political system, as chapter after chapter bears witness. Open and accountable administration remains a powerful force in Hong Kong's core values as it struggles for survival.

## Notes

1.  On the distress of these vulnerable groups, see Leo F. Goodstadt, *Poverty in the Midst of Affluence: How Hong Kong Mismanaged Its Prosperity*, 2nd ed. (Hong Kong: Hong Kong University Press, 2015).
2.  Urban Renewal Authority Steering Committee on Review of the Urban Renewal Strategy, 'Report on the Building Conditions Survey' (SC Paper No. 18/2009, 30 June 2009), 2–3.
3.  These warnings appear to have started with the doubts expressed by Michael Suen Ming-yeung, Secretary for Education, *Hong Kong Hansard* (*HH* hereafter), 12 March 2008, 5275.
4.  On these developments, see Leung Chun-ying, Chief Executive, *Government Information Services* (*GIS* hereafter), 19 January 2015; John Tsang Chun-wah, Financial Secretary, *GIS*, 8 April 2015; Matthew Cheung, Chief Secretary, *GIS*, 15 June 2017.
5.  The productivity figures are for 2002–2011. Economic Analysis Division, *First Quarter Economic Report 2012* (May 2012), 'Chart 1: Hong Kong's Labour Productivity Growth Outperformed Many Other Economies', 13.
6.  Research Office, 'The 2017–2018 Budget March 2017', Research Brief, Issue No. 3 (2016–2017) (Hong Kong: Legislative Council Secretariat, 2017).
7.  Tung Chee Hwa, Chief Executive, 'Inaugural Speech', *GIS*, 1 July 1997.
8.  Carrie Lam Cheng Yuet-ngor, Chief Executive Elect, *GIS*, 26 March 2017.

9. Carrie Lam, 'We Connect: Connecting for Consensus and a Better Future: Manifesto of Carrie Lam Chief Executive Election 2017' (Campaign Office of Carrie Lam, February 2017), 8.

10. It should be noted that, by Hong Kong's normal standards, industrial disputes had been unusually high in 2007.

11. Paul Chan Mo-po, Financial Secretary, *HH*, 22 February 2017, 4591. The Budget Speech took place a few days before the launch of Carrie Lam Cheng Yuet-ngor's manifesto.

12. Tung, Chief Executive, *GIS*, 30 October 1998.

13. State Councillor Tang Jiaxuan reported in Albert Au-yeung, 'Tung Best Choice in Upholding Stability', *China Daily*, 16 September 2003.

14. Tung, Chief Executive, *HH*, 12 January 2005, 3263.

15. Tung, Chief Executive, *GIS*, 10 August 2000.

16. Tung, Chief Executive, *GIS*, 29 May 2004.

17. These postings gave Donald Tsang Yam-kuen considerable experience of highly sensitive negotiations in unfavourable environments. In 1989, he was given charge of organising the issue of United Kingdom passports to 50,000 selected Hong Kong families, a scheme denounced by the Chinese government and unwelcome to the British immigration authorities, who did as little as possible to facilitate him. He then took charge of Hong Kong's external trade at a time when the final stage of international discussions to create the World Trade Organisation was under way. The consequences of blunders on his part in either role could not have been concealed and would have had severe consequences both for Hong Kong and for its government's credibility.

18. The plan to introduce political appointees with the rank of ministers to head government bureaux had been outlined publicly in 2000 by Tung, Chief Executive, *GIS*, 11 October 2000.

19. Donald Tsang, Financial Secretary, *HH*, 6 March 1996, 84; Dr Margaret Ng Ngoi-yee, *HH*, 28 March 1996, 240.

20. Matthew Cheung Kin-chung, Permanent Secretary for Economic Development and Labour, *GIS*, 8 March 2005.

21. Donald Tsang, Chief Executive, *HH*, 12 October 2005, 24.

22. Donald Tsang, Chief Executive, *HH*, 12 January 2006, 3880–81.

23. Donald Tsang, Chief Secretary, 'Statement on Housing', 3 September 2001, http://www.info.gov.hk/gia/general/200109/03/0903236.htm.

24. Donald Tsang, Financial Secretary, transcript of BBC interview, *GIS*, 23 June 1998; *HH*, 24 October 2001, 809–10.

25. Office of The Ombudsman, 'Direct Investigation Report: "Special Procedures" of Buildings Department for handling UBW cases involving celebrities' (OMB/DI/316, January 2014), 2–3, 15–16.

26. Donald Tsang, Chief Executive, *HH*, 15 October 2008, 56.

27. His business friendships were explained in Donald Tsang, Chief Executive, *HH*, 1 March 2012, 6926, 6942, 6950, 6052.

28. Donald Tsang, Chief Executive, *GIS*, 30 July 2011.

29. Donald Tsang, Chief Executive, *HH*, 1 March 2012, 6926–27, 6929.

30. For details, see Buildings Department, *GIS*, 1 June and 7 September 2011.

31. A striking example of this characteristic was recorded in 'Q&A: CY Leung on What It Takes to Run Hong Kong', *South China Morning Post*, 28 June 2016.

32. Leung Chun-ying, 'The Transition and Unexpected Changes', in *Hong Kong's Transition a Decade after the Deal*, ed. Wang Gungwu and Wong Siu-lun (Hong Kong: Oxford University Press, 1995), 138–39, 150–51.

33. The political and commercial struggles at the local levels during the 1990s are described at length in Yasheng Huang, *Capitalism with Chinese Characteristics: Entrepreneurship and the State* (New York: Cambridge University Press, 2008), chapter 3.

34. Leung was appointed to prestigious posts in the organisations which the Mainland established to manage the creation of post-colonial political institutions, e.g., Secretary General, Basic Law Consultative Committee (1988–1990); Leader, Preliminary Working Committee Political Sub-Group (1993–1995); Vice Chairman, Preparatory Committee (1996–1997).

35. Leung, Chief Executive, *GIS*, 22 March 2013.

36. Leung, Chief Executive, *GIS*, 6 December 2012.

37. The Chief Executive had to struggle to provide a positive interpretation of the new arrangements for Beijing visits. See the coverage in *Ta Kung Pao*, 17 December 2013.

38. See, for example, the comments of Qiang Shigong, Director of Peking University's Research Centre for the Rule of Law, reported in *Ming Pao Daily*, 13 December 2013.

39. Leung, Chief Executive, *GIS*, 23 December 2015. A Hong Kong Macao Affairs Office spokesperson took the same line. The media showed considerable confusion as to why Leung had been treated in this way. See, for example, the different reporting and analysis in *Ta Kung Pao, Hong Kong Economic Times* and *Sing Tao Daily*, 24 December 2015.

40. Leung's income figure was expressed as US$1,800. Keith Bradsher and Chris Buckley, 'Hong Kong Leader Reaffirms Unbending Stance on Elections', *New York Times*, 20 October 2014.

41. Ambrose Leung and Eva Wu, 'Exco Chief Says City's Development Has Slowed', *South China Morning Post*, 25 September 2009.

42. *Report on the Work of the Fourth-Term Government of the Hong Kong Special Administrative Region June 2017*, 83.

43. Ibid., 56.

44. Carrie Lam, 'We Connect: Connecting for Consensus and a Better Future; Manifesto of Carrie Lam Chief Executive Election 2017' (Campaign Office of Carrie Lam, February 2017), 5.

45. This snapshot of Carrie Lam relies heavily on Professor Charles Kwong, 'Mrs Carrie Lam Cheng Yuet-ngor, GBS, JP, Doctor of Social Sciences, *honoris causa*, Citation', https://www.ln.edu.hk/poccb/hac/citation/2013-carrielam.pdf.

46. Professor Charles Kwong, 'Mrs Carrie Lam Cheng Yuet-ngor, GBS, JP, Doctor of Social Sciences, *honoris causa*, Citation'.

47. Carrie Lam, Director of Social Welfare, 'Role of Welfare in a Laissez-Faire Society', Speech to the Hong Kong Democratic Foundation (18 April 2001), http://www.hkdf.org/newsarticles.asp?show=newsarticles&newsarticle=120. She repeated these views at other public forums. See also Raymond

M. H. Ngan and Mark K. Y. Li, 'The Dilemma and Crisis for Public Welfare Payments in Hong Kong', in *The July 1 Protest Rally: Interpreting a Historic Event*, ed. Joseph Y. S. Cheng (Hong Kong: City University of Hong Kong Press, 2005), 418.

48. Carrie Lam, Secretary for Development, *GIS*, 26 February 2009.

49. Carrie Lam, Secretary for Development, *GIS*, 30 January 2010.

50. Donald Tsang, Chief Executive, *HH*, 27 June 2005, 8944.

51. Lam Woon-kwong, Secretary for the Civil Service, 'International Conference on Public Management and Governance in the New Millennium', *GIS*, 10 January 2000.

52. Edward Yau Tang-wah, Secretary for Commerce and Economic Development, *GIS*, 1 August 2017.

53. The planned increase in the size of the civil service would not come into effect until 2018–2019 and was not Carrie Lam's own proposal but an item left over from the previous administration. On this issue and the overall manpower situation when she assumed office, see 'Report of the Panel on Public Service for submission to the Legislative Council' (CB(4)1294/16-17, 23 June 2017), 2.

54. Barry Cheung Chun-yuen, 'Chairman's Statement', in Urban Renewal Authority, *Annual Report 2012–13*, 7.

55. Consumer Council, *How Competitive Is the Private Residential Property Market?* (Hong Kong: Consumer Council, 1996), 2–4, 5, 8, 3–9, 5–3, A 3–2, Annex 4.

56. An excellent legal and historical survey of the system of land ownership and administration inherited from the colonial era, together with its complexities, is Roger Nissim, *Land Administration and Practice in Hong Kong* (Hong Kong: Hong Kong University Press, 1998).

57. Press release, *GIS*, 29 August 2017.

58. Press release, *GIS*, 30 June 2003.

59. 'Breaking Barriers: China's "Nationalization" Drive', *Renmin Ribao*, 1 July 2000.

60. 'China Moves to Clear Blockades for Unified Market', *New China News Agency* (*NCNA* hereafter), 10 December 2013.

61. 'Full Text of Speech by President Xi Jinping at Welcome Dinner in HK', *NCNA*, 1 July 2017.

62. Zhang Dejiang, National People's Congress Chairman reported in 'HKSAR Basic Law Meets Test of Practice: Top Legislator' and 'HKSAR Political System Is Not Separation of Powers: Top Legislator—Xinhua', *NCNA*, 27 May 2017.

63. The Census and Statistics Department revises many of its statistical series from one edition of its publications to another. An effort has been made to use the latest revised figures that are accessible.

# 1
# The Basic Law: Rights denied

The people of Hong Kong are fortunate that the Basic Law is such an outstanding model of a constitutional statute. It is clear, comprehensive and fair and continues to command community-wide respect. It has proved highly successful as the blueprint for Hong Kong to preserve its separate identity, its successful economy, its rule of law and its personal freedoms.

Chief Executives and their ministers have constantly invoked the Basic Law and repeatedly pledged their commitment to it. In practice, however, they regarded some articles of the Basic Law as requiring the strictest observance, while others were ignored. Arguably, the most frequently cited and the most faithfully observed has been Article 107:

> The Hong Kong Special Administrative Region shall follow the principle of keeping expenditure within the limits of revenues in drawing up its budget, and strive to achieve a fiscal balance, avoid deficits and keep the budget commensurate with the growth rate of its gross domestic product.

Hong Kong's rulers have insisted that this Article justified them in minimising government spending as a matter of principle, regardless of the real state of the economy or the damage that financial restrictions would cause to the community as a whole—with one important exception. In the name of maximising economic growth, Chief Executives and their Financial Secretaries felt free to be generous in funding infrastructure projects and promoting business interests. But they ignored the way in which the limits they imposed on funding for government departments and agencies reduced their efficiency and restricted their ability to improve services and enforce laws and regulations.

The consequences have been very costly. The most visible victims included hospital patients, school and post-secondary students and low-income families. But the refusal to provide adequate government funding also aggravated a crisis faced by the private housing sector which endangered the public's safety. This mismanagement of public finances began with the selective enforcement of the Basic Law.

The policies of Chief Executives and their Financial Secretaries were also in conflict with the views of Wen Jiabao who, when still Premier, insisted that ample public funds were available to finance improvements in the social services, for example. His statements were a clear rejection of claims that Hong Kong's public finances were on the verge of disaster.

## An unconditional right

On social issues, the Basic Law addresses the well-being of the community as a whole. It does not authorise, directly or indirectly, a reduction in the quality of the publicly-financed social services or of access to them from their 1997 standards. It sets out the government's duty 'to develop and to improve medical and health services', for example, and the government's responsibility for 'the development and improvement of education'. These social services are to be available on terms no worse than those which were provided or subsidised by the government before 1997.[1] The government has failed to fully comply with these obligations.

There is one further provision, Article 36, which the government openly and consistently refuses to respect. This lays down that 'Hong Kong residents shall have the right to social welfare in accordance with law'. The importance to be attached to this unconditional entitlement is obvious from its listing among the human and civil rights of the people of Hong Kong. It comes immediately after the Basic Law articles protecting personal liberty, namely the right to independent legal representation and to sue government agencies in the courts. The promise of 'social welfare' is followed by the guarantee of 'freedom of marriage' and a 'right to raise a family freely'. 'Welfare' was to be part of the foundations for the future well-being of the people of Hong Kong.

The clear intention of the Basic Law Drafting Committee was to provide Hong Kong with a constitutional guarantee that the pre-1997 standards of social services would be maintained as the legal minimum. This objective was subsequently explained by Professor Xiao Weiyun, a member of the Committee who later became known as one of the 'Four Guardians' of the Basic Law.[2] He has recorded how committee members took it for granted that, after 1997, the new administration would seek to improve the range and quality of Hong Kong's welfare services. Thus, Article 145 states: 'On the basis of the previous social welfare system, the Government of the Hong Kong Special Administrative Region shall, on its own, formulate policies on *the development and improvement* of this system in the light of the economic conditions and social needs' (emphasis added). No scope was left for dismantling or curtailing the pre-1997 system.

Indeed, the drafters had concerns that the post-colonial adminis-tration might be excessively ambitious in seeking to expand the social services. They called for 'a prudent approach' in their 'development and improvement', Professor Xiao has noted. Nevertheless, maintenance of existing rights and their future expansion was deliberately enshrined in the Basic Law, he pointed out.

> The provision in the Basic Law on residents' social welfare is mainly to provide legal protection for the present level of social welfare that Hong Kong residents are already enjoying. Other kinds of social welfare benefits that are not enjoyed by the residents yet could be gradually introduced in light of economic developments.[3]

The drafters made it clear what new services should be introduced, identifying, for example, the need for measures to provide for 'the retirement protection and welfare benefits of the labor force'.[4]

## The Beijing view

These clear provisions have been ignored, almost universally, because of the government's incorrect interpretation of Article 107's conservative financial prescription. This has been made possible because the people of Hong Kong retained a trust in the expertise and the integrity of their rulers when dealing with matters of law and finance. As a result, political parties, welfare agencies, professional and academic specialists and the media have generally accepted the government's restrictive view of the public's rights to decent social services under the Basic Law.[5] If a legisla-tor or a voluntary agency (a non-governmental organisation or NGO) challenged the legality of government cuts in services or increases in fees and charges, an official spokesperson would reply that these were necessary precautions to comply with the Basic Law's budget require-ments.[6] Even when such official statements were based on a misinter-pretation of the Basic Law's provisions, government explanations were respected as authoritative.[7]

Special interests were also involved. The business sector was active in the campaign against any increase in government spending on social services because such expenditure was regarded as the first stage in creating a welfare state. For example, a member of a leading business dynasty and chairman of a political party told fellow legislators that workers in 'low-skilled jobs' must face facts. 'If they fail to meet the needs of society', he said, 'it is a matter of course that they will unfortunately be eliminated by society'.[8] That sentiment was entirely contrary to the Basic Law.

China's leadership did not accept this state of affairs. In commenting on Hong Kong affairs after the annual session of the National People's

Congress in 2011, Premier Wen Jiabao rejected the criteria adopted by Chief Executives and their Financial Secretaries in assessing the affordability of social services. His message was clear and simple.

> With sufficient government revenue and ample foreign exchange reserves, Hong Kong needs to make the most of the favorable conditions to improve its social safety net, in particular, to take good care of the vulnerable groups, thus making people in Hong Kong live a better life.[9]

His statement was an obvious rebuke to the ruling élite: existing social services were inadequate. This state of affairs was unacceptable, in the Premier's opinion, because the usual claims of Chief Executives, Financial Secretaries and the business community that a comprehensive programme of social reforms would bring financial ruin were grossly exaggerated.

The following year, the Premier found it necessary to repeat his message: 'Particular efforts should be made to solve such major issues as social justice, price stability, housing, education and medical care of the people'.[10] On the Premier's analysis, there was no justification for government claims that the costs of an adequate supply of social services and decent housing would be in conflict with the Basic Law. His comments were ignored by Hong Kong's rulers, however. Not until 2017 did a Premier's views prevail after Li Keqiang made it clear to Hong Kong's fourth Chief Executive that the quality of life must be given priority, as this chapter later explains.[11]

## The Court of Final Appeal: Government found guilty

For years, the courts, too, were reluctant to condemn government policies on social services. Judges assumed that they could take at face value government presentations and statistics on 'affordability' when social rights were raised. As a result, the courts tended to rule in favour of the government if it claimed in its defence that Hong Kong's financial stability would be endangered by an increase in spending on such services.[12]

Eventually, a case against the Social Welfare Department reached the Court of Final Appeal in 2013. Its verdict ruled against the government's practice of depriving individuals of their rights in the name of fiscal stability. 'The Government might simply state that it is cutting expenditure with the aim of "saving money"', the Court declared, '[b]ut saving money would not in itself be a legitimate aim'. 'If the cut in expenditure meant that the Government was abdicating an important responsibility which the government ought to discharge in the public interest', its verdict continued, 'The saving of money by that means would not be a legitimate aim'. The Court also reviewed Hong Kong's budget record and concluded there was no evidence that the costs of adequate social services would lead to dangerous deficits.[13]

The government reacted to the Court of Final Appeal's findings with warnings that the expenditure on social welfare would increase to a level which would cause serious financial burdens. Expressions of alarm followed from a broad range of legislators and much of the media. There were even calls for the government to request the National People's Congress Standing Committee to use its constitutional powers to overturn the Court's decision. In the end, the government concluded that such drastic measures were unnecessary. Ministers assumed that, in practice, the Court of Final Appeal's verdict would make little difference to the government's freedom to shrink social services or to raise their costs to the public. Chief Executives and their ministers would be able to continue to interpret the Basic Law to suit their own convenience— just as they had done in the past—as long as they invoked forecasts of impending financial doom.[14]

## Broken promises

Rejection of the Basic Law as a defining feature of social policy had begun with Tung Chee Hwa. As he prepared to take office in 1997, he had presented the public with an attractive vision of what his government would achieve. He promised to satisfy all the community's aspirations. 'Hong Kong will become a stable, equitable, compassionate and democratic society', he declared, 'based on equal opportunities and fair competition'. There would be, he pledged, 'a social welfare system that promotes self-reliance while protecting the aged, disadvantaged and unfortunate'.[15]

He was proposing a 'new deal' that would transform the lives of every level of society. His promises were specific:

- 'to give each person in Hong Kong a modern and well-balanced education';
- 'to enable more citizens to realize the dream of home ownership . . . in as short a time as possible'; and
- to 'develop a comprehensive policy for our ageing population, [and] provide our elderly with a sense of security, belonging and worthiness'.[16]

His pledges seemed very much in line with the Basic Law's prescriptions for the development of the social services after 1997. Very quickly, however, the people of Hong Kong were to discover that Tung did not expect these commitments to be taken literally. 'Equitable' and 'compassionate' were to be given very restricted interpretations.[17] Eventually, all three of his original goals were discarded. The quality of education that an individual received very soon came to depend on the parents' financial status. The public housing programme had been largely dismantled by the end of 2002 in order to end its alleged competition with private developers. The production of public and private housing dropped, while the supply of building sites shrank. By 2011, the results of this misguided policy had become so serious that it had to be reversed. In 2017, the government was still struggling to restore public housing programmes and the supply of building sites to their pre-2002 levels. As for the elderly and their security, 20 years on, the government was still busy conducting public consultations on pension arrangements, while business interests were successfully blocking reforms to the Mandatory Provident Fund (MPF) established to finance post-retirement life.

Tung had also come into office 'appealing to Hong Kong people to rediscover Confucian ethics'. He defined these as 'consensus, modesty, harmony, obligation, familialism and collectivism rather than confrontation, rights and individualism'. The community would be motivated by 'a cultural call to duty rather than the pursuit of individual interests'. Care of the elderly, infirm, the disabled and the sick was to be a family responsibility.[18] Tung's insistence that, in effect, these vulnerable groups must find their own means of survival was a view widely shared by the business and professional élite. Their dominant belief was that if state benefits were available, the costs involved would undermine business efficiency, reduce profits and increase taxation. As Tung himself explained, 'in addressing the question of alleviation of poverty, the Government will adhere closely to the free market principles which have underpinned Hong Kong's success all these years'.[19] In other words, the government saw no reason to extend to those in need the protection which the Basic Law had sought to provide.

## Hopeless cases

The second Chief Executive, Donald Tsang Yam-kuen, followed Tung's example, with one important difference. His objection to expenditure on social services was not just affordability. Indeed, he admitted on one occasion that 'the Government does not need money' and faced no budget difficulties. A better quality of life for all was a goal within reach. 'We are able to balance the budget and the community should focus on the best way to ensure we have the resources to do the things we all wanted to do—cleaner air, better hospitals, longer life expectancy, better social welfare, better roads, better everything', he admitted.[20] But he was also convinced that spending on those in need would achieve nothing. 'The Government must never try to assist the poor using its own resources, for this is doomed to failure', he declared, 'just like pouring sand into the sea to reclaim land'.[21] This assertion was a total rejection of the Basic Law's declaration of the Hong Kong people's right to social welfare services.

That Hong Kong could not expect to eliminate poverty was a message Donald Tsang preached throughout his administration. All the world's advanced cities attracted immigrants, he argued in 2006, who were impoverished and destined to remain so.[22] It made no sense to expect either an early or easy solution, he claimed on a later occasion.

> No one has ever been able to truly solve this problem. We can only hope that this gap can be filled by employment and promotion and through education, and we also hope no single sector in society will remain in poverty forever. We hope that people can improve their lot and incomes after a certain period of time.[23]

In 2011, he was still trying hard to convince the public that this gap between rich and poor was an unavoidable and incurable feature of capitalism.[24]

In fact, immigration into Hong Kong was very tightly controlled by the Mainland authorities. There was thus no question of an unlimited influx of the poor and destitute, as there was in so many Asian cities. Furthermore, Tsang's claims that Hong Kong was importing intractable poverty were not supported by census data. These statistics showed that by 2011, new arrivals from the Mainland were much better off in terms of average household income than immigrants had been in 2001. In addition, Hong Kong was importing individuals from the Mainland whose average educational qualifications had improved impressively by 2011 and now matched the average for the overall population.[25]

Tsang seemed to be convinced that spending on social services, especially for those unable to become self-supporting economically, was some sort of fraud on the community. He saw Hong Kong, it seemed, as a city under siege from a rising flood of welfare applicants whose entitlement to benefits was very doubtful.[26] A particularly striking example of Tsang's biased outlook was his mistrust of the aged. He suspected elderly citizens of seeking medical treatment without genuine cause. They queued up at outpatient clinics before dawn, he claimed, in order 'to meet up with their "buddies" [for] morning tea in a Chinese restaurant'. He called on the Health Minister to investigate whether 'our health care resources have been abused' by the older generation.[27] These comments were astonishingly lacking in respect for the aged in a community which he himself described as 'steeped in Chinese culture'.[28] Not only did the Chief Executive fail to protect the Basic Law rights of the elderly, they found themselves blamed in official reports for overloading clinics and hospital facilities.[29]

## Maintaining a tradition

The next Chief Executive, Leung Chun-ying, was in many ways a throw-back to the Tung era. Leung, too, took office promising 'a fair, just, caring and harmonious society [where] every one can live and work in peace and contentment'. All the sick would receive the treatment they needed. The elderly would be assured of adequate support. Students would all find jobs to match their educational attainments.[30] Sadly, even those programmes where he seemed to have the expertise to achieve success were to prove too difficult for him to manage, both politically and administratively. This was particularly true of housing, a sector which his professional background should have made him highly qualified to oversee. The mystery was why he proved so handicapped, especially since as the former Convenor of the Executive Council, he should have been no political novice. He had been personally involved in discussing and approving all major government policies for more than a decade.

Leung proved as insistent as his predecessors were on the perils of spending commitments for social and related services and showed no awareness of social rights as a legal entitlement of Hong Kong people. Instead, he shared the élite's paranoia about a potential rise in public demand for social services. Universal suffrage, he told foreign journalists in 2014, was very worrying. If elections were 'entirely a numbers game and numeric [*sic*] representation', then those earning less than $13,400 a month (the average employee's monthly earnings), the poorer half of the population would dominate 'politics and policies'.

To avoid this danger, there needed to be 'screening' of candidates for the post of Chief Executive, he said, which 'would insulate candi-dates from popular pressure to create a welfare state, and would allow the city government to follow more business-friendly policies'. His analysis implied an on-going class struggle in which each class would fight to protect its own special interests, and he was convinced that the business class and its interests were best for Hong Kong. Thus, 'contain-ing populist pressures was an important reason for resisting the protest-ers' demands for fully open elections', Leung said. At the same time, he was aware of the social tensions that his attitude provoked. 'Lack of social mobility and affordable housing' had led to widespread protests, he stated.[31]

His political analysis ignored the Basic Law's political as well as its social provisions. The rejection of universal suffrage was in direct conflict with the principle for constitutional development set out in Article 45: 'The ultimate aim is the selection of the Chief Executive *by universal suffrage* upon nomination by a broadly representative nominating com-mittee *in accordance with democratic procedures*'. (emphasis added) Leung's argument that the government should discriminate against those whose monthly earnings were low and in favour of business interests was contrary to this Article. His failure to recognise the Law's provisions for better social services was an additional violation of its provisions.

Leung worried about the community-wide resentment that his policies provoked. He had revived the Poverty Commission on taking office in 2012, but poverty in terms of inadequate incomes remained serious, with 14 per cent of the population classified as living in poverty in 2015. The government prided itself that the figure had been held below the one million level for the third consecutive year. (That year's total was 970,000.)[32] Overall, Leung tried to make as few long-term welfare commitments as possible. Instead, he adopted a plethora of short-term initiatives, which were recited in the Legislative Council and elsewhere in a bid to silence criticism of the inadequate funding for the long-term programmes urgently required by so many of those in need of health and social welfare services.

This strategy failed. Future Chief Executive Carrie Lam Cheng Yuet-ngor, but then still Chief Secretary, was responsible for the general management of the Poverty Commission. She found herself facing attacks in 2016 that 'the poverty alleviation measures this year[were] only piecemeal hand-outs' and that 'welfare efforts were spin and of no substance'. In reply, she listed the Commission's activities. But there was a note of desperation about her attempt to find concrete achievements to quote. In her effort to demonstrate 'the commitment the Government has to assisting the poor and the needy', she was reduced to citing the Commission's public relations: 'Apart from establishing a dedicated webpage, [it had] issued over 110 press releases'.[33]

To Leung's credit, at the end of his five years in office, he abolished one of the most demeaning conditions imposed on applicants for social security benefits: the 'bad son statement', a formal declaration of refusal to provide help for one's parents. But his concession was also a move to hold down public spending. He linked it to a reduction in the number of elderly people who would qualify for social security as the minimum age for applicants was to be raised from 60 to 65.[34] This sort of trade-off seemed inconsistent with the provisions of the Basic Law.

## A faithful disciple

When Carrie Lam was campaigning for selection as Hong Kong's fourth Chief Executive, she paid considerable respect to the Basic Law. 'All the advantages of our system, rights and freedom that we enjoy are protected by the Basic Law', her election manifesto correctly declared. But she made no mention of its provisions for the rights to welfare and other social services.[35]

On this policy area, her manifesto set out the vaguest of principles:

> Whether in poverty alleviation, care for the elderly or support for
> the disadvantaged, the Government should adhere to the following
> principles in formulating policies: pro-child, pro-family, pro-work,
> and pro-user.

This list should have been expanded to include a 'pro-business model'. Her commercial outlook was made plain by the way that instead of 'the caring professions', her manifesto referred to 'the care services industry'. Behind the jargon, her goal was very specific: to give the private sector a larger role than ever before and to reduce public spending. For example, her manifesto declared: 'We will consolidate and enhance the overall medical and healthcare services through cross-sector, cross-profession collaboration as well as public-private partnership'. This 'enhancement' would include a drive 'to reduce the need for specialist and hospital services', even though these had been grossly underfunded and inadequate for the last 15 years.

Carrie Lam also promised more generous treatment for the elderly than Donald Tsang had thought they deserved. 'The ageing population should not be considered a threat or a burden to our public finances', her manifesto stated. But, once again, the policy commitment was vague and consisted mainly of pilot schemes and limited innovations rather than full-scale programmes to end, for example, the acute shortage of care places in homes for the elderly. She faithfully incorporated these restricted manifesto proposals into her 2017 Policy Address.[36]

There should have been no surprise about Carrie Lam's caution over public spending on the social services. She had adopted this outlook when she was appointed Director of Social Welfare in 2000 and had retained it as her career prospered. In dealing with policy for the elderly the year before her appointment as Chief Executive, for example, she had issued a dire warning about the costs to the community of caring for an aging population. Among the most serious deficiencies in providing for old age had been the government's failure to set up a comprehensive retirement scheme. But in a discussion of possible solutions, she suggested that the community had to choose between 'a costly universal pension scheme' and 'the consequences of inadequate funding for enhancing medical and welfare services to meet the needs of the elderly'.[37] Her comment meant, in effect, that the government had washed its hands of finding a practical and comprehensive solution for ensuring the well-being of the elderly.

## The death and burial of social rights

The process of drafting the Basic Law and then publicising its contents had created considerable community awareness by 1997 of the individual's social rights, so much so that the well-known social work professor, Nelson Chow Wing-sun, forecast a surge in welfare expectations among the community. He believed that because the Basic Law gave the people of Hong Kong 'the right to social welfare', there was 'not the slightest chance that the trend of an increasing demand for social welfare from the government will be reversed'.

Professor Chow found it difficult to see how Tung Chee Hwa could achieve his target of making the families of 'the weak and the frail' share the burden of protecting the vulnerable. An alarming situation would develop, he argued, because the supply of social services would be incapable of meeting demand. Yet the government could not provide the funding needed because of its duty under the Basic Law to maintain the low tax system, he declared. In 1998, he urged the government to warn the public that the right to enjoy social welfare would be confined to the very poorest members of the community.[38]

Professor Chow was not alone in his fears for the future. A prominent businessman and member of the Legislative Council looked back to a golden age long before the Basic Law was drafted.

> There used to be no CSSA [Comprehensive Social Security Assistance], no job referral service or Employees Retraining Scheme in Hong Kong, for the whole community attached importance to continuous self-improvement . . . Even if they became unemployed, Hong Kong people would try again in the belief that they could always make a living if they did not shrink from hardship. However, Hong Kong people have got into the habit of blaming society and refusing to find out the cause in themselves. They have become passive and rely only on the Government instead of themselves.[39]

The government lost no time in crushing hopes that the spending on social and related services would increase as the Basic Law drafters had expected. In 1997, a team from Harvard University was hired to make an assessment of Hong Kong's current health care system and its long-term affordability. Its findings, published in 1999, forecast financial difficulties ahead. The government had new ammunition for arguing that in framing social policies, conservative budgets were its most important duty under the Basic Law.[40] The assault on social rights intensified.

The following year, a high-status government advisory body whose members included leading business personalities claimed that Hong Kong's long history of sustained economic growth had undermined the work ethic of segments of the labour force. Employees had acquired a 'get rich quick' mentality and 'a dependency culture' with 'unrealistic expectations' about the government's obligations towards them.[41] There was no statistical evidence of any kind to support the allegations. The suggestion of spoiled workers was absurd in a community where trade

unions were so weak and strikes so rare. Furthermore, labour productivity had reached impressive levels in the pre-1997 period, even when
wages stagnated and income inequality had worsened.[42] But the smear
was useful ammunition in the government's campaign to limit social
services.

Chief Executives and their ministers often invoked unfavourable
economic conditions in world markets and setbacks to local business as
the justification for failing to adopt far-sighted programmes to create the
educational, medical and social welfare services which a community with
Hong Kong's proud record of self-generated prosperity deserved and
ought to be able to afford. In 2002, for example, the Financial Secretary,
Antony Leung Kam-chung, claimed that Hong Kong could suffer the
same financial catastrophes as Argentina, one of Latin America's most
troubled economies. He invoked its financial misfortunes in his Budget
Speech that year as a warning to Hong Kong and felt it necessary to
repeat the call for austerity. The absurdity of the comparison with a
Latin America state was all the more obvious because, previously, he
had explained quite clearly why Hong Kong faced no risk of suffering
similar misfortunes. But his motive in now turning to scare-mongering
was explicit: he was seeking an excuse to cut public spending.[43]

Occasionally, ministers would reveal a determination to openly defy
the Basic Law. Thus, early on, a Health and Welfare Minister had quoted
the Basic Law and its requirement that pre-1997 policies could be
modified on condition that the changes promoted '"development and
improvement" of the social welfare system'. Nevertheless, he set about
reducing government subventions to welfare agencies across the board.
These cuts were not being carefully tailored in order to minimise the
adverse effects on dementia patients, children with special needs or
those with severe disabilities. If the Basic Law were 'construed narrowly',
he openly admitted, the changes he was making to the system for financing NGOs with government grants were unlawful.[44] The minister went
ahead, anyway, with unfortunate consequences.

NGOs depended on these subventions in accepting responsibility
for delivering 80 per cent of the Social Welfare Department's services.
They warned that 'the quality and sustainability of welfare services' were
under serious threat, a danger aggravated by the economic downturn
that Hong Kong was then experiencing, which had been accompanied by 'the increasing complexity of social problems'. An additional
problem was that NGOs were labour intensive. They had little scope
for making personnel redundant because staffing standards were frequently set by legislation or licensing regulations. By 2008, the plight
of the social services had become acute, in gross disregard of the Basic
Law's provisions.[45] The government had won the battle to convince

virtually all sections of the community that social services were inherently unaffordable.

In 2009, the Legislative Council's legal team argued the case for social security cuts with generalisations about budget constraints which, as usual, were unsupported by evidence of any kind.

> While we are committed to providing an effective and sustainable safety net for the financially vulnerable, we also need to strike a reasonable balance among the interests of various sectors of the community, having regard to the long-term sustainability of our social services and the need for a rational basis on which our public resources are allocated in the light of fiscal constraints and ever-rising demands.

The legislature's legal specialists seemed to be aware that this rhetoric would not stand up to serious forensic examination. So, they invoked public opinion. But once again, their argument was based on generalisations unsubstantiated by any data.

> There is growing public disquiet about the burgeoning welfare spending and a general consensus in the community that there is room for tightening the existing residence requirement for CSSA, which is considered too lax.[46]

In any case, the provisions of the Basic Law are not supposed to be suspended because of 'public misgivings', particularly when these had been fuelled by, among other things, government television advertisements to denigrate applicants for social security, even though government data revealed no justification for these attacks.[47]

## The government fights back

The government's position seemed impregnable until 2013 when the Court of Final Appeal found it in breach of the Basic Law. As explained earlier, the Court declared that the Law's promise of social welfare rights, adequate education and other social services could not be disregarded. The following year, however, the Financial Secretary, John Tsang Chun-wah, appeared to be successfully burying the Court's decision under a mountain of statistical data. He had set up a small Working Group on Long-Term Fiscal Planning which included two prominent academic economists and two well-known accounting professionals. It prepared a portfolio of econometric and social forecasts which were published and promptly became part of conventional wisdom on budgetary affairs.[48]

Thanks to the Working Group, John Tsang was able to deliver an alarming forecast of impending financial catastrophe if the government did not immediately halt the growth of its spending on the three social services: education, health services and social welfare. Their rising costs would bring to an end Hong Kong's traditional balanced budgets, the Working Group claimed. This advisory body produced three scenarios, each of which would lead to long-term deficits. It also forecast how quickly the reputed crisis would begin. Tsang summarised their predictions in his 2014 Budget Speech. Financial catastrophe would start within:

- *seven years*, if the past pattern continued of an annual average increase of three per cent in funding for the expansion of the three social services;
- *eight years*, if the annual average increase in funding for the expansion of the three social services were cut to one to two per cent;
- *fifteen years*, if the current programmes of the three social services were frozen at their current level.

In fact, the Working Group's recommendations were not beyond challenge. They were based on the assumption that Hong Kong's economy was fragile and particularly vulnerable to fluctuations in the global economy. The Financial Secretary himself faced potential embarrassment—which he skilfully evaded—from official statistics which demonstrated Hong Kong's current prosperity and its unmatched resilience throughout its modern history. His 2014 Budget Speech, for example, had to admit that there was no real threat of financial or economic disaster. 'With per capita GDP at US$38,000, Hong Kong is now a mature economy', he said, 'Over the past three decades, the annual real GDP growth averaged 4.6 per cent'.[49] The government's accumulated reserves were equal to one-third of total GDP and were enough to finance all the government's activities even if it received no taxes, rates, fees, charges or other revenue for 22 months. There was no significant public debt. The Financial Secretary's pessimism about the future was bizarre when it was hard to identify any other advanced economy whose public finances were so robust.

Nevertheless, John Tsang set about implementing his Working Party's recommendations without delay. He shrewdly avoided launching a direct assault on the social services alone, which would have provoked considerable public alarm. Instead, he launched a general, three-year, 'efficiency enhancement' programme. All government departments were required to reduce their operating costs by two per cent over the next three years. The hardest hit would inevitably be the social services, where the public's need for schools, hospitals and related services could not be cut arbitrarily. They were labour intensive as well, which meant that smaller budgets led inevitably to staff or wage cuts. The quality of these services would come under pressure, and waiting times for the sick and the vulnerable would lengthen. The supply of social services would shrink in line with their funding, thus repeating the past policies of both Tung Chee Hwa and Donald Tsang Yam-kuen.[50] Once again, the Basic Law was being ignored.

## Business promotion

Year after year, individual Financial Secretaries had claimed that welfare was unaffordable, yet in their annual Budget Speeches, they still gave tax concessions to salary payers despite the fact that with the maximum rate set at 15 per cent, these were among the most lightly taxed group in the world. Similarly, property owners were frequently given rebates on rates. The truth was that budget surpluses had grown so large that they had become a political embarrassment. The solution was to grant tax cuts from 2007 labelled 'one-off relief'. These became permanent concessions from 2018 as surpluses continued to grow unremittingly.

From the start, it was apparent that in distributing these budget handouts, the disadvantaged were to have the lowest priority. The outcome for 2008, for example, was that cuts and waivers for profits, property and salaries taxes were worth $28 billion. The increased benefits for the disadvantaged amounted to just over half that figure. In addition, 'the government [was] to collect $6.5 billion less a year from the rich on a long-term basis'. However, 'long-term allocations' to disadvantaged groups totaled a mere $287 million.[51] In 2017, the Legislative Council's Research Office reported that of such 'one off relief' payments announced in that year's Budget Speech, 64 per cent were allocated to 'returning the surplus revenue to payers of salaries tax, profits tax and rates'. Only 16 per cent went to aiding 'grassroots families and disadvantaged groups', such as social security beneficiaries.[52]

There was seemingly endless funding available for purposes other than social and related services, especially for business projects which had potential political benefits. These handouts began with an allocation of $7.8 billion in 1999 in support of the Cyberport project which was intended to attract global IT investment.[53] Its results did not live up to original expectations, and the project was attacked by the business sector itself.

Direct subsidies for small and medium enterprises (SMEs) also started in that era even though there was ample evidence that this financial assistance had little commercial justification. These subsidies have continued ever since in spite of the original opposition from the banking industry, the Hong Kong Monetary Authority and the Treasury because of serious dangers of fraud and misuse of public funds.[54] These fears proved well-founded. Widespread abuse of subsidised loans by SMEs was uncovered in two reports by the Director of Audit.[55] Yet, in 2012, the Financial Secretary renewed a $100 billion commitment to the SME loan guarantee programme even though only a relatively small number of firms and employees were expected to benefit from this funding.[56]

By 2017, Hong Kong's SME subsidies had taken on international dimensions. They were evidence of Hong Kong's innovative economy, the minister responsible proudly announced at a Paris meeting of the Organisation for Economic Co-operation and Development (OECD). Hong Kong had recently launched a $500 million 'pilot program to help SMEs improve productivity and upgrade business processes by using cutting-edge technologies', he said.[57] No indications were provided of the actual benefits which could be expected from the latest subsidies for SMEs.

Carrie Lam's Chief Executive election manifesto promised to maintain this generosity. She planned to establish 'a two-tier profits tax system with tax reduction of 40 per cent for tens of thousands of enterprises'. 'Small, medium and startup enterprises' would pay 10 per cent instead of 16.5 per cent on the first $2 million of their profits. In addition, there would be tax concessions designed to 'attract internationally well-known and recognized leading companies to set up in Hong Kong'.[58] These latter tax incentives were hard to justify as necessary in an economy as open and sophisticated as Hong Kong, and which already had minimal tax rates. Furthermore, the local market was not the target for the international firms she wanted to attract. The largest share of their profits would be generated offshore and would be automatically tax free in Hong Kong anyway.

## Taxing truths

Although Financial Secretaries have invoked the Basic Law and its call to avoid budget deficits as the primary explanation for clamping down on funding for the social services, the real priority has been personal and commercial interests: to hold down taxation and, where possible, to reduce it. In this context, almost always ignored is the flexibility of the tax environment before 1997. By current standards, it was by no means either fixed or even low. The rate of corporate profits tax varied considerably during the two decades before reunification. During the 1980s, it stood at 18.5 per cent for three years, while the high for the 1990s was 17.5 per cent. These fluctuations allowed Financial Secretaries to adapt to changing business conditions. Uncertainties about the rate had caused no business panic, and the economy had continued to flourish.[59]

Rarely quoted are the statistics on the tax paid by individuals. In this century, the average taxpayer has paid less than 7.5 per cent of total earnings in tax. The top 20 per cent of Hong Kong's earners, which receives 60 per cent of total household incomes, has paid less than 10 per cent of its incomes in tax on average.[60] These low tax bills for the top earners—and not just the average household—are only part of Hong Kong's remarkable tax concessions to the affluent. Capital gains, dividends and inheritances are entirely untaxed. Profits and salaries earned outside Hong Kong are not subject to taxation.[61] It seems obvious that tax rates for the highest earners could be raised without breach of the Basic Law's low taxation principle.

As for complying with the Basic Law's provisions for maintaining the pre-1997 tax system, the government showed little hesitation about introducing a completely new type of taxation which had not been envisaged by the Law's drafters. Financial Secretary Henry Tang Ying-yen maintained a determined drive between 2003 and 2007 to introduce a goods and services tax (GST). The case made for this innovation was that higher-income groups were making an excessive contribution to salaries tax. Introduction of a GST scheme would offer an excellent solution, the government argued. It would be 'based on the "capacity to pay" principle' and would expand the tax net, thus 'enhancing the community's sense of civic responsibility'.[62] Almost unanimously, the public rejected the proposal, with business leaders among the most vocal opponents of GST.

Also overlooked in discussions of financial policy have been the budgetary consequences of a refusal to finance social services which the Basic Law had identified as of special importance. Education provides a striking example of this problem. The colonial administration and its business collaborators stubbornly resisted the introduction of compulsory education. In 1964, for example, the Financial Secretary claimed that the introduction of free and compulsory education would require direct taxation to more than double, which turned out to be the grossest exaggeration.[63]

A significant number of children were receiving full-time secondary education in the 1970s, even before it was compulsory.[64] Business leaders saw this trend as a threat to their profits. In 1978, a member of the Legislative Council (a prominent textile tycoon) attacked proposed legislation to introduce free and compulsory schooling for all up to the age of 16 because of 'a danger that more young people than ever before will choose to continue full-time education rather than employment'.[65] The introduction of free and compulsory secondary school education that year created no such crisis, of course.[66]

In 1998, the government started to face the bill for past defects in the educational system. Official statistics indicate that as Hong Kong's recession started that year, workers who had had no or only limited access to full-time education in the 1970s accounted for a high proportion of the unemployed receiving CSSA.[67] Ill-educated workers who were victims of colonial reluctance to fund schools could no longer find jobs and needed state help to survive.

A similar threat has emerged in this century, although at the other end of the educational spectrum. Chapter 6 describes how the government refused to raise the 1989 ceiling on the number of subsidised first-year university places. Instead, the government encouraged a boom in self-financed post-secondary courses, which lead to qualifications that have little credibility in the job market. The students' future career prospects are doubtful. This situation was not a development which the Basic Law endorses. Carrie Lam's election pledges included a promise of more generous funding for the social services, particularly education, which seemed a significant retreat from the austerity practised by her predecessors. However, her actual proposal proved to be poorly designed and offered only limited improvements to the struggling post-secondary education sector. Thus, in practice, there was to be no radical break with the past.

### The Premier finally prevails

The Working Group's vigorous warnings about the financial damage and economic costs of long-term budget deficits were extremely helpful to the government. Its report had come as close as it dared to suggesting that the government's annual budgets were already on the verge of breaching the Law's requirements for 'the prudent management of the public finances'.[68] But the Group and its role came to a sudden end in 2017.

At the ceremony to mark Carrie Lam's appointment as Chief Executive in April, Premier Li Keqiang listed the well-being of the people of Hong Kong as one of her three major tasks. She must, he said, 'pay attention to improving quality of life'.[69] Unlike his predecessors, Premier Li and his instruction on social priorities had some effect. The Group's policy prescriptions were discarded. But not without reluctance. In August, Carrie Lam was still defending the basic credibility of the Working Group's analysis.[70] Finally, in October, she distanced herself from its pessimistic forecasts and their use in drafting the annual budget.[71]

### Conclusion

Spending on social services was anathema to the business sector which had a dominant position in Hong Kong politics and which played a major role in the selection of Chief Executives. And Chief Executives themselves and their ministers shared the business outlook. Tax concessions for salary earners and property owners and subsidised loans for smaller businesses were continuing evidence that Hong Kong's rulers have long had ample money to spend while crying 'unaffordable' about improved social services, thus denying the public its rights under the Basic Law.

Since 1998, Chief Executives and business leaders repeatedly claimed that Hong Kong was in imminent danger of losing its markets and would face budgetary collapse unless spending on social and related services was cut. The predictions of impending doom ignored completely a defining feature of Hong Kong's open, competitive and resilient economy: a survival culture which has constantly adapted to adverse political and economic conditions. On this alone, its people could validly claim that their right to enjoy the social benefits conferred by the Basic Law was no threat to Hong Kong's prosperity. Furthermore, the glowing history of past achievements left Chief Executives and business leaders with no justification for denigrating the community as likely to abuse these rights. The historical record ought not to have been ignored when predicting how Hong Kong would cope with future challenges.

A striking feature of this chapter is the way that constitutional rights, social justice and caring government disappeared under a tide of government book-keeping. Yet, the community continued to assume that those in power were mostly sincere and the best placed and the best informed to make the right decisions for Hong Kong. In consequence, the Basic Law continued to be enforced on a selective basis which was in direct conflict with the drafters' intentions and which denied the people of Hong Kong important rights clearly conferred by this Law.

## Notes

1. Article 136 states: 'On the basis of the previous educational system, the Government of the Hong Kong Special Administrative Region shall, on its own, formulate policies on the development and improvement of education including . . . the allocation of funds.' Article 137 adds: 'Educational institutions of all kinds may retain their autonomy and enjoy academic freedom.' Article 138 states: 'The Government of the Hong Kong Special Administrative Region shall, on its own, formulate policies to develop and to improve medical and health services.'
2. Professor Xiao Weiyun's status as a leading interpreter of the Basic Law is evident from his career. Prior to 1997, he was Convenor of the Political System Panel of the Basic Law Drafting Committee and was a member of the Preparatory Committee. His key role as an official expert on the Basic Law continued after 1997. On his significance, see Yiu-chung Wong, 'Absorption into a Leninist Polity: A Study of the Interpretations by the National People's Congress of the Basic Law in Post-Handover Hong Kong', in *Trends of Political Participation in Hong Kong*, ed. Joseph Y. S. Cheng (Hong Kong: City University of Hong Kong Press, 2014), 45–46. Professor Xiao's book, *One Country, Two Systems: An Account of the Drafting of the Hong Kong Basic Law*, was originally published (in Chinese) in 1993.

3. Xiao Weiyun, *One Country, Two Systems: An Account of the Drafting of the Hong Kong Basic Law* (Beijing: Peking University Press, 2001), 448, 205.

4. Xiao, *One Country, Two Systems: An Account of the Drafting of the Hong Kong Basic Law*, 206.

5. For an important example of confidence in the government's right to interpret the Basic Law to match official policy, see Legal Service Division, 'Subcommittee on Poverty Alleviation: Paper on the Constitutionality of the One-Year Continuous Residence Requirement for the Comprehensive Social Security Assistance Scheme' (LC Paper No. LS18/09-10), 26 November 2009), 3.

6. See, for example, Anson Chan Fang On-sang, *Government Information Services* (*GIS* hereafter), 30 April 1999.

7. For example, Dr York Chow Yat-ngok, Secretary for Health, Welfare and Food, *Hong Kong Hansard* (*HH* hereafter), 14 June 2006, 8278–89.

8. These remarks were made by James Tien Pei-chun, Liberal Party Chairman and eldest son of one of Hong Kong's most successful textile tycoons, *HH*, 15 February 2006, 4632.

9. Premier Wen Jiabao, 'Hong Kong's Traditional Advantages as Int'l Financial Center Unchanged: Premier Wen', *New China News Agency* (*NCNA* hereafter), 14 March 2011.

10. 'Premier Wen Jiabao Attends Press Conference of the 5th Session of the 11th NPC', *NCNA*, 14 March 2012.

11. Premier Li Keqiang, 'Premier Li Grants Appointment Certificate to Incoming HKSAR Chief Executive', *NCNA*, 11 April 2017.

12. For a review of the courts' record in handling such cases, see Karen Kong, 'Adjudicating Social Welfare Rights in Hong Kong', *I•CON* 10, no. 2 (2012): 588–99.

13. Mr Justice Ribeiro PJ in *Kong Yunming vs Director of Social Welfare* FACV No. 2 of 2013, 18, 41–42, accessed 18 December 2013, http://legalref.judiciary. gov.hk/lrs/ common/ju/ju_frame.jsp?DIS=90670&currpage=T

14. See Matthew Cheung Kin-Chung, Secretary for Labour and Welfare, *HH*, 8 January 2014, 5157–59.

15. Tung Chee Hwa, Chief Executive, *GIS*, 1 May 1997.

16. Tung, Chief Executive, *GIS*, 20 September 1997.

17. During his first month in office, the labour force, for example, was warned not to expect improvements in wages and working conditions. Tung, Chief Executive, *GIS*, 31 July 1997.

18. Eliza W. Y. Lee, 'The Politics of Welfare Developmentalism in Hong Kong', *Social Policy and Development Programme Paper No. 21* (ISSN 1020-8208, August 2005), United Nations Research Institute for Social Development, 6.

19. Tung, Chief Executive, *GIS*, 19 September 2000.

20. Donald Tsang Yam-kuen, Chief Executive, *GIS*, 17 October 2006.

21. Donald Tsang, Chief Executive, *HH*, 27 June 2005, 8944.

22. Donald Tsang, Chief Executive, *HH*, 12 January 2006, 3881.

23. Donald Tsang, Chief Executive, *HH*, 14 January 2010, 4247.

24. Donald Tsang, Chief Executive, *HH*, 12 October 2011, 29.

25. The average household income of new arrivals from the Mainland in 2011 was 30 per cent lower than the overall average for Hong Kong, but these

newcomers were 20 per cent better off on average than the arrivals in 2001. Ironically, the Welfare Minister used this census information to counter complaints in the legislature from pro-Mainland members against Mainland immigration. (Matthew Cheung, Secretary for Labour and Welfare, *HH*, 22 January 2014, 5798.) Only 68 per cent of new arrivals in 2001 had completed secondary or higher education. The 2011 figure was 85 per cent, significantly higher than the average of 77 per cent for the overall Hong Kong population. For educational attainments, see 2011 Population Census Office, *2011 Population Census Main Report: Volume I* (Hong Kong: Census and Statistics Department, 2012), 81.

26. Donald Tsang, Chief Executive, *GIS*, 7 April 2006.

27. Donald Tsang, Chief Executive, *HH*, 27 June 2005, 8942.

28. Donald Tsang, Chief Executive, *GIS*, October 2005.

29. Health and Medical Development Advisory Committee, *Building a Healthy Tomorrow: Discussion Paper on the Future Service Delivery Model for Our Healthcare System* (Hong Kong: Health, Welfare and Food Bureau, 2005), 8 n1; Food and Health Bureau, *Your Health Your Life Healthcare Reform Consultation Document* (Hong Kong: SAR Government, 2008), 14–15.

30. 'C Y Leung Makes Opening Remarks at Chief Executive Candidates' forum 19 March 2012', http://www.ceo.gov.hk/eng/pdf/speeches_elect/sp20120319.pdf

31. Leung's test of who should not qualify for full political rights was all those with monthly earnings of US$1,800 or less. Keith Bradsher and Chris Buckley, 'Hong Kong Leader Reaffirms Unbending Stance on Elections', *New York Times*, 20 October 2014.

32. The 2016 figure was 995,800. It was not published until after Leung had left office. Matthew Cheung, Chief Secretary, *GIS*, 17 November 2017.

33. Carrie Lam, Chief Secretary, *HH*, 18 February 2016, 5454–58.

34. Leung, Chief Executive, *HH*, 18 January 2017, 3136–37.

35. Unless otherwise indicated, quotations that follow are from Carrie Lam, 'We Connect: Connecting for Consensus and a Better Future: Manifesto of Carrie Lam Chief Executive Election 2017' (Campaign Office of Carrie Lam, February 2017), 6, 35, 38.

36. Carrie Lam, Chief Executive, *HH*, 11 October 2017.

37. Carrie Lam, Chief Secretary, *GIS*, 12 April 2016.

38. Nelson Chow, 'Social Welfare and the Challenges of a New Era', in *Hong Kong Economy and Society: Challenges in the New Era*, ed. Wong Siu-lun and Toyojiro Maruya (Hong Kong: Centre of Asian Studies, University of Hong Kong, 1998), 146–47.

39. Hui Cheung-ching, *HH*, 10 May 2000, 6265–66.

40. For examples of this overriding government priority, see Anson Chan Fang On-sang, Chief Secretary, *GIS*, 30 April 1999.

41. Commission on Strategic Development, *Bringing the Vision to Life: Hong Kong's Long-Term Development Needs and Goals* (Hong Kong: Central Policy Unit, 2000), 16–17.

42. On productivity and income distribution during this period, see John Dodsworth and Dubravko Mihaljek, *Hong Kong, China: Growth, Structural Change, and Economic Stability During the Transition* (Washington, DC:

International Monetary Fund, 1997), 6; Hon-Kwong Lui, *Income Inequality and Economic Development* (Hong Kong: City University of Hong Kong Press, 1997), 46–49.

43. Antony Leung Kam-chung, Financial Secretary, *HH*, 6 March 2002, 4141 and *GIS*, 2 February, 14 and 22 May 2002.

44. Dr Yeoh Eng-kiong, Secretary for Health and Welfare, *HH*, 5 April 2000, 5631.

45. Lump Sum Grant Independent Review Committee, 'Review Report on the Lump Sum Grant Subvention System December 2008', 4, 8, 12, 13, 38, 46.

46. The quotations are from Legal Service Division, 'Subcommittee on Poverty Alleviation: Paper on the Constitutionality of the One-Year Continuous Residence Requirement for the Comprehensive Social Security Assistance Scheme' (LC Paper No. LS18/09-10), 26 November 2009), 3, 5.

47. For comprehensive, long-term data demonstrating that social security benefits in Hong Kong had not created a dependency culture and how a majority of those qualified for benefits did not receive them, see Leo F. Goodstadt, *Poverty in the Midst of Affluence: How Hong Kong Mismanaged Its Prosperity*, 2nd edition (Hong Kong: Hong Kong University Press, 2014), 175–76.

48. The Working Group's report was far from complete. See its reasoning, for example, for excluding public housing from social spending. The Treasury Branch, Financial Services, and the Treasury Bureau, 'Report of the Working Group on Long-Term Fiscal Planning (Phase 2)', 116.

49. John Tsang Chun-wah, Financial Secretary, *HH*, 26 February 2014, 8310.

50. John Tsang, Financial Secretary, *GIS*, 9 October 2014 and *HH*, 25 February 2015, 7195.

51. The detailed analysis was undertaken by a legislator, Dr Fernando Cheung Chiu-hung, *HH*, 16 April 2008, 6109–11.

52. Research Office, 'The 2017–2018 Budget March 2017', Research Brief, Issue No. 3 (2016–17) (Hong Kong: Legislative Council Secretariat. 2017), 12.

53. For details, see Press Release, *GIS*, 3 August 2000; Rahul Jacob, 'Hong Kong in Cyberport Deal', *Financial Times*, 17 May 2000; 'Secret Deal on Cyberport Dismissed', *GIS*, 16 March 1999.

54. Tung, Chief Executive, *GIS*, 2 December 1999; Market Research Division, 'Survey of the Financing Situation of Small and Medium-Sized Enterprises', *Hong Kong Monetary Authority Quarterly Report*, October 2000, 38; Donald Tsang, Chief Executive, *GIS*, 8 December 2008.

55. The determination to meet requests for loans regardless of the borrowers' merits was documented on almost every page of Audit Commission, *Report 39*, 'Chapter 5: Special Finance Scheme for Small and Medium Enterprises' (Hong Kong, 15 October 2002). The persistence of abuses was well illustrated in Audit Commission, *Report No. 47*, 'Chapter 4: Four Small and Medium Enterprise Funding Schemes' (Hong Kong, 23 October 2006), especially 13, 15, 31–32. The Audit reports uncovered abuses not only in schemes guaranteeing bank loans but across a range of business support initiatives.

56. An estimated 29,800 enterprises, each employing an average of four workers might benefit from the HK$100 billion loan guarantee according to the

Commerce and Economic Development Bureau, *Item for Finance Committee*, HEAD 152 Subhead 700, 'New Item "SME Financing Guarantee Scheme— Special Concessionary Measures"' (FCR(2012-13)12, April 2012), 2, 7.

57. Gregory So Kam-leung, Secretary for Commerce and Economic Development, *GIS*, 8 June 2017.

58. Quotations are from Carrie Lam, 'We Connect: Connecting for Consensus and a Better Future; Manifesto of Carrie Lam Chief Executive Election 2017', 19. See also Chief Executive-elect, *GIS*, 23 June 2017.

59. Financial Bureau, *Profits Tax Review Consultation Document* (Government Secretariat, July 1997), Appendix A: 'Changes in Profits Tax Rate'.

60. Census and Statistics Department, *2011 Population Census: Thematic Report Household Income Distribution in Hong Kong* (Hong Kong: Census and Statistics Department, 2012), 'Table 7.4 Summary Statistics on Households in the 9th and 10th Decile Groups', 122; Census and Statistics Department, *2016 Population By-Census: Thematic Report Household Income Distribution in Hong Kong* (Hong Kong: Census and Statistics Department, 2017), 'Table 7.4 Summary Statistics on Households in the 9th and 10th Decile Groups', 130.

61. Property taxes and rates, together with minor excise duties, are light. (Tobacco is the exception in modern times and for health reasons.) On the tax system and its history, see Michael Littlewood, *Taxation without Representation: The History of Hong Kong's Troublingly Successful Tax System* (Hong Kong: Hong Kong University, 2010).

62. 'Reforming Hong Kong's Tax System Consultation Document' (2006), 4, 6, 16, 25. http://www.taxreform.gov.hk/eng/document.htm. See also Financial Services and the Treasury Branch, 'Public Consultation on Tax Reform Final Report' (June 2007).

63. John (later Sir John) Cowperthwaite, Financial Secretary, *HH*, 26 February 1964, 52.

64. For a fuller account of the background, see Goodstadt, *Poverty in the Midst of Affluence: How Hong Kong Mismanaged Its Prosperity*, 121-2.

65. Francis Yuan-hao Tien, *HH*, 30 March 1978, 696; Kenneth J. Topley, Director of Education, *HH*, 12 April 1978, 737.

66. See Philip (later Sir Philip) Haddon-Cave, Financial Secretary, *HH*, 1 March 1978, 542.

67. On age distribution of the unemployed, see 'Statistics on Comprehensive Social Security Assistance Scheme, 1996 to 2006', *Hong Kong Monthly Digest of Statistics July 2007*, 'Table 4 Percentage distribution of unemployed CSSA recipients by sex and age group as at end-2006', FA10. On their inadequate educational backgrounds, see Dr York Chow Yat-ngok, Secretary for Health, Welfare and Food, *HH*, 29 June 2005, 'Table 3 Number of CSSA Recipients by Educational Attainment, 2001 to 2004', 9066.

68. The Treasury Branch, 'Report of the Working Group on Long-Term Fiscal Planning (Phase 2)', 118, 161.

69. The three tasks the Premier gave the new Chief Executives were: 'developing the economy, improving quality of life and enhancing exchanges and cooperation with the Mainland'. Premier Li Keqiang, 'Premier Li Grants Appointment Certificate to Incoming HKSAR Chief Executive', *NCNA*, 11 April 2017.

70. Carrie Lam, Chief Executive, *GIS*, 4 August 2017.
71. She revealed this change of heart in an exclusive interview with a newspaper. Interestingly, most of the political and media attention was captured by the low limit she proposed in the same interview for the supply of public rental housing. Carrie Lam, Chief Executive, *Ming Pao Daily*, 27 October 2017.

# 2
# From public service to ministerial mismanagement

Tung Chee Hwa began his term as Chief Executive with an assertion of his high opinion of the civil service.

> Providing consistent financial management, high quality regulation and forward looking infrastructure planning is only part of what Hong Kong's civil service provides. Overall, it is a model for open, accountable, forward looking public administration, headed by people of the very highest calibre. Anywhere would count themselves fortunate to have them: I can assure you that I am keeping them. Maintaining the quality of the civil service is vital to the confidence that we in Hong Kong and our partners overseas have in our prospects.[1]

From 1998, however, this prestigious status evaporated rapidly. The civil service was to be severely tested in the next two decades by the mismanagement of public administration caused by the political inexperience and incompetence of Chief Executives and their teams, their lack of administrative skills, their misguided policies and their inability to manage relations with the Mainland effectively.

Most serious of all was the deliberate misinterpretation of the Basic Law and its financial provisions. Financial stringency became the foremost dogma of those in power, as the previous chapter explained, and the civil service became a prime target for financial cutbacks and redundancies. This chapter demonstrates the damage done to the effective functioning of the civil service and the painful consequences for the overall well-being of the community. It highlights how policymaking became dominated by the pursuit of business-based models rather than how to provide the high standards of public services to which the people of Hong Kong were entitled in a city they had made so prosperous.

The chapter begins with Chief Executives themselves. Initially, Tung had assumed that after the reunification with the Mainland, the public would lose interest in politics because patriotism, the national interest and the sheer excitement of the new era would take command. He was proved wrong. In response to an increase in political activism, he was induced to introduce a ministerial system to provide a degree of accountability for the new Special Administrative Region government. Career civil servants were replaced by political appointees who would be responsible for making policy, mobilising public support and overseeing government departments. This initiative proved a failure. The ministerial system was to remain flawed under the leadership of all four of the first Chief Executives.

The analysis then turns to the practical consequences for civil service performance of seeking to imitate the business world. Chief Executives felt free to ignore the serious costs—economic as well as social—of failing to ensure that there were enough civil servants to meet the needs of the community. The shortfall began in 1998 when Tung introduced his Enhanced Productivity Programme (EPP). Its objectives were to reduce public expenditure, to privatise as much of the public sector as possible and to make government bureaux and departments adopt business practices. In the process, the EPP was to leave them acutely short of the funds and staff needed to carry out their basic duties, including enforcement of the law.

For the next two decades, the civil service had to struggle with demands to deliver new and improved services without being granted additional financial resources, even when supplying essential social services where the profit motive and short-term planning should have no place.[2] Among the long-term consequences was a forced tolerance among government departments of unlawful behaviour—including corrupt practices and damage to public property and safety. Staff shortages created scandals in almost every branch of the government. These were reported in the media, investigated by the Director of Audit and the Ombudsman, deplored by the Legislative Council and confessed to by helpless heads of government departments. However, they were mostly disregarded by Chief Executives and rarely acknowledged by the ministers responsible.

Finally, this chapter examines the fate of the Social Welfare Department which proved to be, arguably, the most serious casualty of the EPP. The Department's inability to survive intact brought severe, long-term suffering to very large numbers of Hong Kong families. The irony was that the Department had never sought to use a bureaucratic or a 'statist' model to supply its services. On the contrary, it had developed highly efficient partnerships between the Department's professionals and non-government organisations (NGO) in the voluntary sector (formerly called 'charities'). These partnerships were deliberately dismantled from 2000, and their place was taken by a system based on business practices even though social services require long-term planning and training and NGOs should be motivated not by profits and bonuses but by professionalism and personal dedication.

## The transfer of power

As the first Chief Executive took office, a key question was how Hong Kong's administration ought to adjust to the new political environment. The Basic Law seriously curtailed the powers of the legislature. Legislative Council continued to have a crucial financial veto: its members could refuse to approve government financial proposals, both taxation and expenditure. They could also summon ministers and officials to give an account of themselves. But they ceased to be 'legislators'. The Basic Law stripped them of the right to propose legislation relating to 'government policies' and the 'political structure or the operation of government'. These restrictions were extremely far-reaching. Legislators could review and criticise the government's legislative proposals and recommend amendments, and they could debate government performance. But they had lost most of their former law-making function.[3] Over the years, this limited role was to lead to a loss of trust between ministers and directly elected legislators in particular, leading to increasing disruption of Legislative Council business by filibustering and similar protest tactics.[4]

The crucial importance to good government of a legislative council with elected members had become clear in 1997–1998 when it had been replaced by a temporary 'provisional legislature' (ten of whose members had failed to win seats in the 1995 elections for the Legislative Council). This unelected body marked 'a massive return to the politics of patronage and clientelism' of the colonial administration's pre-election era, according to a leading constitutional expert.[5] Its appointed membership was dominated by representatives of business and professional groups. Despite their financial and commercial expertise, members showed themselves to be thoroughly confused about the economic situation during the 1997–1998 Asian financial crisis and the recession which Tung Chee Hwa's policies were creating.[6]

As deflation hit the economy, Donald Tsang Yam-kuen, the Financial Secretary, insisted that there was no alternative: 'The hard truth is that in this world in which we live, there is no easy path, no economic Promised Land . . . even if it did, I am not the Moses who can lead our community to it'.[7] But after direct elections to the Legislative Council were held in May 1998, there was a dramatic change in the political environment. The newly elected legislators rejected claims that nothing could be done to halt economic disaster. The differences between political parties were shelved for the time being as they cooperated in drafting proposals to compel Tung and his Financial Secretary to take active measures to counter the downturn. Within a month, the government had produced two packages of economic recovery measures.[8]

In parallel, the government was being hit by a series of scandals which were seen as evidence of administrative and professional incompetence within the civil service.[9] The list of these highly embarrassing management failures was alarming. The normal measures for controlling epidemics had not been implemented fast enough to deal with an outbreak of avian flu in 1997.[10] The new airport's facilities were not fully operational on the official inauguration date in 1998, at which China's President, Jiang Zemin, had agreed to officiate.[11] The Housing Authority uncovered a construction racket which dated back to 1996. Public outrage mounted as a Legislative Council investigation in 2000 identified considerable management failures by the Authority. Official responses to controversial events often seemed misleading or downright deceptive. For example, officials at first tried to play down the airport's problems but were quickly induced by the new Legislative Council to be far more forthcoming.[12]

## Excessive expectations

As the Provisional Legislature was discrediting itself and civil service scandals proliferated, Tung Chee Hwa came under increasing political pressure. A consensus developed among legislators and political parties, business leaders and senior civil servants themselves that the most effective remedy for deteriorating standards of administration would be to increase the government's accountability. The simplest way to achieve this goal, it was widely believed, would be the introduction of a ministerial system. Government bureaux should be headed by suitable persons who were not part of the bureaucracy. They would take personal responsibility for the programmes and services under their control and for developing new initiatives to meet changing conditions and public expectations. This ministerial system seemed simple and straightforward. It had been adopted by most advanced economies and seemed to foster accountability.

Initially, Tung Chee Hwa was sceptical about whether ministers would be the right solution. He worried that, for Hong Kong, the introduction of a ministerial system would not be so simple. For a start, he said, Hong Kong's political system was incomplete, and the introduction of universal suffrage had still to be achieved. In 1999, he tried to counter demands for the appointment of ministers with a warning that 'it is not the opportune time for taking this idea into consideration'. Considerable caution would be required in making such a move, he stated, because 'the implementation of a ministerial system entails the reform of the entire constitutional system'. A more urgent priority according to the Basic Law, he went on, was its 'blueprint . . . for the political development of Hong Kong' through democratic initiatives which needed to be implemented and allowed to operate before considering other 'major changes'.[13]

But demands for increased accountability continued to grow. In late 2001, Tung announced that he was hard at work seeking a formula for turning senior officials into politically appointed ministers.[14] The following year, he announced that ministers would be appointed under a 'Principal Officials Accountability System' (POAS). These would be political appointees, selected by him and answerable to him. They would replace civil servants as heads of bureaux, he explained, and would take over the power to 'formulate policies, explain policy decisions, market policy proposals and gain the support of the Legislative Council and the public'.[15] In short, civil servants were no longer responsible for running the government. The new status of senior civil servants was summed up neatly by Donald Tsang, now Chief Secretary: 'The simple fact of the matter is if [an official] is not delivering what the [minister], who is the boss wants, the [official] will be removed, at least sent sideways'.[16]

Nevertheless, the radical restructuring of Hong Kong's administration was a dangerous gamble. It was far from clear that political appointees answering to the Chief Executive would lead to the sort of open and accountable government that the people of Hong Kong were seeking or that a ministerial system would avoid the civil service fiascos that had been so embarrassing in the first years of Tung's rule. Almost immediately, the fundamental weaknesses of the new system became all too apparent. Tung and his political appointees failed the most important test of good government: crisis management. One incident after another left new appointees discredited or humiliated.

- In 2002, a contentious proposal to delist low-value shares from the Hong Kong Stock Exchange was approved, which promptly provoked market outrage. At first, the Financial Services Minister was reported to have said that he had not been informed of this decision in advance. But he then agreed that he had been given a written briefing which he had not read. The proposal was withdrawn.
- Later that year, the Education Minister, a prominent academic, unveiled a plan to amalgamate the Chinese University of Hong Kong with the Hong Kong University of Science and Technology, whether they liked it or not. The proposal was withdrawn after a wave of protests. He claimed that he had only been expressing a personal view, not government policy.
- The following March, the Financial Secretary in his Budget Speech proposed a steep increase in the tax on first registration of motor

vehicles. The media discovered almost immediately that he had
bought a new car ahead of the tax's announcement. He resigned.

• The Security Minister was determined to introduce new and
unpopular security legislation. In July 2003, a 500,000-strong
public protest took place. She had to resign.[17]

• When the severe acute respiratory syndrome (SARS) epidemic
began in 2003, Tung's administration had no 'clear chain of
command [or] contingency plan' for dealing with such an emergency. Government 'at the highest levels' ignored warnings from
front-line professionals about the mounting crisis. The introduction of measures to halt the epidemic was hindered by the inability of Tung and his political appointees to understand that in the
health sector, the government must comply with laws and regulations.[18] The Health Minister became the scapegoat and had to
resign despite his personal endeavours to halt the epidemic.

POAS was to prove no deterrent to ministerial inadequacy and misconduct as scandals were uncovered among the appointees of later
Chief Executives. In 2011, for example, it became widely known that
Donald Tsang had felt compelled to warn ministers and other Executive
Council members to rectify illegal building works in property which they
owned.[19] Tsang himself was an offender, it was later reported.[20] Media
revelations followed of continuing disregard for the legal ban on unauthorised modifications by the ruling élite and, in some cases, by their
wives.[21] This property scandal resulted in considerable loss of public
respect for Tsang's administration.

By the time the third Chief Executive took office, it had become
extremely difficult to find individuals willing to accept invitations to
head bureaux because of the low prestige with the community that a
ministerial post conferred. In addition, there was a growing realisa-
tion that accountability was not solely to the Chief Executive and that
he was not free to hire and fire ministers. Mainland officials played the
major role in vetting a Chief Executive's recommendations for ministerial appointments. Mainland officials' approval was also required in
deciding who could be dismissed. Chief Executives did not have the
undisputed control over membership of their ministerial teams that
Tung had seemed to expect when introducing POAS in 2002.

Thus, the ministerial system never managed to establish its credibility
with the community. The appointees had been entrusted with almost
undisputed authority (apart from a duty of obedience to the ruling
Chief Executive), but few possessed the qualifications for a ministerial
post. Several came into office ignorant of the responsibilities and legal
duties of the bureaux and departments they were to control. Not many
had much talent for lobbying the Legislative Council or mobilising

community support. All were unelected and thus enjoyed limited public esteem.

## Joined-up administration

The ministerial system, it had been believed originally, would free the Chief Executive from a civil service bureaucracy that was accused of hindering his personal direction of the government. In future, he would take direct control of policymaking and government priorities and of coordinating implementation across bureaux. Because Tung's team of ministers answered to him alone, he had to deal personally with every minister on every policy issue where serious problems might arise.[22] Nothing in his past had equipped him for coping with this gargantuan challenge. To add to his burdens, where were the qualified 'political' ministers to be found for a society as complex and sophisticated as Hong Kong and with such an advanced, global economy?

In fact, Tung was dismantling the former coordinated system of government. Before the ministerial system was adopted, there had been an integrated administrative structure designed to ensure a high degree of cooperation between bureaux and departments. In future, there would be no clear arrangements to ensure cooperation between them. Instead, the management of government was being shared among self-contained 'silos', a management model which may have a useful role in the business world but which made 'joined-up government' increasingly unattainable.

Tung's successors were caught in this trap on an even larger scale. Responsibilities for the same policy issues were often divided among several ministers, and many bureaux were given oversight of several services which had nothing in common. To take the more striking examples:

- In 2006, there was a Secretary for Health, Welfare and Food, which seemed to have some logic. By 2017, there was a Secretary for Labour and Welfare. The roles, the challenges and the statutory duties for which the Labour and the Social Welfare Departments were responsible did not overlap. For example, a high percentage of the Social Welfare Department's clients were excluded from the labour market because they were elderly or had disabilities.[23]
- In 2007, there had been a Secretary for Housing, Planning and Lands, which seemed a rational combination of duties. By 2017, there was a Secretary for Transport and Housing. In that order, with no apparent justification for combining these two responsibilities or giving transport pride of place. Responsibility for Planning, Lands, Buildings had been assigned to the Secretary for

Development, together with oversight of the management of the private sector's housing stock. In handling this last responsibility, the Secretary for Home Affairs also had an important role.

The third Chief Executive, Leung Chun-ying, had made the restructuring of public administration an item in his 2012 Election Manifesto. He entrusted this task to Carrie Lam Cheng Yuet-ngor, his newly appointed Chief Secretary and future successor.[24] She seemed to regard the assignment as daunting even though she took pride in her 30 years of public service. 'These days government businesses are very complicated', she said', and 'you cannot have one bureau or one department that is capable of handling [an entire] issue'. She was sure, nevertheless, of the underlying principle to be followed: 'It has to be different parts of the Government being pulled together in one direction, in one heart, in one mind, to serve the people of Hong Kong,' she declared. How such unison was to be achieved remained obscure. 'We have to be more or less like [a] federal government', she insisted, without clarifying how the ministerial system should be amended to achieve this goal.

An important item on Carrie Lam's agenda for restructuring the administration was 'more livelihood projects that would touch the hearts of the people'. Her immediate plan of action focused on areas where a high proportion of the population lived in public housing. 'Many of [them] are on social security, so they have very low buying power', she said, and could not afford to buy in regular retail outlets. This was an unintended indictment of the welfare system: the Chief Secretary was admitting that a significant proportion of those on social security could barely afford a subsistence existence. Her solution did not include increasing the inadequate welfare benefits, however. Instead, she wanted to subsidise the rents of 'hawkers, small businesses, individual entrepreneurs . . . to provide more shopping outlets'. She also suggested that some shops were using monopolistic practices to keep prices up. She made no mention of the fact that two months later, the Competition Ordinance would come into effect, which would protect the people of Hong Kong from unfair trade practices and thus weaken the case for the subsidies she had proposed. This was 'gesture' politics. It might 'touch hearts' but the daily burdens of low-income groups were not significantly lightened.

Carrie Lam also tried to show how delegation of authority would improve administrative performance. The example which she cited with pride was public lifts. After extensive consultations at district level, she had already begun work, she said, on 'co-ordinating with the various departments' for a programme to install lifts 'throughout the territory' to enable those with mobility difficulties to have access to footbridges and pedestrian walkways.[25] The project seemed admirable from a welfare point of view, although the high priority assigned to this proposal was open to dispute.

In practice, this initiative to provide more open and responsive government proved to be another example of 'gesture' politics. Public involvement was minimal and limited to an invitation to District Councils to submit suggestions for additional lifts, the Transport Minister later reported. Actual decision-making could not be delegated to the Councils themselves because the technical feasibility of their proposals depended on highly complex factors (which the Minister explained in detail). It was plain that although District Councils would be allowed to recommend locations for three additional lifts each (initially, at any rate), the Highways Department must continue to have full control over Hong Kong's lifts.[26] In 2017, there was embarrassing criticism of the failure to implement the lift programme, with the media pointing out that the delay was all the more deplorable because, in fact, Carrie Lam's programme had not been truly original. It had first been launched in 2009.[27]

Carrie Lam was still struggling to find the formula for joined-up government when she took over as Chief Executive in 2017. She continued to offer such vague generalisations as 'bureaux and departments should refrain from operating from their own silos' and must 'get together to resolve problems faced by the people'.[28]

In this environment, the civil service was what held the administration together and ensured, as far as funding allowed, the supply of services which the community needed. Ministers were able to shelter behind the fact that the public did not fully realise that civil servants no longer had responsibility for policymaking or for policy mistakes and that they were unable to resist ministerial decisions, no matter how misguided. In addition, the public's misconceptions included a belief that government departments could find their own sources of funding, if necessary, and there was only limited understanding of the total control which the Legislative Council had over public spending. Inevitably, the credibility of the civil service suffered as its members took the blame for government pledges which were not achieved, for policies that proved defective and for laws that were enforced selectively.

The legislature added to this misconception. When Legislative Council's panels and committees met with bureaux and departments for public discussions and inquiries, civil servants did much of the talking for the government. The impression given to the public and to the media was that civil servants were still responsible for making policy and ensuring its implementation and, therefore, must take the blame for whatever went wrong. Thus, political appointees were well sheltered except when a major crisis or catastrophe occurred.

## Government on the cheap

The biggest challenge for the civil service was Tung Che Hwa's introduction of minimally financed administration. This initiative was to shape government policy and affect the living standards of the entire population for the next two decades. In his Policy Address in 1998, he had embarked on sweeping changes to Hong Kong's public administration that amounted to a rejection of its past organisation and performance. This assault on what he had so recently described as a civil service of the highest quality by international standards came via the EPP. At its heart was a ruthless determination to cut payrolls. He might have invoked the 1997–1998 Asian financial crisis to justify this cost-cutting, but he did not. Quite simply, EPP's goal was to transform the civil service. Tung specified three key targets.

- 'We will require departments and agencies to put forward proposals for new or improved services without giving them additional financial resources'.
- 'Managers will be required to deliver productivity gains amounting to 5 per cent of their operating expenditure by 2002'.
- 'Managers [must] make more use of appointments on contract, rather than permanent appointments'.[29]

Tung presented these targets as if they were dogmas which the people of Hong Kong were to respect without further discussion. And his successors in office never discarded his model.

## Borrowing from the past

In Tung's defence, it must be said that his belief that the public sector should adopt a business-based model was not original. Decades earlier, the colonial administration had joined forces with the business sector to defend the concept of 'small government' and to resist pressures from the Colonial Office and the Labour Party in London to raise taxes and expand social services. In 1967, senior officials defied a more liberal-minded governor, Sir David Trench, to protect business interests by blocking implementation of an official report recommending the introduction of sickness, health care and retirement benefits.[30] His Financial Secretary, Sir John Cowperthwaite, personally sabotaged the Governor's support for a compulsory universal retirement scheme on the completely false grounds that it was part of a plot by anti-business forces from the United Kingdom. Cowperthwaite's victory was so total that, for the rest of the colonial era, all later proposals for some form of compulsory provident fund or state pension scheme were turned down.[31]

Hong Kong's 'small-government' outlook was reinforced in the 1980s by the growing belief in Western countries that state intervention should be minimised. The upper ranks of the colonial administration followed this fashion. They became keen fans of the 'New Public Management' philosophy which was remodelling public services worldwide in the expectation of making them more competitive, creative and cost conscious. These senior officials watched Hong Kong conglomerates adopting an advanced business culture which was regarded as driving global modernisation and growth. Officials became convinced that the public sector must follow suit. The first concrete step towards adopting a business model came in 1987. The Governor, Sir David (later Lord) Wilson, announced that future growth of the civil service would be cut back, while international management consultants had been hired to review the senior levels of Hong Kong's administration.[32]

This call for a leaner civil service was welcomed with considerable enthusiasm.[33] There was some awareness at the top of the colonial administration, nevertheless, of how carefully the target of zero growth for the civil service would have to be managed as Hong Kong's sustained prosperity raised the expectations of this increasingly post-industrial society. 'New schools, new housing estates, and new hospitals' would need more personnel, the Chief Secretary, Sir David Ford, warned in 1991. They could only be hired under a 'zero growth policy', he pointed out, by 'cutting back on existing services'.[34]

In launching the EPP, Tung, consciously or otherwise, was building on that legacy. He offered no facts or figures to justify his targets although there were data available on civil service efficiency. These statistics provided evidence that the drastic EPP austerity measures were unnecessary. Between 1991 and 1997, the population had increased by 23 per cent, but the size of the civil service had fallen by 5 per cent. Civil service emoluments fell from 28 per cent to 21 per cent of total government expenditure over the same period.

These achievements reflected the superior managerial abilities of the Hong Kong personnel who were replacing expatriates in senior government positions in the 1990s and the rising educational standards of new recruits. These changes generated a sustained surge in the government's professionalism and productivity very similar to the dynamism driving the transformation of Hong Kong from reliance on light industry into a world-class financial services centre during this period. Civil service managers were obviously delivering value for money, and their ability to improve productivity while cutting costs and staff had been remarkable.[35] But this boost in efficiency could not be expected to continue indefinitely.

None of this was of much concern either to Tung or to his successors. He himself was convinced that his business experience had given him the leadership qualities as well as the experience to personally transform the civil service into a streamlined, innovative organisation totally at his service. He took for granted that the civil service must have a significant amount of waste and unproductive personnel that could be easily eliminated. After all, the business community firmly believed, civil servants were not subject to the same sort of pressures to perform as the private sector. Civil servants' pay, pension and housing benefits, it was assumed, did not provide incentives to maximise efficiency. And unlike the private sector, government 'managers' were not easily dismissed for failing to cut costs and improve output.

## Civil service collaboration

The civil service itself helped to embed Tung's doctrines in the culture of the Special Administration Region government. Although it was widely rumoured that Anson Chan Fang On-sang, the Chief Secretary, and her senior colleagues constantly opposed Tung's initiatives, the evidence is overwhelming that they wholeheartedly endorsed the EPP, its staff cuts and outsourcing. Furthermore, they genuinely believed that the major objective of these measures was not a reduction in government spending but improved performance. For a start, said the Chief Secretary, the money saved through EPP staff cuts 'will allow us to launch new initiatives, meet past pledges and increased demands on our social safety net for people in need'.[36] In 2000, she was advocating further cuts in personnel. Through this policy, she insisted, 'government departments are [being] encouraged to provide better and more effective public services through wider private sector participation and information technology application . . . [and] uphold the principle of "small government"'.[37] These claims were to be soon discredited.

Senior officials were convinced that the measures were generally popular. As they were with the business sector, of course, which believed that the EPP and its business-based targets would lead to lower taxation. In fact, a government study of a reduction in the rate of profits tax was already under way.[38] According to the Treasury Secretary, the entire civil service was in favour of the programme. 'EPP is now a household name in the public sector', she declared, 'All Government bureaux and departments as well as the Government-subvented sector have responded positively to this challenge'. The results would be entirely beneficial. The EPP was 'not about expenditure cuts,' she insisted but 'part of the Government's long-term effort to improve the management and delivery of public services'.[39] From her commanding position in managing public finances, she should have known better.

Where Tung went wrong in his attempt to remodel the civil service was his obsession with minimising public spending. He was convinced, for example, that, somehow, the community and its families would find means of their own to improve Hong Kong's educational standards and care for the elderly or infirm even if they had only limited financial resources. The mindset introduced by Tung in 1998 was to become a permanent influence on policymaking and was faithfully implemented by his successors in office.

When Donald Tsang took over as Chief Executive, he had much the same remoteness from the realities of life for the average family. He was to claim in 2005, for example, that he had been unaware that the severe cuts in funds and staffing which, as Financial Secretary, he had imposed on the social services meant waiting times for services would increase and some programmes come to a halt.[40] Like Tung, he wanted to keep public spending as low as possible regardless of its purpose. In 2006, for example, he held discussions on how to make Hong Kong 'Asia's world city'. But to every suggestion made about how this could be done, his response was the totally negative 'where does the money come from?', reported one of the discussants.[41]

## The civil service under attack

Tung's EPP policy had revealed his administrative and political limitations. To launch his reforms with an arbitrary, across-the-board austerity campaign was grossly misconceived. His demand for a 5 per cent reduction in funding from every part of the public services did not distinguish between departments which were already operating at their optimal efficiency from those government units in which management performance was only average. The 5 per cent cut also hindered departments whose responsibilities were increasing significantly and needed extra resources. For Tung, all that mattered was a reduction in the numbers employed in the public sector. Payroll was for him the real indicator of over-staffing and inefficiency.

Tung faced no opposition. His Chief Secretary, Anson Chan, for example, seemed mesmerised into believing that better schooling, elderly care services and public housing could be achieved without spending money. She declared that Tung had shifted the government's focus 'from promising to spend more money to promising to achieve results'. 'His promises to the community on [these] livelihood issues' had made a major contribution to better government, she went on.[42] Unfortunately, his promises did not improve performance. Chapter after chapter in this book will illustrate that the results of his civil service 'reforms' were to prove highly damaging for the people of Hong Kong.

Tung pledged that the public would not be adversely affected. 'In making these changes', he declared, 'we will not accept any deterioration in our level of service to the community'.[43] This was a promise which could not be honoured, and his inability to understand the crucial difference between public services and the business world was to prove disastrous. A business firm has a straightforward test of performance and popular ranking: does a product or branch make a profit? If not, it can be terminated. Public services, however, cannot be allowed to fail. A community faces collapse if they do. Despite Hong Kong's commitment to 'small government', there is a lengthy list of essential services which the public expects the government to maintain. To name only a sample, they include health and hospitals, the police and fire services, the ICAC, civil aviation safety, supervision of banks and financial and stock markets and international trade negotiations.

Tung's misguided view that the business model should prevail was the product of his own limited managerial qualifications. He would have had some useful preparation for the wide range of his future government responsibilities if, previously, he had been chief executive of a global bank or a pharmaceutical firm—or even a senior civil servant. In all three roles, he would have been trained to handle a complex institution with an extremely large work force, producing a diverse range of products and services and subject to tight legal and regulatory controls. Instead, his business background was with a shipping company, where his biggest challenge had been to save his father's firm from bankruptcy. As Professor Lau Siu-kai, a well-known academic and future head of Tung's Central Policy Unit, observed, Tung lacked the necessary experience to mobilise a bureaucracy. Nor did he have the required political skills, as Tung himself confessed shortly before stepping down from office.[44]

## Quality control collapses

As contracting out of government activities increased and privatisation gathered momentum, measures should have been taken in advance to maintain quality, particularly for services for which the public had no alternative source of supply. The most vulnerable departments and agencies were responsible for health, welfare, housing and educational programmes. 'Monitoring' and 'training' were the solutions promised, but when government departments and agencies found their budgets being cut, their staff made redundant and their role denigrated by comparison with the business world, the capacity to maintain standards shrank.

This danger was under-estimated initially because the momentum of improvement in the government's performance in the decade before the launch of the EPP had been too strong to be brought to a sharp halt. As a result, senior officials were misled about the benefits of the EPP by impressive data of rising professional standards and reduced waiting times reported in its earliest years. But adverse outcomes were inevitable. The EPP sought to apply the methods of the business world—which were profit-driven—to the public sector. The results, according to a carefully researched review, turned out to be detrimental to the community's well-being. 'The main services such as regular hospital care and conventional academic programs are often squeezed or put aside', this investigation by a well-known academic pointed out. 'As citizens have to pay more under the user-pay principle', he noted, 'Many people could not afford expensive social services based on economic calculations'.[45]

The attempts to reform the civil service through the EPP had come with heavy costs that were carefully concealed by a mantra of business rhetoric. His investigation summed up the exercise in scathing terms.

> First, the EPP neglects a proper balance between social and economic values. Second, the EPP decreases political accountability. Third, the EPP demoralizes civil servants. It must be pointed out that the EPP has enabled the government to save money and to provide a similar level of public service under budget and financial constraints. Yet, it should be equally noted that the EPP provides more expensive social services, that citizens have less say on the provision of public services, and that civil servants are less committed. These three side effects, if unchecked, could jeopardize the stability of society and the legitimacy of government.[46]

No one in power seemed to worry about the correlation between government performance and the availability of human and financial resources. One Legislative Council Panel drew attention to how, over the years, strains on government employees had intensified because the available personnel could not cope with the growing demands made on them. The panel made the obvious point that the population had increased considerably since 2000 but the original staff cuts had not been reversed. The official response dismissed the suggestion that more people was the solution. Instead, a string of clichés was put forward as to the proper remedy: 'redeployment of manpower resources, streamlining of work procedures, re-engineering of operations, etc'.[47] These empty generalisations reflected the remoteness of Chief Executives and their ministerial teams from the day-to-day realities of government administration in Hong Kong.

Nor did anyone in power appear to care about the damage that could be done to the private as well as the public sector by inadequate staffing. A particularly important example was a disregard for accurate statistics. These are the lifeblood of good government. Without them, policy-makers draft their plans blindfolded, and monitoring the outcomes becomes a matter of guesswork. A regular supply of reliable and comprehensive data from the government is no less essential to efficient performance by the business world. In 2013, accusations surfaced in the media that, for the previous ten years, Census and Statistics Department personnel had been faking their survey data.[48] This accusation was taken very seriously as it put the credibility of virtually all government reports at risk.

A full-scale investigation was launched. Among its findings was the revelation that the government had demanded increasing quantities of statistical information over this period which were beyond the capacity of the available personnel to generate accurately. To make matters worse, a specialist fieldwork team for a key survey programme had been disbanded in 2003 as part of a government-wide campaign to raise output by abolishing the distinction between specialists and generalists. The investigation found no evidence of fraud or misconduct on the part of the statistical personnel but recorded, nevertheless, the potential threats to the integrity as well as to the quality of the government's collection of statistical information.[49]

Even when public safety was at risk, staff cuts were enforced. By 2013, for example, technical and survey officers with the Buildings Department had run out of patience and organised a rare public protest. They were responsible for inspecting buildings, enforcing safety measures and removing unauthorised structural works. The programme was beyond the capacity of the Department's work force to handle effectively. The Department's statistics showed how the backlog of work had grown between 2001 and 2012. In this period, around 320,000 orders had been issued to remove unauthorised building works. In almost 20 per cent of the cases, the property owners had not yet complied, and the dangers had not been rectified.

The Department's only solution for coping with the increasing number of outstanding cases was to promise 'prioritisation of enforcement'. It could not pretend that it had the resources to achieve prompt compliance with legal orders for urgent maintenance. Interestingly, the Department did not admit outright that it was short of staff. Instead, its spokesperson explained that it had 'applied for additional people and creation of more posts through the current resources allocation mechanism'. In plain language, this statement meant that the Department needed more people and had applied for them, but that the necessary funding had been refused by the Treasury.[50]

Only very occasionally was a government agency able to reverse mistaken policies and resume normal operations. The Housing Authority was among the few exceptions. Even before Tung assumed office in 1997, the government's senior housing official had decided to privatise as much as possible of the management of public rental housing because he was convinced that the private sector model would be more efficient. Responsibility for building maintenance was transferred to the tenants in 1999. This decision made no sense. As he himself had publicly acknowledged in 1997, most of the Housing Authority's tenants

came from 'the oldest, most dilapidated properties, in bed-space apartments and the like, or squatter shacks'. They could not be expected to
know how to find their own plumbers, electricians and repair workers.
Privatisation went ahead nevertheless. Maintenance of public rental
housing promptly collapsed, and many tenants were left living in unacceptable conditions. By 2006, the Housing Authority had no choice but
to take back responsibility for repairs.[51]

## Falling foul of the EPP

In the original round of staff cuts by the colonial administration, private
sector consultants were brought in who drafted a blueprint for the
Social Welfare Department to cut its budgets, and its payroll in particular, through outsourcing and privatisation.[52] The government's own
investigation had already shown that the level of social security benefits
and the supply of welfare services were barely adequate to meet basic
needs.[53] But its budgets were to be constantly attacked as unaffordable
and as the first step towards a dependency culture.[54] As a result, nowhere
in Hong Kong's public services did the pursuit of business models and
self-financing do more damage than in the welfare field. Yet, ironically,
the Social Welfare Department had been the one government agency
which from the 1970s, had developed a highly successful model for outsourcing services provided to the public.

The first foundations for a modern social welfare system in Hong
Kong had been laid as early as the 1950s. Medical, social work and education professionals pioneered programmes for children with special
needs and for the disabled and the elderly. To deliver them, they created
NGOs. These were not just 'charities' run by good-hearted volunteers.
By the 1960s, a large number were highly professional organisations
pioneering the modern practices that guaranteed a high quality of care.
The Social Welfare Department's professional social workers actively
collaborated with the NGOs, and a working partnership was to develop
between them based on 'five-year plans' drafted by the Department in
consultation with the non-government sector.

By 2000, five-year planning had been abandoned, and the partnership was being wound up.[55] A new system of competitive tenders for government funding for individual projects was introduced, which, over the
years, reduced the government's accountability for service shortfalls and
for quality issues.[56] Initially, officials had been confident that monitoring
of performance would be enhanced under the EPP.[57] NGOs warned that
this optimism had been misplaced and that the quality and sustainability
of welfare services were now in serious danger just when Hong Kong
faced social problems of increasing complexity.[58] But their protests were
ignored.

The partnership and its forward planning had created a very efficient subvention system which allowed the Department to finance the
outsourcing of vital services to NGOs safely and efficiently. The drive
to dismantle this arrangement was maintained for years to come by the
government's Efficiency Unit (which had played a key role in coordinating the EPP). 'Best practice suggests that contracts with NGOs and charities should be similar to contracts with the private sector', the Efficiency
Unit claimed in 2009, although 'best practice' was not defined.[59] This
assertion ignored how radically the role of NGOs in delivering social
services for the vulnerable differed from private enterprises. NGOs were
not profit-making.

NGOs could no longer depend on a professionally designed system of
government subsidies. Instead, they were forced to rely increasingly on
competitive bids for government projects and on their own, uncertain
fund-raising. The government steadfastly refused to make planned commitments to the development of welfare services and to the solution of
the most acute shortfalls, which reduced its direct involvement in the
welfare sector and its public accountability.[60]

Creation of a new business-inspired model was finalised in 2004
to provide 'new strategic directions to achieve the paradigm shifts
from "service provision" to "social investment"', the Welfare Minister
announced. And he looked to partnerships with the business sector as
a replacement for public funding.[61] Meanwhile, the number of elderly
people who died while waiting for a place in a residential home increased.
The queues lengthened for admission to facilities for the mentally and
physically disabled.[62] Children with special education needs were given
no priority.[63]

By 2011, the values and standards of the caring professions seemed
to have no place in policymaking to judge from an official committee's
recommendations on long-term planning.

> In the past, the business/professional sector used to play a sup-
> plementary role in resource provision in our social welfare system.
> However, in recent years this role has changed and diversified to
> include experience and knowledge sharing with the welfare sector,
> mentorship/tutorship for welfare services/programmes, and
> promotion of volunteerism among their staff . . . Engagement of
> the business sector in welfare services can inspire new thinking in
> welfare services, enable knowledge transfer and shift, enhance staff
> relations and loyalty, and improve corporate social responsibility
> and corporate image.[64]

It is difficult to understand what 'mentorship/tutorship' a business
executive would be qualified to bring to 'welfare services/programmes'
or how a business career would confer any credible capacity to inject 'new

thinking in welfare services' superior to the experience and expertise of the professionals in the field. It did not seem to matter any longer that the adequacy of services would deteriorate once the drive began to force professional social workers, in both the government and their former NGO partners, to adopt business-based management styles. Ironically, a fundamental flaw in this report's promotion of business as a model was the complete absence of any 'market' analysis. No data were given on the gaps between current and forecast future demand for social services and their supply. In the absence of statistical information, there could be no fact-based analysis of the priorities needed for long-term planning of expenditure on new institutions and facilities or the expansion of staff training and recruitment programmes.

The rise of future Chief Executive, Carrie Lam, was to reinforce this misguided belief that the market would prove superior in delivering social services. After her promotion to Chief Secretary in 2012, she gave a high priority to the increasing elderly population. She insisted that a business model was the way to overcome the acute shortfalls in the provision of residential care for the aged, which were causing considerable alarm to the community.[65] But this commercial approach had already been discredited by the government's Elderly Commission. It had uncovered an alarming failure by the private sector to provide proper standards of residential care for the elderly. One-third of private accommodation was left unoccupied because the public had become very reluctant to use these unsatisfactory commercial facilities, according to the Commission. By contrast, the subvented, voluntary sector maintained professional standards of care, and the accommodation available could not keep up with demand. Waiting times for admission ranged from 22 to 40 months (according to the type of institution).

The Elderly Commission refused to accept the argument that lower charges had encouraged the long queues for the government-subvented places. 'The elderly (and probably their family members) have better confidence in the quality of subsidised [institutions]', the report diplomatically explained.[66] Families had been given good reason to feel nervous about the quality of care for ageing relatives in the private sector as scandals increased and legislation to end poor standards in private homes had been delayed for five years before coming into force in 2011.[67]

## Conclusion

The wonder was that the civil service survived its mismanagement over the years so well. The worrying question is: For how much longer? Productivity cannot be forced up indefinitely. As challenges worsened from crisis to catastrophe, particularly in the housing and social service sectors, the volume of work increased relentlessly. Departments and other government agencies had no alternative but to find a coping mechanism: duties were 'prioritised' to match the limited personnel and other resources at their disposal. Which laws and regulations could be enforced effectively, the senior civil servants involved had to decide, and which public complaints could be ignored? What risks to health and safety were tolerable and how could sensible decisions be made without crucial statistical and other data?

Senior officials frequently tried to warn the legislature and the general public that the civil service lacked the human and financial resource to find solutions. But neither they nor legislators were able to induce Chief Executives to face the reality that without enough funds and personnel, their policies and promises to the community could not be implemented.

These truths became very evident following the dismantling of the partnership between the Social Welfare Department and NGOs. In this case, the government was not motivated solely by EPP targets. The government also gained a substantial political advantage. Welfare projects were now allocated to NGOs through competitive tenders. 'Goodwill' was believed to be important in this new 'commercial' relationship. Many NGOs felt it was no longer safe to question official policies or to campaign for more and better services. NGO board members worried about being classified by senior officials as 'trouble-makers'.[68] The NGOs' power to act as advocates for those in need of social services was diminished.

There is a resilience in Hong Kong's institutions, nevertheless, that somehow generates unexpected remedies that promote survival. In the civil service's case, it managed to maintain a high degree of credibility, despite the sustained criticism from politicians, academics and the media. This achievement owed a great deal to its contribution to the higher degree of accountability that was surprisingly achieved in this century. Political appointees and the entire operations of the government were brought under continuous public scrutiny, thanks to a working partnership that developed between the civil service, Legislative Council panels and committees and the Director of Audit and the Ombudsman.

Officials in bureaux and departments provided these bodies, freely and frankly as far as can be judged, with whatever evidence they sought about blunders and deficiencies in government performance. As a result, Chief Executives and their ministerial teams were continually open to close public scrutiny on a far greater scale than before 1997, regardless of how politically embarrassing the outcomes might be. That has been an invaluable reassurance to the people of Hong Kong because it enables them to monitor the threats to the survival of Hong Kong as a modern, flourishing community.

## Notes

1. Tung Chee Hwa, Chief Executive, *Government Information Services* (*GIS* hereafter), 5 September 1997.
2. The precise wording of Tung's edict was: 'We will require departments and agencies to put forward proposals for new or improved services without giving them additional financial resources'. Policy Address, *Hong Kong Hansard* (*HH* hereafter), 7 October 1998. This policy is discussed below.
3. See Yash Ghai, *Hong Kong's New Constitutional Order: The Resumption of Chinese Sovereignty and the Basic Law*, 2nd ed. (Hong Kong: Hong Kong University Press, 1999), 252–55, 263–64.
4. For an excellent overview, see Ray Yep, '"One Country, Two Systems" and Special Administrative Regions: The Case of Hong Kong', in *China's Local Administration: Traditions and Changes in the Sub-National Hierarchy*, ed. Jae Ho Chung and Tao-chiu Lam (Abingdon: Routledge, 2009), 94–97.
5. Ghai, *Hong Kong's New Constitutional Order*, 279.
6. Provisional Legislative Council, *Financial Affairs Panel*, 6 October and 17 November 1997; *Proceedings*, 13 January 1998.
7. Donald Tsang Yam-kuen, Financial Secretary, *GIS*, 12 February 1998.
8. For details, see Press Releases, *GIS*, 26, 28, 29 May and 22 June 1998.
9. This troubled environment is well summarised in Wilson Wong, 'From a British-style Administrative State to a Chinese-style Political State: Civil Service Reforms in Hong Kong after the Transfer of Sovereignty', *The Brookings Institution* (June 2003): 1, 6 in particular.
10. For details on the seriousness of this incident, see Tung, Chief Executive, *GIS*, 31 December 1997.
11. See *Report of the Legislative Council Select Committee to Inquire into the Circumstances Leading to the Problems Surrounding the Commencement of the Operation of the New Hong Kong International Airport at Chek Lap Kok since 6 July 1998 and Related Issues* (Hong Kong: January 1999); *Report of the Commission of Enquiry on the New Airport* (Hong Kong: Government Information Services, 1999).
12. Compare Donald Tsang, Financial Secretary, *GIS*, 8 and 16 July 1998.
13. Tung, Chief Executive, *HH*, 14 January 1999.
14. Tung, Chief Executive, *GIS*, 11 October 2001.
15. Tung, Chief Executive, *HH*, 17 April 2002, 5490, 5493.
16. Donald Tsang, Chief Secretary, *GIS*, 25 April 2002.
17. For a well-documented review of these incidents, see Timothy Ka-ying Wong and Shirley Po-san Wan, 'The Implementation of the Accountability System for Principal Officials: Efficacy and Impact', in *The July 1 Protest Rally: Interpreting a Historic Event*, ed. Joseph Y. S. Cheung (Hong Kong: City University of Hong Kong Press, 2005), 195–200.
18. 'Report of the Select Committee to Inquire into the Handling of the Severe Acute Respiratory Syndrome Outbreak by the Government and the Hospital Authority, July 2004', 234.

19. Dennis Chong, 'Chief Executive Orders Home Checks after Education Chief Is Embroiled in Scandal', *South China Morning Post*, 26 May 2011.
20. 'Buildings Department Statement on Unit at 64 MacDonnell Road', *GIS*, 7 September 2011.
21. Hon Kam Nai-wai and a written reply by Carrie Lam Cheng Yuet-ngor, Secretary for Development, in *HH*, 29 February 2012, 6455–57.
22. Li Pang-kwong, 'The Executive', in *Contemporary Hong Kong Politics: Governance in the Post-1997 Era*, ed. Wai-man Lam, Percy Luen-tim Lui and Ian Holliday (Hong Kong: Hong Kong University Press, 2007), 26–27, 34.
23. It is true that reassigning responsibilities and restructuring ministries is common among many democratic governments. But in their case, ministers are genuine 'political' appointees who are accountable through universal suffrage to the public at large. Where their portfolios are not consistent with efficient administration, there is a price to pay at the ballot box. It should be noted that 2007 did not mark the date on which overlapping and confusion began. These were features of the ministerial system from early on.
24. The quotations that follow are from Carrie Lam, Chief Secretary, *GIS*, 27 September 2012.
25. Carrie Lam, Chief Secretary, *GIS*, 27 September 2012.
26. Anthony Cheung Bing-leung, Secretary for Transport and Housing, *HH*, 22 May 2013, 12119–21. The department was already operating 78 such lifts.
27. This failed initiative was highlighted in extensive reporting and editorial comment in *Ming Pao Daily*, 19 May 2017.
28. Carrie Lam, Chief Executive-elect, *GIS*, 21 June 2017.
29. Tung, Chief Executive, *HH*, 7 October 1998.
30. *A Report by the Inter-Departmental Working Party to Consider Certain Aspects of Social Security* (Hong Kong: Government Printer, 1967). The personal commitment of Sir David Trench, Governor, to social insurance is recorded in (7) 'Notes of a Meeting with the Governor on 15th April 1966 by D. S. W.'. HKRS890-2-31, 'Correspondence with the Governor and notes of discussion with H.E.'.
31. For fuller details of this successful defiance of Trench by his senior officials, see HKRS163-3-264, 'Coordination of Social Service Policies'; (7) 'Notes of a meeting with the Governor on 15th April 1966 by D. S. W.'. HKRS890-2-31, 'Correspondence with the Governor and Notes of Discussion with H.E.'; M. 7 Governor to Financial Secretary, 22 June 1967; M. 24 Financial Secretary to Governor; (11) 'An Appreciation of the Report by the Inter-Departmental Working Party on Social Security', 10 October 1967. HKRS163-9-486, 'Social Security—Implications of Change in HK Status-Quo . . .'.
32. Sir David (later Lord) Wilson, Governor, *HH*, 7 October 1987, 46.
33. Sir Piers Jacobs, Financial Secretary, *HH*, 7 March 1990, 958.
34. Sir David Ford, Chief Secretary, *HH*, 9 May 1990, 29 May 1991.
35. Civil Service Bureau, 'Legislative Council Panel on Public Service General Overview of the Civil Service Strength, Retirement and Resignation' (CB(1)1817/07-08(01), June 2008), 1–3; Legislative Council Secretariat, 'Panel on Public Service Meeting . . . Updated Background Brief on the Overview of the Civil Service Establishment, Strength, Retirement, Resignation and Age Profile' (CB(4)963/14-15(11), 15 May 2015); 'Civil

Service Bureau, 'LegCo Panel on Public Service Supplementary Note on Containing the Size of the Civil Service' (CB(1)1290/01-02, March 2002). See Annexes C and D.

36. Anson Chan Fang On-sang, Chief Secretary, *GIS*, 29 September 1999.

37. Anson Chan, Chief Secretary, *HH*, 5 April 2000, 5661.

38. Financial Bureau, 'Report on the Profits Tax Review' (1998).

39. Denise Yue Chung-yee, Secretary for the Treasury, *GIS*, 19 October 2000.

40. Joseph Li, 'Election is "an Education on HK"', *China Daily*, 11 June 2005.

41. Joseph Li, 'Education Can Bridge Income Gap', *China Daily*, 11 August 2006; Commission on Strategic Development, 'Summary of the Views Expressed at the Fifth Meeting of the Executive Committee of the Commission on Strategic Development Held on 10 August 2006' (Secretariat, September 2006).

42. Anson Chan, Chief Secretary, *GIS*, 26 April 1999.

43. Tung, Chief Executive, *HH*, 7 October 1998.

44. Lau Siu-kai, 'Government and Political Change in the Hong Kong Special Administrative Region', in *Hong Kong the Super Paradox: Life after Return to China*, ed. James C. Hsiung (London: Macmillan, 2000), 49–51; Tung, Chief Executive, *HH*, 12 January 2005, 3262.

45. Jermain T. M. Lam, 'Enhanced Productivity Program in Hong Kong: A Critical Appraisal', *Public Performance & Management Review* 27, no. 1 (September 2003): 63.

46. Lam, 'Enhanced Productivity in Hong Kong', 68.

47. Legislative Council Secretariat, 'Panel on Public Service Meeting . . . Updated Background Brief on the Overview of the Civil Service Establishment, Strength, Retirement, Resignation and Age Profile' (CB(4)963/14-15(11), 15 May 2015), 5–6.

48. *Ming Pao Daily*, 7 and 24 January 2013.

49. 'Report of Investigation Task Force on Statistical Data Quality Assurance' (March 2013), 28–29.

50. Buildings Department Spokesperson, *GIS*, 31 October 2013. See also the coverage in *Ming Pao Daily*, 30 October and 1 November 2013.

51. Tony Miller, Director of Housing, 'Becoming Stakeholders of Hong Kong: Home Ownership', speech to the Hong Kong Institute of Real Estate Administration (19 February 1997); Lau Kai-hung, Deputy Director of Housing, *GIS*, 30 January 2006.

52. This account draws heavily on Anthony B. L. Cheung, 'Civil Service Reform in Post-1997 Hong Kong: Political Challenges, Managerial Responses?'. *International Journal of Public Administration* 24, issue 9 (2001): 930–33, 939, 940–41. The Housing Department suffered very similar treatment.

53. On the gap between the department's provision of services and growing demand, see Social Welfare Department, *The Five-Year Plan for Social Welfare Development in Hong Kong: Review 1998*, 103–6.

54. On the hostility towards improved social services and the dominant role of business leaders in framing post-colonial political arrangements, see Alvin Y. So, 'Hong Kong's Problematic Democratic Transition: Power Dependency or Business Hegemony?'. *Journal of Asian Studies* 59, no. 2 (May 2000): 370, 373, 377.

55. The practical difficulties created by abandoning the former five-year planning exercises were summarised in Hong Kong Council of Social Service, 'Response to SWAC's 2nd Stage Consultation Exercise on Long-Term Social Welfare Planning in Hong Kong', 3–4.

56. The explanation given for this change focused on the control of 'inputs' in the planning exercise, which, of course, created long-term obligations for the government which it now found inconvenient. Dr Yeoh Eng Kiong, Secretary for Health and Welfare, *GIS*, 20 June 2000.

57. A striking feature of the positive reaction to Tung's EPP initiatives was that the end of the planning regime was seen as the start of performance monitoring rather than the reverse, as was the case in reality. Lam, 'Enhanced Productivity Program in Hong Kong: A Critical Appraisal', 60.

58. Ivy Cheng, 'Impacts of the Lump Sum Grant Subvention System on the Subvented Welfare Sector: Information Note', Legislative Council Secretariat (IN14/07-08, 8 May 2008), 4–5, 12, and 'Table 1: Chronology of Major Events in Relation to the Introduction of LSGSS', 8.

59. Efficiency Unit, 'Serving the Community by Using the Private Sector—Policy and Practice', 2nd ed. (January 2007), 15.

60. Gary Ma Fung-Kwok, *HH*, 1 June 2000, 7161.

61. Dr Yeoh, Secretary for Health and Welfare, *HH*, 5 February 2004, 3097, 3098.

62. See Leo F. Goodstadt, *Poverty in the Midst of Affluence*, 161–63.

63. See, for example, Panel on Education Subcommittee on Integrated Education, 'Report September 2014' (CB(4)1087/13-14(01).

64. Labour and Welfare Bureau, 'Legislative Council Panel on Welfare Services: Long-Term Social Welfare Planning', Annex 1; Social Welfare Advisory Committee, 'Report on Long-Term Social Welfare Planning in Hong Kong' (LC Paper No. CB(2)2279/10-11(03), July 2011), 29–30.

65. Carrie Lam, Chief Secretary, *GIS*, 24 November 2012.

66. Ernest Chiu Wing-tak et al., *Elderly Commission's Study on Residential Care Services for the Elderly Final Report* (Hong Kong: University of Hong Kong, December 2009), 15.

67. Legislative Council Secretariat, 'Provision of Residential Care Places for Persons with Disabilities' (CB(2)1149/09-10(02), 23 March 2010), 5–6.

68. These adverse consequences had been identified very early on by Kenneth L. Chau and Chack-kie Wong, 'The Social Welfare Reform: A Way to Reduce Public Burden', in *The First Tung Chee-hwa Administration: The First Five Years of the Hong Kong Special Administrative Region*, ed. Lau Siu-kai (Hong Kong: Chinese University Press, 2002), 215–27.

# 3
# Private homes under threat

'Everyone has a dream', Hong Kong's Housing Minister, Professor Anthony Cheung Bing-leung, wrote in 2013, and 'to many Hong Kong people, this is having their own home for their children to grow up happily and healthily'. In the 1990s, the Minister went on, that dream seemed about to be fulfilled, and Hong Kong had 'a housing story that people took pride in'. Even for 'grassroots families', the sustained government housing programmes since the 1950s had transformed their living conditions.[1] The private sector showed an equally dramatic improvement as owner-occupancy had risen from 18 per cent in 1971 to 52 per cent in 1997.[2] The community appeared well on the way to having an adequate supply of decent homes for the first time in its history.[3]

It seemed safe to assume that the appalling housing conditions of the past had been consigned to the dustbin of history. However, in this century, there was to be a dramatic reversal of fortunes, which hit the private sector hardest. Owner-occupiers and tenants alike found that their homes were under threat because of a lack of maintenance of the building stock on a scale which had not been foreseen. In 2010, the threat was being officially described as 'urban time bombs waiting to strike and cause injuries and fatalities'.[4] Large numbers of families found themselves living in private housing which was dangerous, unhealthy and not fit for human habitation. The number of 'dilapidated, over-crowded and neglected' buildings with 'dreadful standards of accommodation' was officially forecast to increase.[5]

The crisis had been made possible by weak political leadership, administrative confusion and the reluctance of the government to take responsibility for halting the destruction of the private housing stock. But even more important was the maladministration caused by the refusal of Chief Executives, their political appointees and a majority of legislative councillors to recognise that public administration is 'labour intensive'. The community's housing problems could not be solved unless the civil service had enough administrators and professionals to handle the volume of work required. But no one in power seemed to worry about the correlation between government performance and the availability of human and financial resources.

## Dilapidation and decay

Urban decay has become the biggest single threat in this century to the quality of life for a million families with homes in the private sector. By 2010, at least 110,000 families were found to be living in privately owned buildings described by an initial Urban Renewal Authority (URA) study as neither healthy nor safe. Their dilapidation had reached an alarming state, and the standards of accommodation they provided were dreadful. The typical flat in this category had an average space of around 500 square feet and was 'home' to three or more families. Defective electrical wiring and fittings meant there was a serious risk of fires. The common areas were filthy, and leaking pipes meant that flooding was frequent.[6]

Why were these frightening conditions accepted in a prosperous, post-industrial community as sophisticated as Hong Kong? An important part of the explanation for the community's tolerance was that many of its members were born or brought up in even worse conditions. As the industrial takeoff in the 1950s achieved an astonishing export growth rate of over 100 per cent a year, the private property sector enjoyed seemingly unlimited demand from families who were prospering in the new manufacturing era. Construction expenditure on new private housing between 1955 and 1965 rose by 110 per cent a year. Initially, the housing surge seemed to promise a substantial improvement in the quality of Hong Kong's homes. The over-crowded, insanitary, three to four-storey tenements built before the Japanese invasion in 1941 were being replaced by large-scale, multi-storey developments.[7] In 1959, a prototype of the skyscraper blocks that were to define the future Hong Kong landscape came on to the market. It contained nearly 1,000 residential units averaging just over 500 square feet each, and it became a standard model for Hong Kong homes.[8] The boom accelerated in the 1970s and continued, almost uninterrupted, until the end of the century.

But from the very start, these massive new high-rises were at risk. They were quickly subject to gross overcrowding and to dilapidation on a scale well beyond all normal wear and tear, as a 1963 government Working Party warned.

> . . . it is not unknown for 60 or 70 persons to be living in a three-room flat . . . the W.C.s are as few as the builder could get away with installing; and on many if not most floors the water taps can stay empty even in a good water year because of the inadequacy of the internal supply pipes. The people in these buildings may well present a more serious health hazard, and bring up their children mentally, socially and physically more handicapped or stunted than if they had been in . . . squatter shacks on the hillsides.[9]

## Shameful statistics

The standards of public sector homes were to be transformed in the decades that followed, but the private sector was not so fortunate despite the overall prosperity of Hong Kong and its rising incomes. Almost all Hong Kong buildings have used reinforced concrete, and, in consequence, they have a very finite life.[10] Builders had no concept of design life until relatively late in the last century. Even now, the design life is only 50 years. As a result, high-quality maintenance is essential to protect buildings from serious deterioration.

In 2013, the URA estimated that 4,000 private residential buildings were worn out. They were over 50 years old, 'with three-quarters of them already classified as substandard'. Another 12,000 buildings had been built between 30 and 50 years ago 'which had substandard or no property management at all'. As a result, maintenance was minimal, and they deteriorated relentlessly, posing a growing threat to the safety and health of their residents, to say nothing of their comfort. The struggle to slow down the rate of dilapidation was to become more arduous because by 2020, the number of buildings which would exceed their design life span of 50 years was forecast to reach 16,000.

If anything, these statistics underestimated the magnitude of the decay and dilapidation. They were derived, it was openly admitted, from data which had been collected 'more than 15 years ago' and which were not based on comprehensive surveys. A similar warning applied to government statistics on unlawful building works which were aggravating the deterioration of the housing stock. A 2015 report by the Director of Audit listed a catalogue of deficiencies in data collection by the Buildings Department and its computer systems which meant that the full dimensions of the private housing crisis were concealed by the limited coverage and dubious accuracy of the available statistics.[11]

## Public sector lessons ignored

The large stock of public housing meant that the government's housing professionals had become aware of the limited life expectancy of concrete buildings, and they had acted early to protect the public sector from dilapidation. In 1988, the Housing Authority began renovation works on the 560 buildings constructed before 1973. This programme took 21 years to complete, and then a new monitoring and renovation cycle had to begin.[12] The government had thus acquired considerable experience of the complexity of the programmes needed to prolong the life of high-density residential buildings in Hong Kong.

It had also learnt from its own experience the serious limitations of owners and tenants in overseeing the management and maintenance of the buildings in which they lived. In 1999, the Housing Authority had followed the fashion of the Tung Chee Hwa era. It privatised as much as possible of the management of public rental housing because it was convinced that the private sector model would be more efficient. Maintenance standards collapsed almost immediately, with large numbers of premises becoming unfit for use. By 2006, the Authority had no choice but to take over maintenance once again.[13]

But these lessons were not applied to the private sector. The government ignored the deteriorating quality of the private sector housing stock until much later, and it did not start the launch of measures to improve safety and enforce building regulations in privately owned buildings until 1998, ten years after the Housing Authority had begun work on the renovation of the public housing stock.[14] Furthermore, the Authority's experience did not offer an accurate indication of the much more serious scale and speed of dilapidation that would overtake the private sector and of the active role which the government would have to play to halt the crisis.[15]

## Reluctant remedies

The government's lack of enthusiasm for direct involvement in finding a solution for the increasing threat to private housing had become very clear at the start of the century. In 2001, the 'Implementation Plan for the Comprehensive Strategy for Building Safety and Timely Maintenance' was launched, but it proposed only a limited solution. In 2003 and 2005, public consultations took place with 'an aim to mapping out further initiatives to arrest the long-standing problem of building neglect'. The initiatives that followed were limited in scope although dilapidation was accelerating. A vaguely worded commitment by the government to 'suitably assist building owners to conduct repair and maintenance works' was announced, but it would be implemented 'in collaboration with other partner organisations'. The limited value of these initiatives was highlighted by the government's 'Voluntary Building Inspection Scheme'. This could have done a great deal to identify neglected maintenance and the appropriate remedial measures. But the government was afraid of public resistance if owners were legally liable for financing the scheme. Because neither the Chief Executive nor the ministers involved possessed the political credibility to market this programme for safeguarding private property, it was made voluntary and had little success.[16] The message to the average family had been clear: if the government did not think that the situation was serious enough to warrant compulsory measures, there was no immediate crisis, and maintenance could continue to be postponed.

The government's reluctance to get involved also reflected maladministration, notably the absence of clear lines of responsibility and the serious overlapping of chains of command. In 2009, there were three separate policy bureaux, five different departments and two public agencies involved in housing and land issues, a daunting display of administrative confusion. The total was soon to be increased by one more bureau and two more departments.

It seemed at first that this desire to keep clear of the property management and renovation crisis would remain a permanent policy. But during Donald Tsang Yam-kuen's term in office as Chief Executive, his Financial Secretary, John Tsang Chun-wah, became worried that the economy was going into recession. In response, a mixed bag of 'targeted measures to provide various types of jobs and internship opportunities' was announced in the 2009 Budget Speech, among them 'Operation Building Bright'. This measure would enable the URA to give cash grants to flat owners for urgent repairs in 1,000 of Hong Kong's most dilapidated buildings. This funding was a one-off, temporary initiative, it was made clear, inspired solely by fear of rising unemployment in a downturn.[17] Carrie Lam Cheng Yuet-ngor, a future Chief Executive, was the minister responsible for implementing Operation Building Bright. She, in turn, emphasised that the creation of 10,000 new jobs as rapidly as possible was the dominant reason for providing cash grants to flat owners. [18] The programme was to be an emergency measure and not a long-term cure.[19]

The scheme achieved impressive results which, legislators argued, justified making it a major model for housing rehabilitation. It seemed possible that Donald Tsang might agree. He had begun to show some interest in the problem of dilapidated buildings in 2007 and had introduced measures to preserve heritage buildings. But his real interest was in political prestige rather than in halting the growth of slum homes.[20] By 2010, however, the URA had established a remarkable level of autonomy which was inspired by the social consciousness of its Chairman, its Board and senior staff and their awareness of the worsening crisis. The URA thus took the initiative to disregard the reservations at ministerial level and mounted a campaign which awoke the public to the severity of the physical decay of Hong Kong's building stock.

Donald Tsang could not ignore the new public mood, and his Policy Address in 2010 admitted that increasing the building supply was not enough. Rehabilitation of the existing stock should be given a new priority. He promised legislation 'to tackle the problems of building dilapidation and unauthorized building works' and to reform the management of private buildings, together with 'comprehensive assistance to building owners who lack organizational ability or financial resources'. However, Tsang's conversion was strictly political rhetoric.

His Policy Address made no commitment to any early implementation of his pledges. An extensive programme of legislation, monitoring and financial aid was urgently needed, he admitted. But first of all, there would have to be further consideration and public consultations, he was careful to explain, for which he set no timetable. Thus, his proposals could be delayed indefinitely.[21] Practical measures to end the destruction of the housing stock through neglect, malpractice and corruption were not introduced.

Nevertheless, between 2009 and 2016, the URA and Operation Building Bright succeeded in rescuing a total of 2,000 buildings at risk which contained 100,000 flats.[22] Special grants had been made available for elderly owner-occupiers with limited means.[23] These statistics demonstrated that large-scale measures to reverse dilapidation and to improve management were affordable, and the results were impressive.

When Leung Chun-ying took office in 2012, he was prepared to continue Operation Building Bright but not to make it into a permanent programme, regardless of its past achievements. Leung and his minister ran out of enthusiasm for subsidising the protection of safety, health and living standards in dilapidated buildings. Operation Building Bright was wound down in 2016, and staff from the Buildings Department were laid off.[24]

## Market forces fail

Operation Building Bright had uncovered the alarming scale of dilapidation in Hong Kong housing for the first time. No less important, the scheme had revealed the urgent need to convince property owners themselves that they had an obligation to do much more than manage the interior decoration of their own flats and the cleanliness of the common areas. Despite seven decades of Hong Kong's families making their homes in multi-storey dwellings, it could not be taken for granted, the Home Affairs Department warned in 2016, that owners understood the complexity of the services and facilities on which the quality of their housing depended. And for which they were financially responsible. The Department found it necessary to explain in the simplest terms what was involved.

> Many owners of private buildings may not be aware that the properties they own include not only the flats they live in. When they buy a flat in a building, they also purchase the common parts of the building. The water the family consumes every day is provided through the water supply system and water pipes of the estate. Every day when the family go out, they use the lift of the building. Furthermore, the estate has external walls, ground foundation, pillars, beams, etc. All these facilities, fixtures and structures form

the common parts of the building, which are jointly owned by all owners of the estate.[25]

The limitations of owners as property managers were understandable. In the early years of a building's life, owners can generally take it for granted that structural repairs will rarely be needed and that the building's amenities are designed to last. It is tempting, therefore, to delay significant expenditure on maintenance indefinitely. Furthermore, most of the damage being caused by the lack of maintenance remains virtually invisible for years: out of sight under floors, within ceilings and behind party and partition walls. As a result, the protection of the physical fabric and the essential fittings and amenities gets postponed or ignored.

Eventually, the lack of regular repairs and servicing creates fire risks, health hazards and structural dangers. The individual owner often suffers a sharp financial shock when informed that extensive maintenance can be delayed no longer without a severe decline in the quality of the premises. In buildings where there are larger numbers of older, lower-income owners, the bills for essential maintenance often cannot be met. Thus, for a substantial number of buildings built 30 or more years ago, owners are unable to cover the costs of urgent renovation works.

Out of Hong Kong's total stock of private residential buildings, 40 per cent were built half a century ago or longer. In most cases, their structures have long since deteriorated, and fittings and fixtures have become obsolete or worn-out.[26] The simplest solution would be to demolish dangerous and unhealthy premises and redevelop the sites. But the government has been unwilling to do so. Their evicted occupants could not be rehoused, it was argued. Private supply already lagged well behind market demand, and there was an acute shortage of public housing into which the lower income families could be transferred. Furthermore, for the owner-occupiers, these homes were usually their biggest lifetime investment, which they could never hope to replace if they were evicted.[27]

The proper solution, as far as both the government and the business world were concerned, was for property owners to shoulder their legal responsibilities. They should pay for renovation caused by past neglect plus whatever maintenance and management fees were required to keep their buildings in good repair for the future. The URA and Operation Building Bright, however, had uncovered clear evidence that the challenges of managing and maintaining Hong Kong's very mixed housing stock were beyond the capacity of free market forces.

To make matters worse, even when a building's owners were prepared to spend money on maintenance to protect the value of their assets, they faced serious practical obstacles. The contribution that professionalism could make to managing buildings was not widely recognised, even though the responsibilities involved were considerable in Hong Kong's multi-storey residential buildings, and the damage done by poor management was severe. Until 2016, proposals for a licensing system had got nowhere, and there had been no standard requirements for property management companies nor formal qualifications for practitioners. Developing training programmes and enforcing professional standards had been extremely difficult under these circumstances.[28]

## Not the government's business

In this dire situation, the extent to which government neglected its statutory duties and postponed reforming the law to improve the standards of management and to clarify owners' obligations was disgraceful. Reform of the legal framework, without which adequate maintenance and management could not be guaranteed, was repeatedly delayed despite mounting evidence of the desperate need to halt the tide of dilapidation. The following timeline speaks for itself.

- 2006: The Legislative Council passed a motion calling for property management companies to be licensed. The government took no action.[29]
- 2007: The Building Management Ordinance was amended, but the opportunity was missed to create greater transparency, accountability and professional oversight of managements and owners' representatives.
- 2011: A Review Committee was appointed 'to identify common building management problems' and to recommend how the Building Management Ordinance should be updated.[30]
- 2014: A public consultation on this issue was announced.
- 2015: A Legislative Council Panel called for the Building Management Ordinance to be amended in order to tackle fraud and corruption. The government declined to change the existing, defective legal and administrative arrangements.[31]
- 2016: The government released a briefing paper 'on the outcomes of the public consultation on . . . the review of the Building Management Ordinance' two years after it had been launched.[32]

The 2016 document was a shocking response to ten years of petition and complaint. It was not a plan of action but another effort to avoid legislating. Suggestions that breaches of the Building Management Ordinance should be punishable by law were countered by the government with the argument that because members of management committees were volunteers, it would be unfair to punish them for breaking the law. The widespread complaints of dishonest bid-rigging for works contracts were not taken seriously. The government decided that changes to existing legislation to eliminate opportunities for fraudulent and corrupt behaviour would not be made. Thus, maintenance contracts, which were supposed to be awarded on an open and competitive basis, would continue to be in danger of going to parties linked to members of management committees in return for financial rewards.

The government stated that a range of legal and other professional groups had been organised to help managements improve their performance—another stratagem to minimise the government's direct involvement in overcoming the threats to such a large proportion of the community's homes. The only significant concession was a pledge that the police and the Independent Commission Against Corruption (ICAC) would investigate more thoroughly reports made by the public. The private sector was being told to find its own solutions. The professional resources available were totally inadequate. There were 800 property management companies in Hong Kong, supplying services to 24,000 private sector residential buildings, 60 per cent of the total. Properties in this category could be enormous, 'with many buildings containing as many as 10,000 or more flats'.[33] Some 9,000 buildings were managed by owners' corporations and other residents' organisations without professional assistance. Another 7,000 were old tenement blocks which had no formal management arrangements.[34]

The government could not completely ignore the political costs of leaving 40 per cent of the private housing stock entirely unaided. As a stopgap measure after Operation Building Bright was wound up, a Home Affairs Department briefing paper in 2016 promised that the number of its 'liaison officers' recruited for 'building management duties' would be increased 'from about 120 to 128 (an increase of about 6.7 per cent)'. In the past, they had been given 'about 80 hours of training', which would now be increased to 90.[35] This increase in staffing and training could do almost nothing to provide the volume of services needed. On average, a building with no formal management would get one visit a year from a liaison officer. Visits to a building 'with some form of residents' representation' averaged just over four a year. What could be done in such brief encounters by Home Affairs staff with limited training was in no way a proper substitute for professional management, all the more so because the two categories of buildings being assisted included the oldest and the most rundown.[36]

The need to lay down professional standards for property management was recognised at last in 2016 when the Property Management Services Ordinance was passed. The new law was full of potential loopholes, however, and was neither universal or compulsory.[37] A Property Management Services Authority started work the following year to create a regulatory system for professional standards covering both management firms and personnel, although the staff and the funding to be made available to the new Authority remained unclear. The standards to be imposed by a new Code of Practice on Building Management and Maintenance seemed likely to be far from stringent, however.[38]

## Conclusion

This chapter has explored why housing conditions deteriorate, why maintenance standards remain inadequate and how the limited legal obligations of both government and property owners have not been properly enforced. The discussion has shown that the multi-storey housing which dominates Hong Kong created unusual challenges for owners and property managers which could not be left to 'market forces' to solve. Nevertheless, the government tried first to avoid and then to delay direct intervention, a strategy which proved catastrophic.

It was not just the safety of Hong Kong families' homes which was at risk. The integrity of the government itself was in danger. The government's austerity policies combined with the deficiencies of the political system allowed the rise of corruption and malpractice in the property and land sectors. Public complaints were ignored or minimised, even by the ICAC, as Chapter 7 will explain.

On the government's part, the struggle continued to minimise its role in halting dilapidation even in the context of fire hazards. One argument put forward by the Security Minister in 2017 was that it would not be practical for the authorities to take 'direct action to eliminate fire hazards and recover the costs from the owners upon completion'. 'Such decisions taken by the enforcement authorities on their behalf . . . may trigger unnecessary disputes or even litigations', he said.[39] In effect, the Security Minister was disregarding fire hazards and the lives at risk in order to wait for owners and management committees to make up their minds as to what they were willing to do.

Why did this state of affairs persist when owner-occupiers and property-owners suffered such serious destruction of the value of their assets as buildings dilapidated? How had ministers and heads of department been able to brush aside the detailed investigations by the Director of Audit and a stream of reports from the Ombudsman and Legislative Council Panels? The sad truth is that when the same serious deficiencies in government performance had been unmasked year after year to no avail, politicians, pressure groups and the media felt they were wasting their energy in continuing to challenge a government that seemed determined not to reform its plainly misguided policies. A sense of indifference developed among the public as well when, year after year, a host of official reports was highlighted in the media but with the same lack of results. This monotonous process deterred political parties and the media from 'wasting' their time on these housing issues except when a fire or a building collapse caused casualties or some prominent personality was caught out in a breach of building-related laws. As for the owners, many believed that the less said in the legislature or by the media about dilapidation the better. Otherwise, increased public awareness might put the market value of their property at risk.

But also important, for most of the time, the government failed to bring home to the individual homeowner how serious was the damage created by minimising maintenance and postponing repairs. How could there be a real health or safety threat when ministers and officials repeatedly emphasised that it was up to the individual to take action? If buildings were truly in a dangerous condition, it was reasonable to assume that the government would intervene and sound the alarm. In the meantime, the message was: no need to panic.

## Notes

1. Professor Anthony Cheung Bing-leung, Secretary for Transport and Housing, 'Chairman's Foreword Long Term Housing Strategy—Providing Adequate Housing for All?', in Long Term Housing Strategy Steering Committee, *Long Term Housing Strategy: Building Consensus, Building Homes* (Consultation Document, September 2013), v, vi.

2. Long Term Housing Strategy Steering Committee, *Long Term Housing Strategy: Building Consensus, Building Homes*, 9–10.

3. 'Adequate' is used in a very comparative sense: what the Hong Kong community regarded as acceptable was by no means 'adequate' by comparison with housing conditions in Singapore, for example. The following chapter elaborates on this point.

4. Development Bureau, 'Legislative Council Panel on Development Subcommittee on Building Safety and Related Issues: Measures to Enhance Building Safety in Hong Kong', Annex: 'Legislative Council Brief Measures to Enhance Building Safety in Hong Kong (File Ref: DEVB(PL-CR) 12/2010)', (CB(1)681/10-11(01), December 2010), 1.

5. Barry Cheung Chun-yuen, 'Chairman's Statement', in Urban Renewal Authority, *Annual Report 2010–2011*, 5–6.

6. Barry Cheung, 'Chairman's Statement', 5–6.

7. The most important stimulant to this housing boom was the abolition of traditional statutory height restrictions. K. M. A. Barnett, Census Commissioner, 'Introduction', in W. F. Maunder, *Hong Kong Urban Rents and Housing* (Hong Kong: Hong Kong University Press, 1969), 1.

8. *Hong Kong Annual Departmental Report by the Registrar General 1959–60* (Hong Kong: Government Printer, n.d.), 3.

9. 'Report of the 1963 Working Party on Government Policies and Practices with Regard to Squatters, Resettlement and Low Cost Housing' (mimeo 1963), 8. HKRS163-3-219, 'Working Party on Squatters, Resettlement and Government Low-Cost Housing'.

10. Except where otherwise indicated, the analysis, together with quotations and data, in this and the following three paragraphs, is based on Urban Renewal Authority *Annual Reports* and on its 'Steering Committee on Review of the Urban Renewal Strategy, 'Report on the Building Conditions Survey' (SC Paper No. 18/2009, 30 June 2009), 2–3.

11. Audit Commission, *Report No. 64*, 'Chapter 1: Buildings Department's Actions on Unauthorised Building Works', *Report No. 64* (Hong Kong, 2015), ix, 13–15, 44.

12. Anthony Cheung, Secretary for Transport and Housing, *Hong Kong Hansard* (*HH* hereafter), 14 November 2012, 1892–93.

13. Tony Miller, Director of Housing, 'Becoming Stakeholders of Hong Kong: Home Ownership', Speech to the Hong Kong Institute of Real Estate Administration (19 February 1997); Lau Kai-hung, Deputy Director of Housing, *Government Information Services* (*GIS* hereafter), 30 January 2006.

14. Full details of these measures were set out in Development Bureau, 'Panel on Development Subcommittee on Building Safety and Related Issues: Consolidation of Financial Assistance Schemes for Building Maintenance and Repair' (CB(1)2087/10-11(02), May 2011).

15. Michael Suen Ming-yeung, Secretary for Housing, Planning and Lands, *GIS*, 25 October 2003.

16. Urban Renewal Authority, Steering Committee on Review of the Urban Renewal Strategy, 'Study on Building Maintenance' (SC Paper No. 19/2009, July 2009), 1; Development Bureau, 'Panel on Development Subcommittee on Building Safety and Related Issues: Consolidation of Financial Assistance Schemes for Building Maintenance and Repair'.

17. John Tsang Chun-wah, Financial Secretary, *HH*, 25 February 2009, 4995–97.

18. Carrie Lam, Secretary for Development, *GIS*, 26 February 2009.

19. Legislative Council Secretariat, 'Panel on Development Minutes of Meeting Held on Tuesday, 26 January 2010 . . .' (CB(1)1508/09-10), 8 April 2010), 13–16.

20. Donald Tsang Yam-kuen, Chief Executive, *HH*, 10 October 2007, 24–25.

21. Donald Tsang, Chief Executive, *HH*, 13 October 2010, 18, 20–21.

22. Legislative Council Secretariat, 'Panel on Development . . . Updated Background Brief on the Work of the Urban Renewal Authority' (CB(1)1034/15-16(02), 15 June 2016), 7.

23. Implementation of the programme was a responsibility shared among four separate bodies: Development Bureau, Buildings Department, Hong Kong Housing Society, and the Urban Renewal Authority. 'Operation Building Bright', 1, 2.

24. There was a curious ambivalence about the precise timing for ending this programme. Hui Siu-wai, Director of Buildings, 'Examination of Estimates of Expenditure 2016–17 Reply Serial No. DEVB(PL)283'.

25. Home Affairs Department, *A Guide on Building Management Ordinance (Cap. 344)* (8th ed., January 2016), 1.

26. Barry Cheung, 'Chairman's Statement', in Urban Renewal Authority, *Annual Report 2012–13*, 7.

27. Legislative Council Panel on Development, 'Subcommittee on Building Safety and Related Issues: Measures to Enhance Building Safety in Hong Kong', 3.

28. Home Affairs Department, 'Legislative Council Panel on Home Affairs Regulation of the Property Management Industry' (CB(2)457/13-14(06), December 2013), 1, 2.

29. Legislative Council Secretariat, 'Panel on Home Affairs Minutes of Special Meeting Held on Friday, 4 July 2008 . . . ' (CB(2)2850/07-08), 22 October 2008), 10.

30. Legislative Council Secretariat, 'Panel on Home Affairs Background Brief Prepared . . . for the Meeting on 17 November 2014 Review of the Building Management Ordinance' (CB(2)238/14-15(04), 13 November 2014), 1.

31. Home Affairs Department, 'Legislative Council Panel on Home Affairs Review of the Building Management Ordinance (Cap. 344)' (CB(2)238/14-15(03), November 2014), 1, 5.

32. Home Affairs Department, 'Legislative Council Panel on Home Affairs Review of the Building Management Ordinance (Cap. 344)' (CB(2)1502/15-16(03), May 2016), 10–11; 'Annex 3: Efforts of the Relevant Government Departments and Organisations on Preventing and Combating Bid-Rigging in Building Maintenance Works', 1; 'Annex 7: Measures and Schemes Launched by the Home Affairs Department in Recent Years', 2.

33. Legislative Council Secretariat, 'Panel on Home Affairs Minutes of Meeting Held on Tuesday, 17 May 2016 . . . ' (CB(2)2016/15-16), 1 September 2016), 4.

34. Legislative Council Secretariat, 'Panel on Home Affairs Background Brief . . . 2013 Proposed Regulatory Framework for the Property Management Industry' (CB(2)457/13-14(07), 6 December 2013), 1.

35. Home Affairs Department, 'Legislative Council Panel on Home Affairs Review of the Building Management Ordinance (Cap. 344)', 12.

36. 'Written Answer by the Home Affairs Bureau to Mr Cheung Kwok-che's Supplementary Question to Question 1', *HH*, 25 November 2015, A 1.

37. Property Management Services Ordinance (Cap. 626); see sections 6 and 7.

38. For example, starting with relatively low standards of professional qualification. See Legislative Council Secretariat, 'Report of the Bills Committee on Property Management Services Bill' (CB(2)765/15-16), 28 January 2016), 6. Rather than raising standards, the new authority was supposed to respect existing practices and 'duly consider the views of the property management services industry and relevant Stakeholders' in drafting the new regulations and other subsidiary legislation. Lau Kong-wah, Secretary for Home Affairs, *HH*, 7 December 2016, 1980–83.

39. Lai Tung-kwok, Secretary for Security, *HH*, 14 June 2017.

# 4
# From squatter huts to 'invisible' slums

The most serious dereliction of duty by Hong Kong's rulers over the last two decades has been to adopt policies which would inevitably reduce both the housing supply and the quality of the average home. This situation was a disgrace by international standards. A United Nations agency pointed out in 2006 that in Hong Kong's private sector, the slum population was growing far faster than the average rate for other advanced economies. To add to Hong Kong's shame, Singapore, it was noted, had eradicated its slums completely.[1] In 2015, the same agency highlighted another disturbing feature of Hong Kong's housing: its 'invisible urban slums'. In this category were 67,000 sub-divided housing units in the private sector. These were home to 171,300 individuals, who paid exorbitant rents despite 'overcrowding, health and fire hazards'.[2]

In 2013, the Housing Minister frankly admitted that Hong Kong's housing crisis had reached alarming proportions.

> Today, housing tops the livelihood issues of concern to the general public – the proliferation of subdivided units (SDUs), under-supply of housing, rising property prices and rents beyond the affordability of the general public . . . our housing problem has resulted in a divided society and aggravated class conflicts.[3]

This was a catastrophe for which there was no excuse. In the past, the public housing programme had been 'widely acclaimed as a success that helped transform society', providing safe and affordable homes for 866,000 households in 1997 (45 per cent of total households), while owner occupancy in the private sector had reached 52 per cent that year.[4]

From 1998, however, policies changed, and there was a rapid retreat from the government's commitment to maintaining an adequate supply of public housing. Its housing programmes were dismantled as extensively as possible. By 2012, the annual average supply of new public housing units was 62 per cent lower than the 1997 level. Among the explanations given for slashing public housing was the government's desire to create greater scope for the private sector. The result of this policy was not increased supply but higher prices as the private sector's output fell by 45 per cent over the same period.[5]

However, it would be wrong to over-romanticise the past and believe that Hong Kong families were well provided with ideal homes before 1997. The supply of both public and private housing had risen fast enough to have eliminated virtually all squatter and temporary housing by that date and the worst of the slum conditions in the private sector. Safety and affordability had been achieved for the bulk of Hong Kong homes. But this was still bare adequacy, a minimal standard which the contemporary community had been conditioned to tolerate from birth. Most serious of all, the supply was barely sufficient. Any change in government policy that reduced the availability of public housing or failed to maintain a steady rise in its quality would be a severe setback to hopes of improving the occupants' standard of living. As would be any significant fall in the private sector supply or increase in prices or rents.

Thus, in 1997, it remained true that except for the well-off family, the average home, whether in the public or the private sector, was cramped, with restricted facilities and only really tolerable for those who spent most of the day at work and had no mobility problems. Privacy was at a premium. Walls were too thin to provide peace and quiet not only for young people who needed to study but also for the older generation who were easily disturbed by noise. The average living unit's design was not ideal for an ageing population. Wheelchair users usually found doors and corridors too narrow for comfort. Bathrooms and toilets had little space for the safety bars that elderly people needed.

This chapter begins with an overview of how Hong Kong overcame the severe lack of decent homes following the flood of newcomers from the Mainland seeking refuge from civil war and revolution after 1945. This is followed by a review of the dramatic reversal by Tung Chee Hwa, the first Chief Executive, of his own pledge to maintain the successful public housing programmes of the past and the dire consequences that followed. Then comes a discussion of the second Chief Executive's determination that, as far as possible, the private sector should be left to solve the housing crisis without fear of competition from government-subsidised accommodation.

The third Chief Executive's performance is discussed in more detail, since he was left with the task of tackling the disastrous legacy of the dismantling of public housing programmes. This section explains how, despite his public recognition of the catastrophe that had overtaken Hong Kong homes, he shared the same preference for the private sector as did his predecessors. In addition, he lacked the political credibility and the administrative skills to launch effective solutions and to mobilise the public backing they needed.

The fourth Chief Executive was trapped by the mismanagement of the past in which she had taken part as the minister responsible for key building issues. The best she could offer as a remedial policy for her first term in office was to increase supply. This involved toleration of the rising tide of illegal and generally unsafe homes in deteriorating residential buildings and vacant factory premises with a chance that some form of monitoring for health and safety might be possible. She hoped, too, that with her creation of more consultative bodies, some solution would emerge although, in practice, what the government needed to do was already very plain, as this chapter will demonstrate in detail.

## From squalor to affordable homes

The community was able to tolerate this century's deterioration in the quality of its homes without mass protests and political unrest because so many families had survived dreadful accommodation in the colonial era. Hong Kong's intractable housing woes had begun in the 1940s with the influx of a tide of newcomers. The population was around 600,000 at the end of the Japanese Occupation in 1945. By 1956, it was estimated to have reached 2.5 million. A very high proportion were making their homes in squatter huts erected mostly on hillsides but also on rooftops, roadsides and anywhere there was a suitable, unoccupied site. But unlike most squatter communities in the world's cities, these makeshift homes were not the result of poverty. The community, including the squatters, was prospering as a result of Hong Kong's industrial take-off in the 1950s and the full employment and rising wages which prevailed in the decades that followed.[6]

Squatters, nevertheless, faced considerable hardships. There were the inevitable dangers caused by winter fires and summer typhoons. There were the deliberate discomforts inflicted by the colonial administration to deter squatting.[7] It decreed that to supply safe drinking water, there would be '1 tap for 500 people'. As for sanitation, the colonial administration rationed public latrines to '1 compartment [per] 100 people' in the squatter areas.[8] These disgraceful 'deterrents' remained in force into the 1970s.[9] Furthermore, official policy in that early era was to clear squatter areas solely to free land for development. There was no intention to improve living standards.

When a full-scale public housing programme began after the Shek Kip Mei fire in 1953, the living units were deliberately designed to provide minimum comfort in order to deter families from becoming squatters by choice in order to qualify for rehousing in a 'resettlement block'. The senior health official said they set a world record for overcrowding.[10] The law specified a minimum of 35 square feet of living space per person, (which was very similar to the Mainland's standards

in 1960).[11] The colonial administration ignored the statutory requirement and allocated only 24 square feet per adult. In practice, as families
grew, the average living space had dropped to '16 sq. ft. for an adult
and 8 sq. ft. for a child', a government report admitted in 1963.[12] There
was virtually no privacy in the communal latrines and washing facilities
which families had to share on each floor of a multi-storey resettlement
block. Cooking had to be done in the corridors. Fortunately, standards
of personal hygiene were very high despite the communal squalor
because it was not until 1965 that the government began to build 'Mark
IV Resettlement Blocks', in which every living unit had its own toilet.[13]

In the 1970s, policies changed, and improving the quality of public
housing became a major goal. Living space per head was increased, and
household amenities improved. A subsidised Home Ownership Scheme
(HOS) was launched to enable public housing tenants to climb on to
the property ladder and join the ranks of the middle classes as their
incomes improved. Public housing finally ceased to be an emergency
policy in the 1980s and was transformed into an efficient, well-planned,
well-resourced and high-priority government programme. But the actual
living standards they provided were still barely adequate.

## Squalor returns

Tung had come into office with a compelling vision of how to put an end
to inadequate housing through a major increase in the annual supply.
'To me and to the community as a whole, housing is the number one
priority', he declared, 'To be able to build these 85,000 [new housing]
units is the absolute priority'.[14] But he rapidly retreated from this commitment when he and business leaders panicked at the start of the
1997–1998 Asian financial crisis. This policy reversal was tragic. His well-
designed public housing programme had developed a momentum so
dynamic that it proved difficult to halt. By 2002, it had overcome the
worst of the housing problems inherited from the colonial era at an
even faster rate than Tung had originally planned.[15]

Waiting times for public rental housing had been halved. The
number of 'inadequately housed' families fell from 170,000 to 100,000.
Overcrowding in public housing was virtually eliminated. All 12,600
families living on makeshift 'temporary housing' sites had been moved
to decent accommodation.[16] The private sector was offering affordable
purchase prices and reasonable rentals. It seemed that, at last, Hong
Kong's perpetual housing crisis was coming to an end. Instead, Tung
capitulated to 'market forces' and pressures from developers. His vision-
ary housing programme was brought to an abrupt halt, and Hong Kong's
much-vaunted public housing policies were discarded.

Tung had assumed, for no convincing reason, that Hong Kong must be engulfed by financial turmoil during the 1997–1998 Asian financial crisis although its economy had survived, almost effortlessly, every previous political and financial crisis in Asia since the defeat of Japan in 1945. He offered no cogent explanation as to why Hong Kong's fate should be any different this time. Indeed, the economy and its financial system's response demonstrated its innate robustness by easily defeating a major assault on the currency and the stock market by foreign speculators in 1998.[17]

But Tung was convinced that almost all public spending was a waste of money. His ambitious housing programme had been a unique exception which seems to have been inspired by political strategists who advised him that the programme was a short and certain path to the community's heart. When the Asian financial crisis began, his business instincts came to the fore, and he believed that he must pursue policies of maximum austerity. For the housing sector, this meant that the government would shelve as much of its building programme as possible. The removal of government 'competition' would then rescue developers from the acute pressures on the property market which Tung's deflation would cause, it was argued. There was a political dividend for Tung personally. The real estate magnates had considerable influence with the nation's leadership and with the Chief Executive Selection Committee and Legislative Council functional constituency representatives. Tung would need their backing for re-selection as Chief Executive in 2002.

Thus, the long-standing public rental housing programme was slashed, and the subsidised home ownership scheme (HOS) terminated. The government suspended normal sales of building sites and liquidated its land bank. In parallel, Tung adopted an austerity programme which imposed an unprecedented deflation on Hong Kong and drove down property values. The hardship caused by Tung's policies affected virtually every family in Hong Kong, as he publicly admitted in 2004.[18] These measures were to remain in force long after economic recovery got underway.[19]

A vicious circle began as Tung abandoned government responsibility for ensuring decent homes for all. His confidence that the market would provide the solution was naive. Because it was more profitable for developers to reduce production and obtain higher prices per square foot for new living units, they cut the supply of new buildings. The volume of construction was no longer large enough to match rising demand and to maintain stable prices for would-be home-owners and to offer reasonable rents to potential tenants. At the same time, the public sector was being dismantled, so that the average lower-income family lost the prospect of being allocated public housing and escaping from the expensive squalor they faced in private rented accommodation. To make matters worse, the public sector no longer had the capacity to tackle another mounting housing crisis: the rehousing of occupants of dilapidated private-sector buildings. The consequences were alarming. Growing numbers had to find their homes in premises which were dangerous and unhealthy.

## Personal property portfolio

Tung's Financial Secretary and future successor, Donald Tsang Yam-kuen, supported an even more complete renunciation of government responsibility for solving the housing shortage. The private sector should be freed from 'unfair' competition from public housing programmes, he proclaimed, and he was unembarrassed about confessing he was protecting the value of his own property investment. The way to achieve this goal, he unashamedly proclaimed, was to create the maximum demand for private sector housing through shrinking the public supply.[20]

Tsang's insistence that market forces could provide Hong Kong with the homes it needed turned out to be hopelessly misguided, and the community was unable to endure the falling supply of housing and rising prices and rents indefinitely. By 2009, public discontent could no longer be ignored. Nevertheless, a stubborn rear-guard campaign was waged to maintain the policy that a competitive market should be left to provide the solution.[21] The government's claims to community support for minimising the supply of public housing in order to protect private sector prices were finally discredited by a research project which its own Central Policy Unit had sponsored. This report advised that an increased supply of public housing was needed to maintain 'social harmony' and declared that the government should revise 'long-term land and housing policies . . . in that light'.[22] Shortly afterwards, the government capitulated.[23] Tsang's 2010 Policy Address began to revive, but on a limited scale, the public housing programmes he had so thoroughly dismantled ten years earlier.[24]

The damage his mistaken policies had done was severe. The end to 'competition' from the public sector, which he and Tung had deliberately engineered, had proved brutally painful for the community although profitable for property interests. As the supply of new private flats dropped sharply between 1997 and 2012, average prices rose by 47 per cent. The developers had discovered that lower output brought higher profits. The longer-term damage was to prove even more disastrous. The government's land reserves had been surrendered to developers, and the government's own highly professional housing development teams had been deliberately dispersed. It would prove impossible to resurrect large-scale public housing programmes in a hurry.

## The professional takes over

The third Chief Executive, Leung Chun-ying, took over in 2012. He appeared to be well qualified to identify how best to solve the housing crisis. He was a protégé of Tung, who had selected him, even before the end of the colonial era, as one of three special advisers who could take charge of crucial, long-term policymaking. Leung was given housing.[25] He had professional qualifications in the property sector, considerable experience in advising Mainland cities on housing issues and a successful career with a well-known real estate corporation. He had taken part in every government policy decision on housing since 1997 because he was serving on the Executive Council, becoming its Senior Member (Convenor) in 1998.

His election manifesto in 2012 reflected considerable familiarity with the housing crisis and its significance to the community. But Leung proved as much committed to relying on free market forces as his two predecessors had been. 'Housing tops the list of livelihood issues that are of public concern', the manifesto read, 'It is also the bedrock of a stable society'. However, sentiment was not translated into any commitment to achieve substantial increases in the output of public housing. The section, 'My Pledge on Housing,' gave almost all its space to the private housing market and how to promote home ownership.[26]

The manifesto also mentioned, but did not promise, special treatment for those families which it classified as living in inadequate housing. There would be a 'comprehensive survey' of 'residents of sub-divided units, caged homes and cubicle apartments', and the government would 'set appropriate safety and hygiene standards and formulate long-term policies to solve the problem'. On taking office, the contrast between sympathy and substance became very plain. Leung seemed very aware of the damage his predecessors had done. The drastic fall in the supply had made decent homes unaffordable for many families, he said. 'Cramped living space in cage homes, cubicle apartments and sub-divided flats has become the reluctant choice for tens of thousands of Hong Kong people', he went on. But he had never intended to give public rental housing a priority on the scale needed to achieve early relief. Instead, 'home ownership by the middle class' was 'crucial to social stability', he declared, a generalisation for which he offered no evidence. It fitted in neatly, however, with his positive attitude towards the private market.

The most he was willing to do to convince the public of his good intentions and to 'demonstrate unequivocally the Government's commitment . . . to resolving the housing problem' was to appoint a Long Term Housing Strategy Steering Committee.[27] A fortnight later, an official release revealed how slowly Leung's public housing programme would gather momentum. It would take five years to restore 'land planning and consultation procedures, as well as design and build'. There could be no significant increase in public sector output before 2018 at 'the earliest'.[28]

There was worse to come. Neither Leung nor his ministers had set unambiguous goals for the Steering Committee. As a result, the Committee's report began with a confession of confusion. 'Our vision is to help all households in Hong Kong gain access to adequate and affordable housing', it declared, which sounded sensible enough. But this simple statement was reduced to the ridiculous by the 181-word footnote which accompanied it. This began with a frank renunciation of responsibility: 'There is no common standard of adequate and afford-able housing'. The lengthy disclaimer ended with an invocation of market forces: 'In terms of affordability, by maintaining a healthy and stable private housing market, people could meet their housing needs in accordance with their means'.[29] The only unequivocal message that committee members had got from Leung, apparently, was to remember the private sector's role.

## Left below the poverty line

As the official warnings first began to reveal that the supply of public housing would remain hopelessly inadequate for years to come, the government's Economic Analysis Division was assembling a document that demonstrated how public rental housing provided more than a decent home. Tenants were actually lifted out of poverty when they moved into a public housing flat. According to this 2013 study, the effectiveness of public rental housing in alleviating poverty was second only to the cash maintenance for families provided by the Comprehensive Social Security Assistance Scheme (CSSA).[30] A follow-up report in 2016 drew attention to 'the visible difference in living quality between [public rental housing] households and low-income households living in private rental housing'.[31]

Reducing the number of families below the poverty line had been a well-publicised aim of Leung's administration, which made his case for limiting the role of the public sector in his search for a housing solution all the more unjustifiable. He was also ignoring the savings to the taxpayer when the families who, thanks to public housing, were lifted above the poverty line no longer needed social security benefits. Furthermore, his focus on making it easier for the middle class to buy flats seemed unlikely to match the 'social stability' dividend from improved living standards that public housing brought to low-income families, contrary to the message in his first Policy Address.

## The market's own solution

Hong Kong's free market knew just how to exploit the situation. It created the successors to the squatter huts and the slum tenements of the previous century. The government offered no resistance to the rise of this 21st century market solution to the desperate shortage of affordable housing: what a United Nations study of Asia's housing problems labelled Hong Kong's 'invisible urban slums'—subdivided units (SDUs).[32] They were created by converting conventional living quarters into tiny homes.[33] These intensified the miserable conditions in older buildings where maintenance had long been neglected. They were overcrowded, frequently dangerous and a gross exploitation of the lower income groups excluded from public housing. The SDUs also increased the strain on worn-out plumbing, wiring and other facilities, which accelerated the deterioration of the older housing stock. But they were the market's profitable response to Hong Kong's mounting housing crisis.

In 2011, the public was outraged by the revelations of unsafe and unhealthy conditions in dilapidated tenements after fires that year got out of hand, killing a total of 13 and injuring another 53. Predictably, it was found that casualties had been aggravated by unlawful modifications to the premises. Legislators, non-governmental organisations (NGOs) and advocacy groups campaigned hard to inform the community of the dangers and defects of SDU accommodation. Surveys, both those officially commissioned and those undertaken by NGOs and advocacy organisations, reported in detail on the unacceptable conditions which they uncovered.[34]

Leung's first Policy Address had shown his familiarity with this scandal. His expressions of concern for these unfortunate tenants were not to be translated into vigorous action to control and curtail the SDU sector, however, and it continued to expand.[35] By 2015, almost 200,000 tenants were estimated to be living in these costly, cramped and ill-equipped homes. The community regarded the creation of these new slums with dismay. But in market terms, they were attractive to a large class of individuals who would otherwise have been homeless. These tenants had not been driven into SDUs by their personal poverty. They were simply the long-term victims of the first two Chief Executives and their decision to reduce the supply of public housing and to leave the private sector free to maximise their profits through their monopoly advantages.

The result was that as the supply of new private flats fell, prices went up and low-income households were left unable to survive except through renting less living space. In 2015, almost 70 per cent of SDU occupants had jobs, and a majority of the rest were homemakers or students. The average SDU household had a monthly income of $12,500. This sum was half the average for the community as a whole, which put the average

SDU tenant just on the poverty line. But less than a quarter of them claimed that they had moved into SDUs because of 'financial difficulties'.

For 60 per cent of these households, the market rent for a regular flat was unaffordable, they reported. They were unable to obtain subsidised public housing. The practical solution was to shrink their living space, which was exactly what an SDU offered. An average living space of 48 square feet per head cost them 32 per cent of their monthly income. This meant that their rent was no higher than the average monthly spending on private sector housing by the community as a whole. And the share of an SDU tenant's income spent on rent was probably some 5 per cent or more below the average for the private housing sector as a whole.[36] SDUs provided 'affordable' homes.

A very worrying issue was disregard for the law. SDUs could only survive if Chief Executives and their ministers ignored breaches of building and other related legislation. Yet, a 2013 government consultation document had recommended that SDUs should continue to be tolerated even if the supply of low-cost housing increased sufficiently to meet demand, provided that safety standards could be ensured.[37] Considerable effort was made to fudge the dubious legal status of this accommodation. The government's 'Long Term Housing Strategy' rejected proposals to control the SDU sector and its growth even though the document identified the proliferation of SDUs as among the worst symptoms of the housing crisis in 2014.

Instead, it tried to bestow a measure of respectability on this widely condemned accommodation and refused to accept that these tenants should be automatically classified as 'inadequately housed'. The only concession made to the critics of SDUs was the promise to take action 'against irregularities relating to building and fire safety' in residential buildings.[38] Since the government had already failed to eliminate these threats in a high proportion of older buildings, it was hard to believe that fire risks and health dangers could be eradicated from the SDU sector very easily.

## Power changes hands

Eventually, the burdens of office became too much for Leung. He appeared to lose control of housing and related land issues in December 2016, with open clashes between him and members of his ministerial team about developments in the New Territories. These events were reported to have left him close to tears. Shortly afterwards, he announced that he would not continue in office because he was unable to give his family the attention which they needed.

In many ways, Leung's downfall had become unavoidable. Despite the respectable professional background which had made him Tung Chee

Hwa's chosen housing expert in 1997, he had offered no visible opposition to Tung's gross mismanagement of housing policy. As the senior member of the Executive Council, Leung had tolerated without protest the even less acceptable approach of Donald Tsang to the housing crisis. He shared the market beliefs of Tung and Tsang and suffered much the same isolation from the community at large. It had not helped his political standing that during his term as Chief Executive, there was a lack of frankness in reporting the waiting times for the Housing Authority's queues of qualified applicants for public housing.[39] The Ombudsman released a report at the end of 2015 complaining that the Housing Department had failed to cooperate in evaluating the reported average waiting times and warning that the Department's statistics could not be trusted. At the end of his term in office, Leung admitted that waiting times had actually got worse.[40]

Leung's unfinished business was summed up by his Housing Minister in December 2016:

> Our "housing crisis" is characterized by a serious supply-demand imbalance, housing prices and rents at a level beyond the affordability of the general public and out of line with our economic fundamentals, the proliferation of inadequately housed households and subdivided units (SDUs), and long queues for public rental housing.[41]

Carrie Lam Cheng Yuet-ngor came into office as Chief Executive with much the same trust in market forces and belief in the importance of the middle-class home owner as her predecessor. She acknowledged the community's 'rightful expectation' that the government should 'provide adequate housing' in order to ensure 'social harmony and stability'. Nevertheless, 'we will focus on home-ownership,' she declared in her 2017 Policy Address, 'to enable our people to live happily in Hong Kong and call it their home'.[42]

Inevitably, the flawed housing policies with which she had been so closely involved, both as a minister and then as Chief Secretary, would continue. But now there would be greater tolerance of more subdivided, overcrowded and illegal premises in the private sector. Her new Housing Minister, Frank Chan Fan, made it his top priority not just to take control of the growing stock of largely illegal SDUs but to increase it judiciously. The intention, Chan told the media, was to ease the private sector's shortfalls by organising an expansion of 'quality subdivided flats'. The use of 'old buildings, especially those waiting to be rebuilt' would be encouraged. 'These will then be revamped into subdivided units which are much more liveable than many currently in use', he went on. He hoped to ensure that they complied 'with the Buildings Ordinance [and] also guarantee safety and sanitary standards', he said, while charging only half the market rate for rents.[43] On past history, that seemed likely to prove an elusive goal. But the government would be able to minimise its own responsibility because this programme would be run by welfare agencies.

Chan's proposal was floated with little attention to the challenges faced in implementing such an ambitious programme. These included dealing with the illegality of most SDUs, arranging the public financing that would be required and mobilising suitable welfare agencies to run the programme. His own apparent confusion over how his proposals would be implemented was widely criticised. But his obvious good intentions moderated the attacks he encountered in the media and from the professionals involved. The new minister was also fortunate in acquiring the support of the well-regarded Hong Kong Council of Social Service, which believed his formula would enable the business world to cooperate with the welfare sector in solving the housing shortage.[44] Chan's plan was inspired by desperation. 'Adequate' housing to meet the public's needs would not be available for the foreseeable future. The best the government could manage was an attempt to control the worst excesses created by the housing shortfall while ignoring buildings and safety legislation.

This was makeshift policy at its most alarming. The government's private sector bias meant that it was failing to provide the volume of new public housing needed to house the lower income groups. As a result, the pressures continued to create private sector slums to accommodate those left to the mercy of the market. In the meantime, this group struggled to find some living space in which to 'squat' while spending years queuing for public rental housing.

## Conclusion

For the government's Long Term Housing Strategy Steering Committee to confess that its members were unsure of what 'adequate and affordable housing' meant was a cry of despair, an admission that no one in the government had any confidence that there could be a solution to the housing crisis. Nothing seemed likely to change in the foreseeable future. In 2017, a new Chief Secretary, Matthew Cheung Kin-chung, summed up the housing environment that confronted the fourth Chief Executive, Carrie Lam, and her team: 'a rapidly ageing population, pressing demand for housing, economic activities and community facilities, as well as a growing aspiration for more living space and better quality of life'. He mentioned several possible initiatives to expand future housing supply. But, in reality, there seemed little chance of meeting the public's aspirations.

The hopelessness of the situation was obvious from the empty formula he put forward as the basis for housing policy under the new Chief Executive: 'Hong Kong needs to respond strategically to meet these challenges and tap into new opportunities'. The challenges were just too daunting, however, and the resources allocated to overcome them remained too limited. 'While we have a rapidly ageing population', he rightly pointed out, 'we have an even more rapidly ageing building stock that poses health and safety risks for the community'. Token assistance had been the government's response in the past. The total number of dilapidated buildings ran to thousands. Yet, between 2011 and 2016, redevelopment of the more dangerous buildings had been extremely slow. The government accepted no blame for this state of affairs. 'Owners are responsible for timely maintenance of their buildings', the Chief Secretary insisted, although he confessed that 'many of them find the relevant procedures rather daunting', which was a cruel understatement.[45]

The underlying policy of the new administration was little different from that of the first three Chief Executives: minimum government intervention in the housing market regardless of the social and economic costs. Under Carrie Lam, there would be a continuation of the overcrowding and squalid living conditions of the past which had been dramatic enough to catch the attention of a United Nations agency, it was noted earlier.

Because of the failure of Chief Executives to recognise the threat to Hong Kong homes, especially in the private sector, the grim housing conditions of a previous era were being resurrected. Misguided convictions about the superior efficiency of market forces in solving the public's needs had led to Tung Chee Hwa's termination of an extremely successful public housing programme. The shortage of affordable homes that followed became so severe that, increasingly, low-income groups could find no other accommodation except makeshift living space. And thus, the SDUs were allowed to proliferate. It seemed incredible that in a city as prosperous as Hong Kong, its government could insist that there was no alternative to SDUs. Yet, Carrie Lam, as the minister originally responsible for this policy, had claimed that if these illegal and often dangerous premises were forced to close down, there was no alternative housing for their tenants.[46] Her solution was to leave things to the market and the SDUs it encouraged and thus reduce the government's responsibility for ensuring a supply of homes for Hong Kong people that met their expectations for health, safety and comfort and the law's requirements.[47]

The increased role of SDUs and their recognition as a 'legitimate' source of homes for lower income groups meant that, once again, the government was taking refuge in makeshift solutions. SDUs actually aggravated the physical deterioration of Hong Kong's private building stock, whose serious costs to the community the previous chapter described in some detail. The probability was high that the lifespan of these 'invisible urban slums'—to use the United Nations agency's term—would be extended far into the future, just as squatter huts had been tolerated for so many decades by the colonial administration. Furthermore, contrary to the Housing Minister's hopes, it was doubtful whether property owners could be prevented from seeking to achieve the full market rental for SDUs unless another feature of the past, the rent controls of the previous century, were reintroduced.[48]

## Notes

1. UN-HABITAT, *The State of the World's Cities Report 2006/2007: 30 Years of Shaping the Habitat Agenda* (London: Earthscan, 2006), 'Table 1: Population of Slum Areas at Mid-Year, by Region and Country; 1990, 2001 and Slum Annual Growth Rate', 181–82; 'Table 2: Slum Population Projections, 1990–2020', 193.
2. UN-Habitat and ESCAP, *The State of Asian and Pacific Cities 2015 Urban Transformations Shifting from Quantity to Quality* (2015), 'Box 3.4: Invisible Urban Slums', 94.
3. Professor Anthony Cheung Bing-leung, Secretary for Transport and Housing, 'Chairman's Foreword: Long Term Housing Strategy—Providing Adequate Housing for All?', in Long Term Housing Strategy Steering Committee, *Long Term Housing Strategy: Building Consensus, Building Homes* (Consultation Document, September 2013), v.
4. Long Term Housing Strategy Steering Committee, *Long Term Housing Strategy: Building Consensus, Building Homes*, 9–10.
5. To be precise: the annual average supply of new public housing units declined from 38,900 units in the period 1997–2002 to 14,600 in 2007–2012. The annual average supply of private sector units declined from 21,900 units in the period 1997–2002 to 9,900 in 2007–2012.
6. For the data recording this breakneck industrial takeoff, see Leo F. Goodstadt, *Profits, Politics and Panics: Hong Kong's Banks and the Making of a Miracle Economy, 1935–1985* (Hong Kong: Hong Kong University Press, 2007), 'Table I: Domestic Exports & Total Exports, 1950–1960 (HKD millions)', 69.
7. Roger Bristow, *Hong Kong's New Towns: A Selective Review* (Hong Kong: Oxford University Press, 1989), 40, 50.
8. (32) 'Note for Executive Council: Provision of Facilities in Resettlement Cottage Areas and Licensed Areas', 1; Annex A: 'Provision of Facilities in Resettlement Cottage Areas and Licensed Areas', XCR(68)302, 14 June 1968. HKRS394-20-8, 'Resettlement Policy Committee'.
9. 'Minutes of 72nd Meeting of the Housing Board . . . 17th January 1973', 3, 4. HKRS156-3-95, 'Squatters on Land Not Required for Development'.

10. (72) D. J. M. Mackenzie, Director of Medical and Health Services, Memo to Colonial Secretary, 'Resettlement Programme', 25 November 1958. HKRS163-3-64, 'Squatter Clearance and Resettlement 1. General Questions of . . . 2. Programmes of . . . '.

11. Nevertheless, in Mainland cities undergoing high-speed industrialisation during the 1950s (as Hong Kong itself was), living space fell to half the national average or less (in Lanzhou, for example). Kang Chao, 'Industrialization and Urban Housing in Communist China', *Journal of Asian Studies* 25, no. 3 (May 1966): 382, 393, 395.

12. 'Report of the 1963 Working Party on Government Policies and Practices with Regard to Squatters, Resettlement and Low Cost Housing', 8–9. HKRS163-3-219, 'Working Party on Squatters, Resettlement and Government Low Cost Housing'.

13. Aggravated by the absence of a communal garbage system, which meant that rubbish proliferated in the open areas. See M. Castells et al., *The Shek Kip Mei Syndrome: Economic Development and Public Housing in Hong Kong and Singapore* (London: Pion Limited, 1990), 19.

14. Tung Chee Hwa, Chief Executive, *Government Information Services* (*GIS* hereafter), 12 September 1997.

15. Shorter waiting times for public housing, for example, for which a 2005 deadline had been adopted originally. Tung, Chief Executive, *GIS*, 16 December 1998.

16. *Review of the Institutional Framework for Public Housing: The Report June 2002* (Hong Kong: SAR Government, 2002), 40–41.

17. Tsang Yam-kuen, Financial Secretary, *GIS*, 23 September 1999.

18. Tung, Chief Executive, *GIS*, 29 May 2004.

19. The official account of housing policy and the relevant data are conveniently summarised in Long Term Housing Strategy Steering Committee, *Long Term Housing Strategy: Building Consensus, Building Homes*, 11–13. See also Roger Nissim, 'A Fresh Look at Housing, Planning and Land Policy', in *Hong Kong's Budget: Challenges and Solutions for the Longer Term*, ed. Tony Latter (Hong Kong: Civic Exchange, 2009), 60–61.

20. Tsang, Chief Secretary, 'Statement on Housing' and Press Conference, *GIS*, 3 September 2001.

21. Government Spokesman, *GIS*, 25 October 2009.

22. Public Policy Research Institute, Polytechnic University, 'A Focus Group Study on Subsidising Home Ownership' (Central Policy Unit, September, 2010), 55.

23. Its surrender was grudging. Transport and Housing Branch, 'Report on Public Consultation on Subsidising Home Ownership' (October 2010), 6.

24. Tsang, Chief Executive, *Hong Kong Hansard* (*HH* hereafter), 10 October 2010, 12–14.

25. Tung, Chief Executive (Designate), *GIS*, 21 March 1997.

26. Leung Chun-ying, 'Manifesto for the Chief Executive Election 2012 One Heart, One Vision', 35–38.

27. Leung, Chief Executive, *HH*, 16 January 2013, 4910–11, 4913.

28. Chief Executive's Spokesman, *GIS*, 30 January 2013.

29. Transport and Housing Bureau, *Long Term Housing Strategy, December 2014*, 2–3. It should not be assumed, the footnote stated, that households 'living in subdivided units are necessarily inadequately housed'. The importance of deciding on a workable definition of 'adequate' had been raised previously by legislators. See Legislative Council Secretariat, 'Panel on Housing Report of the Subcommittee on the Long Term Housing Strategy' (CB(1)1705/13-14), 2 July 2014), 3, 5.

30. Economic Analysis Division, 'Hong Kong Poverty Situation Report 2012' (September 2013), 'Figure 4.14: Effectiveness of In-Kind Benefits in Alleviating Poverty, 2009–2012', 55 and 93.

31. Economic Analysis Division, 'Hong Kong Poverty Situation Report 2015' (October 2015), 'Box 2.2: Poverty Situation after Taking into Account In-Kind Benefits', 34.

32. UN-Habitat and ESCAP, *The State of Asian and Pacific Cities 2015 Urban Transformations Shifting from Quantity to Quality* (2015), 'Box 3.4: Invisible Urban Slums', 94.

33. These were a new version of what the government labelled 'Unauthorised Building Works' (UBW), which, since the start of the century, it had repeatedly promised to eradicate.

34. For the evidence from an officially commissioned private sector study, see Legislative Council Secretariat, 'Panel on Housing: Report of the Subcommittee on the Long Term Housing Strategy', 9. See also Diana Wong, Research Office, Legislative Council Secretariat, 'Information Note: Subdivided Flats in Hong Kong'.

35. Data in the discussion that follows are from Social Surveys Section, *Thematic Household Survey Report: Report No. 60—Housing Conditions of Sub-Divided Units in Hong Kong* (Hong Kong: Census and Statistics Department, March 2016).

36. This conclusion is based on a comparison of data from *Thematic Household Survey Report: Report No. 60—Housing Conditions of Sub-Divided Units in Hong Kong* with information from the 2014/15 Household Expenditure Survey. See Price Statistics Branch, *2014/15 Household Expenditure Survey and the Rebasing of the Consumer Price Indices* (Hong Kong: Census and Statistics Department, 2016), 'Box 1.9: Average Monthly Household Expenditure by Commodity/Service Section by Type of Housing', 18; 'Chart 5: Household Expenditure Patterns by Selected Tenure of Accommodation', 19; 'Box 1.10: Average Monthly Per Capita Expenditure by Commodity/Service Section by Household Size', 21.

37. Long Term Housing Strategy Steering Committee, *Long Term Housing Strategy: Building Consensus, Building Homes*, 65.

38. Transport and Housing Bureau, *Long Term Housing Strategy, December 2014*, 2–3. It should not be assumed, the footnote stated, that households 'living in subdivided units are necessarily inadequately housed'.

39. The one exception was a three-year maximum wait for qualified applicants for public rental housing. As things turned out, Leung did meet this target in his first term of office. (But note the Ombudsman's complaint in the following footnote.) Leung, 'Manifesto for the Chief Executive Election 2012: One Heart, One Vision', 35–38.

40. Leung, Chief Executive, *HH*, 18 January 2017; Office of The Ombudsman, 'Annex 1: Executive Summary Direct Investigation into Method of Calculation of Waiting Time for Public Rental Housing and Release of Information', *Issue No. 3 of Reporting Year 2015/16* (10 December 2015), 1–6.
41. Professor Anthony Cheung Bing-lung, Secretary for Transport and Housing, 'Housing Future at Its Critical Juncture', 3.
42. Carrie Lam Cheng Yuet-ngor, Chief Executive, *HH*, 11 October 2017.
43. See 'Housing chief plans to provide "quality subdivided flat"', *China Daily*, 12 July, 2017.
44. Expressions of scepticism ranged from the Hong Kong Institute of Architects to the government's own Housing Authority. For a good example of editorial anxiety to avoid a negative attitude towards the minister's ambitious initiative while warning of its failure to recognise the challenges in organising, financing and managing such an ambitious programme of urban renewal, see Editorial, '為劏房戶脫苦海　政府須靈活破格', *Hong Kong Economic Journal*, 10 July 2017.
45. Matthew Cheung Kin-chung, Chief Secretary, *GIS*, 5 June 2017.
46. Carrie Lam, Secretary for Development, *HH*, 7 December 2011, 2956.
47. See Wong, 'Information Note: Subdivided Flats in Hong Kong', 1.
48. Rent control legislation of various sorts had been in place from 1921 to 1998. Jackie Wu, 'Information Note: Tenancy Control in Selected Places' (Legislative Council Secretariat IN18/13-14, 2 July 2014), 19.

# 5
# The missing land banks

As the existing stock of housing was being endangered by inadequate management and maintenance, the future supply of housing was threatened by a severe shortage of building sites. Yet, the Special Administrative Region government had begun with the great advantage of a colonial legacy that gave the state far more extensive control over land, its use and occupation, than in almost any other advanced economy. Under government management was nearly 30 per cent of the total land area of Hong Kong.[1] This should have provided adequate land banks, as it had done in the colonial past. But Tung Chee Hwa's retreat from his initial ambitious programme to build more homes was followed by Donald Tsang's initiatives to dismantle the public housing programme. These new policies had drastically cut the Housing Authority's demand for construction sites, and its land bank was quickly sold off. This chapter will trace how government building programmes came to face paralysis and why the shortage of new sites for both public and private developments became so acute.

The full dimensions of this land shortage were not fully acknowledged until 2015 when the Housing Bureau's annual progress report warned of a mounting crisis. 'Providing sufficient land to achieve the housing supply target remains a huge challenge for both the Government and the community', it lamented. Despairingly, it went on, 'there is simply no magic solution'. Attempts to increase the supply of building sites were regularly frustrated because they were so skilfully opposed by local politicians and rural residents. These groups mistrusted the government, and they were determined to prevent their local environment, amenities, public services and transport systems from being swamped by new residential buildings, each containing hundreds or even thousands of flats. The solution, the Bureau continued, would be to persuade the public 'to accept trade-offs in order to cope with the pressing housing needs of Hong Kong people'.[2] To achieve this goal, a superior quality of political leadership at the top would be required, which was not available.

The most important feature of this chapter is the evidence it contains of the crippling costs to the entire community of the staffing policies of Chief Executives and their ministers They starved the relevant government departments of the financial and personnel resources needed to monitor and manage government land resources and to safeguard them from extensive squatting and other illegal uses. Their staff were too few as a result of Tung's austerity programmes at the start of the century. Their IT systems were primitive. The shortfalls were known but not remedied by later Chief Executives. As a result, departments were left with invidious choices about which laws to enforce, how comprehensively and which to ignore. And Hong Kong's urgent requirements for building sites to house its people were not met.

## The land bank disappears

When Tung Chee Hwa and his future successor, Donald Tsang Yamkuen, began their drive to shrink public housing programmes and to make way for private developers, a decision was made to get rid of the Housing Authority's land bank. In 2000, it had an inventory of a thousand or so building sites. These were intended to make possible the construction of almost 750,000 public and private housing units by 2008.[3] The Authority had accumulated sites within the core urban areas where it could continue to provide public housing units highly convenient to their tenants. These sites were viewed with greedy eyes by the private sector because their locations were also very attractive for private residential projects. The property developers lobbied successfully for the Authority's land bank to be liquidated.[4]

In 2011, the government began a limited attempt to resurrect the public housing programme, only to discover, as it publicly complained, there was virtually nowhere to build.[5] It would be impossible to avoid several years of delay in identifying new building sites. There was an added, political complication. Until this century, the Housing Authority had enjoyed widespread support from the community. By now, however, its past achievements had faded from public memory, and the Authority suffered from much the same loss of credibility as other government departments and agencies. Public cooperation with site clearances and rescheduling of open land from recreational to building use would not be easy to mobilise.

## The government abandons control

If the housing supply, both public and private, were to be accelerated, there was no alternative to the New Territories as Hong Kong's largest source of future building sites.[6] In the 1950s, the colonial administration had begun a public housing programme in the New Territories and had then launched 'New Towns' projects in the following decades. These remained self-contained urban enclaves even though they developed into major industrial zones and locations for extensive relocation of families from the city proper to new public housing estates. Here, the government maintained the very high occupation densities to which the Hong Kong community was long accustomed. As a result, the new towns did not sprawl across the countryside as they might in conurbations elsewhere in the world. The Tin Shui Wai project, for example, had a population density of 67,000 persons per square kilometre, 2.5 times the overall average of 27,000 per square kilometre for Hong Kong as a whole.[7] As a result, urbanisation of rural areas was slow, which left the bulk of the New Territories and its communities undisturbed, with a relatively stable population and low population densities.[8]

In this century, however, even closely controlled urbanisation aroused increasing opposition. Groups committed to protecting the environment, national parks and endangered species saw no reason to make way for new homes, while local communities were ready to mount angry protests in defence of their quality of life.[9] These campaigns enjoyed community-wide support because pollution in particular had become a major inconvenience of daily life, which Chief Executives had failed to overcome. The solution to this opposition lay in improved political management to convince the public that new housing programmes would be designed to comply with best-practice environmental standards. This was not forthcoming.

The balance of power had also altered. The Basic Law had given 'indigenous villagers', who retained control over much of the potential building land, a powerful constitutional status from 1997 that went far beyond their true social or economic importance.[10] In consequence, its leaders exercised considerable influence, both with Mainland officials and with Hong Kong's Chief Executives and their ministers.[11] Local rural communities generally saw very little benefit to themselves from environmental and other controls. They wanted to be left free to develop local land as best suited their personal commercial interests, as they had done before 1997, and they felt entitled to disregard legislation and regulations to protect amenities and safeguard the environment.[12]

Exemption of rural areas from the normal rules and regulations applying to land and buildings had been tolerated under colonial rule. 'Male indigenous villagers' were given the right in 1972 to build a small home on village land or, for a concessionary price, on government land. Limits were set to the dimensions of these 'small houses', and subsequent building modifications were subject to legal restrictions.[13] Enforcement was very slack, however. Colonial officials had little inclination to monitor rural property developments. They regarded the New

Territories as a backwater which was most conveniently administered by interfering as little as possible with the Heung Yee Kuk and other rural power-holders.[14]

Under Tung Chee Hwa, rural communities had good reason to assume that they had little to fear from government interference after 1997. The teams allocated by the Planning Department to policing the New Territories suffered very large losses under his civil service cutbacks. The Department claimed that their monitoring was no longer needed because the black spots had been cleared. Thus, when calculating the true level of staffing required to fulfil all the Department's responsibilities, it ignored the danger of land-use abuses reappearing.[15]

## Unenforceable laws

Inevitably, the government departments involved found themselves unable to prevent misuse of the preferential treatment enjoyed by rural residents since 1972.[16] Lands Department staff, in particular, faced a growing challenge from illegal occupation of its property, originally by squatters but, in contemporary Hong Kong, by a range of commercial enterprises as well. Shortage of personnel and other resources crippled the Department's ability to police its land holdings effectively. In 2001, the decision had been made to restrict legal action against illegal structures to new buildings and to ignore old houses unless there was 'obvious or imminent danger to life or property'. Within a year, however, it was felt necessary to make this concession even more generous, and all rural housing was exempted from punitive measures except where safety was directly involved.

In 2002 and again in 2004, the Department had warned the Legislative Council that demands for improved performance in land management were unachievable: it had no spare capacity to cope with any increase in its workload. The Department also pointed out that policing the New Territories was not the most urgent of its duties.

The Ombudsman had refused to close its eyes to the informal immunities given to rural land owners even before the end of colonial rule, and it returned to this growing scandal with an investigation in 2004. Its report confirmed that administrative decisions to suspend the law in the rural areas were still being made because departments did not have enough staff and funding to carry out their legal duties. The Lands Department explained that selective enforcement of the law was unavoidable because of 'the competing demands on its resources'. In the case of the Buildings Department, 'the complexity and magnitude of the territory-wide issue' of illegal building works made 'prioritisation' unavoidable. Compared with the potential dangers involved in multi-storey buildings in the densely populated urban areas, the 'small houses' were of minimal importance, the Department argued, which meant that the Ombudsman's recommendations for solving the 'small houses' issues would not be implemented. This pattern of officials warning that lack of resources made it impossible to comply with the Ombudsman's findings was to be repeated. In 2011, the Buildings Department insisted that a drive to enforce the law would 'entail a disproportionate amount of resources and efforts', and the actual improvement in enforcement was likely to be disappointing.[17]

The Departments involved with housing issues tried to protect themselves from criticism by concealing the extent to which the law was being ignored. The first line of defence was bureaucratic: token enforcement. In handling complaints from the public, 'a standard of proof' was demanded which was excessively high, the Ombudsman noted. If complaints of unlawful building activities were successful, enforcement action by the Buildings Department proceeded as slowly as possible. The Lands Department had abandoned all hope of enforcement and simply sent 'warning letters'.

An additional line of defence for departments was to conceal the facts by suppressing the statistical evidence. The Buildings and the Lands Departments stopped collecting survey data in 2005, the Ombudsman discovered, and ceased to 'systematically collect and monitor statistics'. As a result, there was only limited factual information available which legislators, pressure groups or the media could use to criticise the departments. Subsequent assertions by the Development Bureau, which was responsible for these departments, that the situation was under control were shameless guesswork.

The government confessed to legislators in 2011 that the number of 'small houses' in breach of the law was 'in the tens of thousands'. Nevertheless, the improvements recommended by the Ombudsman were still ignored. 'A pragmatic approach' would continue to be adopted in enforcing the law in rural areas, the government insisted. The Buildings Department remained free to shelve cases as it saw fit, for example. Legislators complained that these special concessions to rural lawbreakers offended 'the principle of fairness' and 'might become a *de facto* amnesty'. Government discussions with legislators made it clear that no significant improvements in the management of land for use by rural residents could take place unless the government allocated the funds for 'a comprehensive data base' and made more staff available.[18] Which was not going to happen.

## Buying immunity

In 2012, the Audit Commission released a devastating report, this time on the Lands Department, revealing that it was so overworked and under-resourced that it had to compromise with law-breakers.[19] The Department had decided that 'granting [short term tenancies] at market rental to the occupiers was a pragmatic way of resolving the unlawful occupation problem'. For the right price, in other words, immunity could be obtained for breaches of the letter of the law. There was no point in prosecuting offenders, the Department claimed, because the penalties were too low to act as a deterrent. The Director of Audit, however, expressed alarm about the rise in public complaints of illegal takeovers of public land, while the annual prosecution rate fell.[20]

The Department's strategy of toleration had been made easier because of the lack of reliable information about the extent of intrusion on to public land and of the action taken to penalise offenders. The Department's so-called 'Land Control Information System' was plagued by misrecording and omissions of essential data. Its computer facilities not only suffered from limited capacity, they were also primitive and obsolete. They were only capable of processing the most basic information and could not handle any data in Chinese. Staff found it faster to prepare reports by hand. As a result, the Lands Department was unable to monitor and manage its land resources. The Department had reported the delays and disruption caused by the dysfunctional computing system in 2010, but a replacement would take four years, the Audit Commission discovered.

There were serious dangers to the public interest in the Lands Department's involuntary pragmatism about how the law should be enforced. Very worrying was the Department's admission that cases were allowed to drag on 'where the occupiers had sought the assistance of local dignitaries and influential bodies'. This statement was an admission that the Lands Department did not feel it had the power to ignore vested interests or overt political pressures. The Department's credibility was in danger, the Director of Audit pointed out, because such cases might be seen by the public as evidence of 'a lack of determination' in enforcing the law. 'They also set undesirable examples', the Director added, 'and undermine the Lands Department's reputation'.[21] His recommendations for improvements were ignored, however, as the minister responsible allowed the Lands Department to continue its defensive strategy.

An even more damning report appeared in 2016, this time from the Ombudsman. The Lands Department had consistently condoned unlawful activities, the Ombudsman complained, 'thus aggravating the problem of illegal occupation and breach of lease conditions'. Processing of complaints was slow and inconsistent, and no accurate records were kept of how they were handled. Significantly, the Ombudsman pointed out that, over the years, the Department's defence against the frequent criticism of its performance had remained unchanged: it lacked the resources needed to carry out its duties.[22]

## Reduced to tears

Leung Chun-ying had taken office in 2012 fully aware that he would have to turn to the New Territories to rebuild the government's land bank in order to meet his ambitious housing targets. Predictably, his plans encountered a series of obstacles: legal appeals against compulsory land acquisitions, protracted negotiation of compensation payments for land resumptions, arranging resettlement of evicted farmers and villagers. There was a desperate need for building sites but there was also a growing public demand to preserve amenities and reduce pollution. These confrontations over rural development were not well managed by Leung's ministerial team, which further weakened his political authority.

An additional threat to his credibility was the way he and his team seemed to have lost control over the financial costs of New Territories housing projects. These ballooned alarmingly. Estimated initially at $40 billion, the government later confessed it had no accurate estimate of what the final bill might be. 'The actual cost can only be ascertained at the implementation stage', it was claimed.[23] Unfortunately for Leung, in Hong Kong, open-ended commitments for government projects are highly unpopular with politicians and the public alike.

Leung's political credibility finally evaporated during a bitter controversy in 2016 over a complex plan to boost the supply of building sites in the New Territories. When this proposal had started to take shape in 2014, public reaction in the districts affected was very unfavourable. Nevertheless, the government persisted, and detailed proposals became public in 2016 about locating an estate of 14.65 hectares to provide homes for 52,000 people on a New Territories site.[24] The reaction from legislators newly elected that year, from New Territories residents and from the media was overwhelmingly unfavourable.

The government's publicity campaign to counter the opposition was disastrous. The release of information about the projected estate was badly botched, with considerable confusion about such basic details as the planned population and the construction schedule. When the Chief Executive and the ministers involved eventually met the media, their statements revealed a governing team that was unclear about what the Chief Executive intended to do and which was suffering from serious administrative confusion because of overlapping ministerial responsibilities and limited mutual trust.

An unsavoury crisis quickly followed. The media reported in detail 'informal' negotiations with rural power-holders of which officials kept no records; misinformation in official statements; concealment of major

amendments to the development plan; the government's alleged concessions to business interests; bitter disputes about the compensation
payable to the property owners and businesses affected; and confusing
errors in official documents. A flood of information was leaked about
dubious measures taken to try to buy off influential New Territories
personalities who opposed the government's plans. Scandals were also
unearthed about illegal occupation of sites which the Lands Department
allegedly had condoned in the area scheduled for development.

The leadership's problems were becoming increasingly difficult to
conceal. Confusion among ministers reached astonishing levels. The
Housing Minister's warning about shortfalls in the supply of sites was
contradicted a month later by the Development Minister, who was
responsible for managing Hong Kong's land resources. There were
ample sites coming forward, he insisted. In fact, the government had to
take steps in 2016 to avoid offering too much land for sale, he added,
for fear that the property market might become nervous.[25] This minister
was contradicted in his turn less than a month later by Leung himself.
The Chief Executive and individual ministers appeared to be both out
of touch and in conflict. The seriousness of this breakdown in political management and public confidence was highlighted by the way in
which Hong Kong's rulers were eventually forced to face a gruelling
public inquisition by the media that was without precedent. Leung, it
was widely reported, was left close to tears.[26]

## Dismal legacy

Leung's Development Minister was to have the last word on land supply
in the final week of Leung's term in office when he faced interrogation
in the Legislative Council about the New Territories. The government's
land holdings were in utter chaos, it seemed. There were 'relatively large
areas of quality agricultural land', the Minister said, whose future use
was to be investigated. But 'the study may take several years to complete',
he went on, and the basic data needed for a survey did not exist. There
were also 'brownfield sites'—'agricultural lands that have been con-
verted to other uses', he continued. The Planning Department had commissioned a study of such sites although 'there is no formal or standard
definition' of what 'brownfield' means.

Worst of all was the case of New Territories land on which structures
had been built. These appeared to range from squatter huts to domestic
housing, and from commercial uses to amenities. The Development
Minister admitted indirectly that effective control over these developments had been lost: 'The government does not have statistics on the
number of domestic and non-domestic structures, the areas involved
and the land ownership of these structures, if any.' Such information as

was available had last been collected in 1982. At this point, the Minister confessed to total despair.

> As the [1982] information is in the form of written records, any attempt to go through these records for compilation of statistics will involve an enormous amount of resources, manpower and time. Such compilation work is not our priority and we are therefore unable to provide the required information.[27]

The Development Minister seemed unaware that Carrie Lam had made an almost identical excuse for the absence of vital data on urban housing when she had occupied the same post in 2010.[28]

Once Carrie Lam took over the post of Chief Executive, she could no longer dismiss her responsibilities for tackling the land crisis so easily. In her Election Manifesto, the acute shortage of building sites had been given high priority. She appeared determined to break the stranglehold which past mismanagement of land resources had created. But turning well-meaning political pledges into practical policies proved very difficult for her even though she had spent five years as the minister dealing with land and related problems.

Instead of presenting a blueprint for the future with specific targets for each sector and a detailed programme of how they would be achieved, her solution seemed an attempt to buy time. She announced the creation of a 30-member Task Force on Land Supply. The chairman and many of the members were well-regarded political and business figures and academics but of diverse views and commitments. It also included three ministers and five senior civil servants. To assist the Task Force, the Development Bureau and its departments had managed somehow to overcome data shortages and had compiled a comprehensive review of Hong Kong's demand, both current and future, for housing and other buildings in a well-structured, easy-to-read format. Every aspect of the problems to be overcome was reviewed, from the shortage of building sites to the frightening rate at which private sector housing was deteriorating with age. This guide to the current situation, the most pressing priorities and the time frames which were involved was ideal for formulating a blueprint for successful management of the land and building crises.[29]

But for Carrie Lam, the major concern was political: the Task Force's success in 'forging the biggest community consensus'.[30] The Force was plainly designed to convince the public to accept the urgent need for large-scale housing developments. The question was whether it included enough members whom the community was likely to believe would have the public's best interest at heart. Inevitably, there would be considerable delays in framing policy proposals as the Task Force launched its public consultation exercises. In the past—and across the whole of government—such exercises almost always led to serious delays in taking action. In the meantime, members of the Task Force included 'making Use of Rock Caverns and Underground Space' on the initial agenda.[31]

Slipping away was the chance to put a rapid end to years of mismanagement. Carrie Lam's first Policy Address admitted the severe restrictions which the lack of building sites was causing. Her many promises for a package of bold initiatives to ease the housing crisis were being blocked by the land shortage for which she could offer only a menu of limited initiatives, of which the public and the media quickly tired.[32] The tragedy was that as the Audit Commission had pointed out in 2012, the government owned 30 per cent of Hong Kong's land, a land bank which it was failing to utilise effectively in the public interest.[33] What Carrie Lam really needed, of course, was a member of the government capable of mobilising public support for a land programme which the people of Hong Kong would accept as the essential foundation for overcoming the mounting housing crisis. Carrie Lam had failed in this role as Development Minister, which did not inspire much confidence when she became Chief Executive.

## Conclusion

The failure to provide an adequate supply of building sites was inexcusable. As Leung Chun-ying had rightly stated in his 2012 Election Manifesto: 'Hong Kong is not short of land'.[34] But Chief Executives and their ministers grossly mismanaged this asset, mainly through knowingly allowing laws and regulations to be ignored. They were also slow to grasp how important to the community were measures to reduce pollution and to protect the environment. As a result, those in power had long since forfeited public trust when it came to housing and land issues. Thus, government's building projects in the New Territories—the government's principal landbank for the future—provoked intense political opposition.[35]

The New Territories offered an important case study of how, over the last two decades, bureaux, departments and other government agencies found themselves unable to enforce legislation and to implement official policies. This drift into lawlessness began in the Tung Chee Hwa era with his determination to slash government spending in general. Donald Tsang remained faithful to this policy as he progressed from Financial to Chief Secretary before ending up as Chief Executive. It had continued under his successor, Leung Chun-ying. Quite simply, the government had failed to spend the money required to hire the professional staff needed to oversee its land resources and to enforce the day-to-day legislation governing land and its utilisation. The community paid the price.

The housing supply was sabotaged, and respect for the law undermined. A shocking outcome for the people of Hong Kong.

## Notes

1. Audit Commission, *Report No. 58*, 'Chapter 7: Lands Department: Unlawful Occupation of Government Land' (28 March 2012), 1.
2. Transport and Housing Bureau, 'Long Term Housing Strategy Annual Progress Report 2015' (December 2015), 12.
3. Dominic Wong Shing-wah, Secretary for Housing, Housing Bureau, 'LegCo Panel on Housing Minutes of meeting . . . 17 October 2000' (CB (1) 121/00-01), 4 November 2000), 2.
4. The private sector's struggle to win control of the Housing Authority's land bank is recounted in Adrienne La Grange, 'Housing (1997–2007)', in *The Hong Kong Special Administrative Region in Its First decade*, ed. Joseph Y. S. Cheng (Hong Kong: City University of Hong Kong Press, 2007), 722–23.
5. Carrie Lam Cheng Yuet-ngor, Secretary for Development, recorded in Legislative Council Panel on Development, 'Minutes of special meeting . . . 14 October 2011' (CB(1)798/11-12), 12 January 2012), 4.
6. The New Territories' potential contribution was summarised convincingly by Paul Chan Mo-po, Secretary for Development, 'The Development Potential of New Territories North', 13 October 2013.
7. Although the 2011 census noted that 'on the whole, the new towns were less densely populated than the urban areas'. Census and Statistics Department, *Hong Kong 2011 Census Main Report: Volume 1* (Hong Kong: SAR Government, 2012), 202.
8. The slow pace of urban overspill into the countryside was summarised in Census and Statistics Department, *Hong Kong 2001 Census Main Report: Volume 1* (Hong Kong: SAR Government, 2002), 183; *Hong Kong 2011 Census Main Report: Volume 1* (Hong Kong: SAR Government, 2012), 'Table 8.10: Domestic Households (1) by Household Size, Whether Internally Migrated and Area of Current Residence, 2011', 196.
9. A summary of the various interest groups can be found in a Central Policy Unit-sponsored report: Li Si Ming, 'Land and Housing Policies in Post-Handover Hong Kong: Political Economy and Urban Space' (Final Report, 31 March 2015), 17.
10. Censuses in the 1970s provided analysis as well as data which tracked the characteristics of the rural New Territories and the New Towns. See Census and Statistics Department, *Hong Kong Population and Housing Census 1971 Main Report* (Hong Kong: Government Printer, n.d.), 10–13, 222; *Hong Kong 1976 By-Census Main Report Volume 1: Analysis* (Hong Kong: Government Printer, 1979), 'Chapter XI Internal Movement'.
11. Leo F. Goodstadt, 'China and the Selection of Hong Kong's Post-Colonial Elite', *The China Quarterly*, no. 163 (September 2000): 738, 740.
12. An important example was reported in Sylvia Chang, 'Land Values Drive Lantau Clashes', *China Daily*, 27 August 2014.

13. For an authoritative summary of the legal background and related policies, see Legislative Council Secretariat, 'Panel on Development Subcommittee on Building Safety and Related Issues . . . Updated Background Brief on Unauthorized Building Works in New Territories Exempted Houses' (CB(1)524/11-12(02), 7 December 2011), 1–3.

14. Resistance to colonial policies by rural interests had a long history. See, for example, Nigel Ruscoe, 'A Conspiracy of Silence', *Far Eastern Economic Review*, 4 May 1961. For a critical overview of colonial management of the New Territories, see Fred Y. L. Chiu, 'Politics and the Body Social in Colonial Hong Kong', in *Formations of Colonial Modernity in East Asia*, ed. Tani E. Barlow (Durham, NC: Duke University Press 1997), 298–302.

15. Spokesman, Planning Department, *Government Information Services* (*GIS* hereafter), 15 September 1999.

16. The historical summary that follows is based on Office of the Ombudsman, 'Investigation Report: The Enforcement Action on Unauthorised Building Works in New Territories Exempted Houses' (August 2004) and Development Bureau, 'Legislative Council Panel on Development Enforcement against Unauthorised Building Works in New Territories Exempted Houses' (CB(1)2530/10-11(05), June 2011.

17. Both versions of the Ombudsman's 2011 report have been used in compiling this summary of the office's investigations and the historical background. Office of the Ombudsman, 'Direct Investigation: Enforcement against Unauthorised Building Works in New Territories Exempted Houses', *Issue No. 1 of Reporting Year 2011/12* (19 April 2011), 'Annex A: Executive Summary' and 'Direct Investigation Report: Enforcement against Unauthorised Building Works in New Territories Exempted Houses, March 2011' (Ref. OMB/DI/203, 31 March 2011).

18. Legislative Council Secretariat, 'Panel on Development Subcommittee on Building Safety and Related Issues . . . Updated Background Brief on Unauthorized Building Works in New Territories Exempted Houses', 5–7, 10.

19. Audit Commission, *Report No. 58*, 'Chapter 7: Lands Department: Unlawful Occupation of Government Land' (28 March 2012), v.

20. By this stage, the government's failure to take remedial action no longer caused any surprise.

21. Data and analysis are from Audit Commission, *Report No. 58*, 1, 2, 4–5, 8, 19–20, 25, 32.

22. Office of the Ombudsman, 'Direct Investigation Report: Lands Department's System of Regularisation of Illegal Occupation of Government Land and Breach of Lease Conditions', *Issue No. 2 of Reporting Year 2016/17* (13 September 2016), 'Annex A: Executive Summary', 1–3.

23. The problems are summarised in Civil Engineering and Development Department, 'Legislative Council Panel on Development North East New Territories New Development Areas Planning and Engineering Study' (CB(1)203/12-13(01) (November 2012), 1–5.

24. For details of the project, see the consultants' report released by the Transport and Housing Bureau (18 October 2016), 'Ove Arup & Partners Hong Kong Ltd, "Planning and Engineering Study for the Public Housing

Development and Yuen Long Industrial Estate Extension at Wang Chau'" (REP-025-01/Final/May 2014).

25. Paul Chan, Secretary for Development, *GIS*, 29 December 2016. He was shortly to be promoted to the post of Financial Secretary.

26. The government's embarrassment can be judged from 'Questions and Answers: What Hong Kong's Leung Chun-ying and John Tsang Told the Press', *South China Morning Post*, 22 September 2016; 'Transcript of Remarks at Press Conference on Wang Chau Development', *GIS*, 21 September 2016; 'Government Response to Media Enquiries on Public Housing Development Plan at Wang Chau', *GIS*, 30 September 2016.

27. Eric Ma Siu-cheung, Secretary for Development, *HH*, 28 June 2017.

28. Carrie Lam, Secretary for Development, *HH*, 10 March 2010, 5776–80. Her statement is discussed in Chapter 7.

29. Development Bureau, 'Task Force on Land Supply Demand for Land' (Paper No. 02/2017, 1 September 2017) and 'Task Force on Land Supply Land Supply Initiatives' (Paper No. 03/2017, 1 September 2017).

30. Carrie Lam, Chief Executive, *GIS*, 6 September 2017.

31. Press release, *GIS*, 7 November 2017.

32. She frankly admitted the policy chaos she faced (partly inherited from her own tenure as minister at the Development Bureau). Carrie Lam, Chief Executive, *HH*, 7 October 2017.

33. Audit Commission, *Report No. 58*, 'Chapter 7: Lands Department: Unlawful Occupation of Government Land' (28 March 2012), 1. But less than 10 per cent of Hong Kong's total land area had been zoned for housing purposes, which seriously obstructed the supply of building sites according to Leung, Chief Executive, *HH*, 18 January 2017, p. 3114. It is a striking indication of the government's political standing that it feels little confidence in seeking to increase the land zoned for housing.

34. Leung Chun-ying, 'Manifesto for the Chief Executive Election 2012 One Heart, One Vision', p. 17.

35. Transport and Housing Bureau, 'Long Term Housing Strategy Annual Progress Report 2015' (December 2015), 12.

# 6
# Students at the market's mercy

Hong Kong began a radical political transformation in 2012. The agenda was being set by a new generation. Young political activists went on to win an impressively large share of the votes in the 2016 Legislative Council elections with a campaign for Hong Kong's future and its core values. This achievement was all the more remarkable because these youthful candidates were not well-known personalities, and the political parties they set up had little experience and limited funding.

The election results intensified the uneasiness of China's leaders about the governability of the Special Administrative Region and the disrespect of the rising generation for the Mainland's authority. Governability was not a new challenge. From the very first months of Tung Chee Hwa's term of office, his administration's public standing had rapidly dropped to the lowest levels ever recorded since official surveys of public opinion began in 1983. The economy was going into severe recession after unbroken annual GDP growth in real terms since 1961. The average family's earnings fell and so did the value of their homes. For the first time since the end of the Japanese Occupation in 1945, parents would no longer have the assurance that their children would be better off than them in terms of schooling, health, housing and lifetime earnings. A firm confidence in Hong Kong's prospects for society as a whole, and not just the affluent, was gone. But Hong Kong coped, as its survival culture took over. Its long-established political maturity and social discipline had prevailed. This pattern was to be repeated throughout the decades that followed. Government-created social hardships caused widespread dismay but public tolerance of those in power was maintained because the community's survival came first.

Political challenges from Hong Kong's youth were thus a new phenomenon in the post-1997 world. Its emergence was first recognised in 2007 by Hong Kong's leading sociologist, Professor Lui Tai-lok. He published a best-seller, *Four Generations of Hong Kong People*, which traced the rise of the 'post-1980s generation' that was reshaping society and its outlook. A flood of research on this topic followed.

In 2010, government-sponsored research was reporting that although the educational standards of the 'post-80s generation' were the highest in Hong Kong's history, their future career prospects were the worst ever in terms of career opportunities and earnings. Nevertheless, they had not developed 'distinctive attitudes towards social justice or opportunities', this study reported, and these young people tended to be neutral towards both the pro-government and the pro-democracy parties.[1] At this stage, the likelihood of a new surge in political activism still seemed limited despite rising social inequality and deteriorating social services.[2]

The evidence was gathering, nevertheless, that the mood could change dramatically.[3] The growing inequality of income distribution across the community as a whole was an issue which had disturbed Hong Kong opinion-makers and embarrassed officialdom throughout this century. A United Nations study had ranked the wealth gap in Hong Kong as the widest among Asian cities and 'relatively high' by world standards.[4] One official census after another showed the gap increasing, while income inequality increased by comparison with the world's advanced nations.[5]

The contrast between the affluent and the average standard of living was worsening sharply. For example, census data highlighted how family income was becoming the key to access to university. In 1991, wealth had not been a factor, and access had been almost equal for both rich and poor in the 19 and 20 age groups. Of the highest income group, 9 per cent were studying for university degrees compared with 8 per cent from the lowest income group. In 2011, the proportion going to university from the richest group had risen to 48 per cent but was only 13 per cent for the lowest group.[6]

The main focus of this chapter is what happened to those who were denied a university place and had to be content with associate degrees and diplomas. These courses were mostly self-financing, and their fees were significantly higher than what a university education cost. The qualifications themselves did not lead to 'a significantly better career prospect, which was a huge disappointment as well as a waste of resources', one prominent think tank claimed in 2016, and 'accounts for a great deal of the current dissatisfaction among the youth in Hong Kong'.[7]

## 'Self-financed' education

In a global, post-industrial society as advanced as Hong Kong, education is of the highest importance, both to the individual and to the economy as a whole. A failure to provide places in universities for all those qualified for admission and to high-quality post-secondary education for those unsuited for degree courses will have serious consequences for an individual's career and for the future prosperity of the community.

In 1997, Chief Executive Tung Chee Hwa had argued strenuously that Hong Kong's economic prospects depended on upgrading the quality of education. But education soon fell victim to his belief that such principles as 'user pays' and 'market forces' should take command. Tung was well aware that compared with the United States, for example, Hong Kong's spending on education was very low ('about three per cent of our GDP', he said). But he saw no reason to increase public spending on schools because, he argued, 'throwing money at things doesn't necessarily solve problems'.[8] Later on, he boasted about giving exceptional priority to education. 'Treat expenditure in education as investment', he had ordered his Financial Secretary, 'Don't treat it as expenditure because we need that investment'.[9]

But this free-spending outlook did not last although Tung remained determined to introduce educational changes. By 2004, a programme had been launched to transform secondary and post-secondary education.[10] This assumed that students' families would fund much of the costs involved through paying higher fees even though average household incomes had fallen below their 1997 levels as a result of government-induced deflation.[11] At the same time, government funding for universities was being reduced, yet they were expected to find the resources to extend their first-degree programmes by a full year. Tung took it for granted that they would be able to maintain standards regardless of the financial cutbacks.[12] The notion of educational spending as an 'investment' had been redefined.

The educational blueprint adopted by the first Chief Executive was embraced by his successors, Donald Tsang Yam-kuen and Leung Chun-ying. Even before he took over from Tung, Tsang had described education as the best solution for the community's challenges. 'We have no greater priority in budgetary, social or economic terms than the education programme', he said.[13] At the same time, he made the surprising claim that Hong Kong was already dedicating more public funds to 'education, training and re-training . . . than in any other developed economy'.[14] So, additional spending was not needed, apart from limited poverty relief to provide help with 'the costs of textbooks and school-related expenses'.[15]

In fact, Tsang's annual Policy Addresses had only one serious educational goal from 2007 onwards: patriotism and how to teach it. 'President Hu Jintao had earnestly advised that "we should put more emphasis on national education for the youth in Hong Kong"', Tsang told the legislature, '"so that they will carry forward the Hong Kong people's great tradition of loving the motherland and loving Hong Kong"'.[16] But setting a new priority for fostering the loyalty of Hong Kong's youth to the nation did not justify ignoring shortcomings elsewhere in the curriculum.

When Leung Chun-ying launched his bid for office in 2012, his election manifesto displayed an unusual awareness of what was wrong with the education system. He paid special attention to how few of those aged 15 or above were able to continue their education after they finished secondary school. Leung seemed poised for a revolutionary change in government policy: 'Access to education is a basic right', he declared, 'Such access underpins the success of our community'.

But Leung Chun-ying's manifesto then made a sharp U-turn. He turned out to be no more willing for the government to pay the costs of exercising this 'basic right' than his two predecessors. In particular, he had no intention of allowing a substantial increase in admissions to university degree courses.[17] Once in office, he maintained the same approach to university funding as Donald Tsang and promoted the same self-financed programmes to fill the degree gap. As a result, under his rule, students and parents continued to pay the costs of expensive sub-degree courses of dubious worth.[18] Nothing of significance had altered since the Tung era.[19]

## Retreat from social responsibility

To begin a drive to reform the structure of the educational system in 1997, Tung Chee Hwa appeared to have found a remarkably well-quali-fied 'chief of staff'. He wanted a businessman for this job because of his conviction that the business model was best. He selected Antony Leung Kam-chung, a banker by profession but who had acquired good creden-tials in the education field. The colonial administration had appointed him to the University Grants Committee during a period of rapid expan-sion of university facilities. As committee chairman, Antony Leung had automatic membership of the Education Commission. Here, he had an overview of every kind of programme, from kindergarten to post-gradu-ate degrees. At the same time, he was highly regarded by the Hong Kong and Macao Liaison Office. He had all the credentials needed to justify his selection to head the Education Commission after 1997 and to direct a very extensive schedule of public and professional consultations.

First of all, however, Antony Leung and the Education Commission had to steer their way through a confrontation with the community provoked by the government's abrupt announcement in 1997 that teaching through English would no longer be allowed in most of the 400 secondary schools receiving government funding.[20] This move was seen by the public as crippling the average pupil's career prospects in the open, international economy of Hong Kong. Not until 2008, did the government back down and allow schools reasonable freedom to teach through the medium of English instead of restricting this right to élite and private sector educational institutions.[21]

By 2000, Antony Leung had overseen the preparation of an ambitious programme of change and improvement. But it did not fully comply with Tung Chee Hwa's doctrine that reform should be achieved free of charge to the government. The Education Commission presented a simple but compelling case for increased public spending on education. The entire community benefitted from improved standards of education and not just the individual graduate or diploma holder, it stated, and the government should accept responsibility for the costs involved. This blueprint for the future saw some scope for an increased contribution from many parents. But the Commission's report believed that this additional funding could be voluntary.

Overall, the innovations recommended in the Education Commission's 'Reform Proposals for the Education System in Hong Kong' were to prove highly conservative by comparison with government policies in later years. Notably, the Commission did not envisage the creation of a large, self-financed post-secondary sector. It took the view that tuition fees in this sector were too low but did not call for the supply of associate degrees and other sub-degree products to be rapidly increased.[22]

Its views soon proved out of date as official commitments to social responsibility began to fade from the educational agenda. In 2002, Antony Leung became Financial Secretary. He had nothing further to do with education, which barely got a mention in his two Budget Speeches. Management of the sector was now in the hands of Professor Arthur Li Kwok-cheung. This new Education Minister was a former Cambridge don and had been Dean of the Chinese University's Medical School before being appointed its Vice Chancellor. Under Li, the Education and Manpower Bureau faithfully pursued Tung Chee Hwa's reform strategy in a new consultation document.

The costs of improved education, especially in the case of post-secondary students, would be unaffordable for the government, the Bureau claimed. The financial choice was either to cut down on other education services, it argued, or force parents to share the bill for studying at post-secondary institutions by paying higher tuition fees.[23] Education at this level was now to be increasingly commercialised. 'Manpower development' replaced the term 'education' for the post-secondary sector. The Bureau described the sector's goals in strictly business terms: 'to enhance the quality and competitiveness of our human resources so as to bridge the manpower gap', to quote an official briefing.[24] What made developments in this sector of unusual importance was its role in meeting the growing demand for academic and professional qualifications which government policy prevented universities from supplying.

## Marketing manpower

Professor Li was to prove an excellent replacement for Antony Leung from Tung's standpoint. The government's funding for universities was being heavily cut.[25] Nevertheless, they were being forced to lengthen the bachelor's degree from three years to four. Tung stuck to his principle that more money did not solve problems, and the additional year was to be implemented free of charge as far as the government was concerned. He expressed complacent confidence that 'core activities and the quality of education' of universities would not suffer as a result, despite their smaller budgets.[26] In practice, money did seem to matter.[27] An Organisation for Economic Co-operation and Development (OECD) report in 2012 indicated that the new first year for Hong Kong's undergraduates had been something of a waste of time because it had been devoted to 'alternative learning experiences' rather than conventional undergraduate studies (which would have required proper financing).[28]

University heads would normally be expected to oppose unreasonable government demands, but Professor Li had both academic credentials and the force of personality to silence opposition. Hong Kong's university presidents and vice chancellors proved very cooperative with him, which further justified his selection by Tung whose ministers rarely managed to overawe potential opponents.

This extension of the bachelor degree to four years was linked to a reduction in the length of secondary education from seven years to six, which would cut the government's outlay for secondary schooling. Students were expected to make up for the lost year by enrolling as university undergraduates or for associate degrees and other post-secondary programmes. But universities could not meet an increase in demand because they were not free to expand their first-year intakes. In 1989, the colonial administration had decided that first-year admissions to a bachelor's degree should reach a total of 15,000.[29] That number had been set as a target rather than a ceiling, and it was achieved.[30] But the figure had remained unchanged ever since despite a growing population, rising educational standards and the increasing sophistication of both society and the economy.

By this century, the origins of the 15,000 maximum had long since faded from public memory. Its rationale as a sensible ceiling on admissions was taken for granted, which helped Chief Executives and their ministers to stifle potential pressure for more public spending on universities. This stubborn policy had unfortunate consequences. Universities were unable to meet the demand for places from applicants who had passed all the relevant examinations. In 2015–2016, for example, 25,782 students met the minimum examination requirements for entry to a university first-degree course, but over half were not were admitted.[31]

For desperate parents and ambitious school-leavers, the associate degree seemed a godsend. This high-sounding qualification, often awarded by institutions with university connections, must surely make a significant difference to employment opportunities and career prospects, the public assumed. But parents and students were being misled, as will be shown later. The post-secondary sector was to be made as 'market driven' as possible, and courses for associate degrees were to be provided by 'self-financing' institutions which charged their students full fees. Business boomed.

## Scandals snowball

The post-secondary education system became ruthlessly commercialised, and nothing was allowed to interfere with the sustained expansion of self-financing programmes for students unable to enter a university. To make commercial investments in self-financed institutions all the more attractive, the government reduced the competition they faced. The government's own superior, subsidised post-secondary programmes for almost 6,000 students were halted.[32] Officials also helped the marketing of sub-degree qualifications by endorsing them publicly as stepping stones to successful futures.[33]

In 2007, Michael Suen Ming-yeung took over as Education Minister in place of Professor Li and seemed ready to take a less commercial view of the post-secondary sector. Suen publicly disclosed his reservations about its breakneck expansion from an annual intake in 2000 of some 2,000 students to over 20,000 a year in 2008. He was not convinced of the quality of education being offered or of whether the size to which the sector had grown was really justified.[34] The media, too, was publishing regular complaints about fees, the quality of the programmes and, most serious of all, the poor view of such qualifications taken by potential employers.[35]

Yet the government continued to refuse to take direct responsibility for the post-secondary sector, and scandals increased. The University Grants Committee in 2010 provided convincing evidence of the sound basis for Suen's earlier misgivings and the media's alarm. The sector's underlying structure was 'complex and fragmented', the Committee warned, 'and the links between different parts are not entirely systematic or transparent'. Students and their parents were very much at risk in this unsupervised business environment. But the most alarming criticism was the Committee's finding that the associate degree was virtually worthless. 'This qualification has neither established a clear identity in the public mind nor much legitimacy as a stand-alone attainment', the Committee concluded. There was some evidence that an associate degree holder earned more than an individual with no further education after secondary school. But 'there is a general perception amongst students and parents . . . that Associate Degree graduates are not yet ready for immediate employment'. Alarmingly, too, the Committee noted that many of the students had been misled into believing that associate degrees were 'stepping stones to full degrees'.[36]

Its investigation recommended concrete measures to end the abuses. These proved too great an interference with market behaviour for the government. Instead, a Committee on Self-Financing Post-Secondary Education was established in 2012 as a 'a pivotal platform'. Its first priority was 'promoting transparency and good practices'. This new body seemed in no hurry to overhaul the sub-degree system that charged students high prices for qualifications of doubtful help to their careers. The Committee's initial goal was to draft 'an Information Framework' and 'a consultancy study . . . [to] pave the way for promoting good practices . . . in due course'.[37] This complacent and unhurried approach was soon discredited by a 2013 Legislative Council research report which warned: 'Self-financing post-secondary education had become merely the massive supply of study places and the indiscriminate admission of as many students as possible'.[38]

Consultants were eventually commissioned by the Committee to review the sector. Their report in 2014 referred to anxieties that 'for private institutions the profit motive is at odds with the values of education and that they may not be able to deliver quality education'. A cautiously worded solution was suggested: 'a carefully balanced approach to regulation' of private institutions 'with some legislative backing'.[39] A year later, the Committee launched its 'Code of Good Practices on Governance and Quality Assurance'. But compliance with its provisions was entirely voluntary.[40] It was not until 2017 that the first results of the new Code were published, and they were described in very positive terms. Nevertheless, the Committee openly admitted that this was no more than 'a good reference document' and not a compulsory code of conduct.[41]

As the Committee took its time to put together even a voluntary code of conduct, sub-degree education seemed to be losing the last of its respectability. But the mounting complaints were ignored because self-financing had become an article of faith with the government. Its multiple merits, according to a new Education Minister in 2014, ranged from 'broadening the opportunities and choices for further studies' to being 'responsive to changing social needs'.[42] Complaints were allowed to continue. The uncontrolled expansion had often been beyond 'the capacity of individual institutions' and came 'at the expense of the quality of learning and teaching', to quote a Legislative Council report in 2016.[43] Not until the end of that year, however, did the University

Grants Committee become directly involved in monitoring standards in the sub-degree sector.[44]

In 2016, a damning report was published by Our Hong Kong Foundation, ironically a policy institute established by Tung Chee Hwa. It condemned the associate degree in brutal terms. The qualification was 'too expensive . . . much higher than the annual full-time tuition in a bachelor-degree program' at the University of Hong Kong and other public universities. Worse still, the associate degree led nowhere in terms of a career. It was of limited value in meeting the entry requirements 'for government civil-service jobs or even government-funded public-service jobs'. Moreover, associate degree holders faced serious difficulties in gaining admission to a university-level programme to complete the final two years required to earn a full bachelor's degree.

The authors of this report identified two practical measures to tackle this problem. The first and most obvious was for the government to pay the costs of expanding access to first degrees.[45] But the reigning Chief Executive had already ruled out this solution in his 2014 Policy Address.[46] Their second suggestion had his approval: to ask Mainland universities to take more Hong Kong students. The report made plain, nevertheless, that something was very wrong if the government was unable 'to satisfy Hong Kong's own local needs for higher education'.[47] There was also a practical obstacle. The Mainland had only a very limited supply of places for Hong Kong students.[48]

## Grim future

Tragically, the youngsters and their parents paying market rates for post-secondary courses faced a high chance of discovering that this had been an imprudent investment. On taking up employment with their associate degrees and diplomas, almost 70 per cent earned less than the average wage for the labour force as a whole, it was reported. They had virtually no hope of catching up with the average university degree holder.[49] The government's Commission on Strategic Development noted that the supposedly superior level of higher educational qualifications did not seem to provide any advantage. 'Many higher education graduates cannot find jobs with a salary commensurate with their qualifications or jobs that offer a clear career structure', it went on. Despite the astonishing growth of this sector, the Commission reported, the average earnings of this group did not improve between 2001 and 2011, while its unemployment rates got worse.[50] In 2016, the Census reported that average earnings of holders of associate degrees and diplomas were only 57 per cent of a university graduate's earnings compared with an average of 62 per cent ten years earlier.[51]

The longer-term prospects of these students were even more depressing. Table 6.1 shows how mistaken were the government's education policies and their assumption that 'market forces' could be relied on to produce the best outcome for post-secondary and higher education growth. The official forecasts were that by 2022, there would be a shortfall of university graduates but an oversupply of individuals with sub-degree qualifications.[52]

What would happen to the surplus workers? The government hoped that 'employers may take this opportunity to enhance their competitiveness and productivity' by hiring individuals with sub-degree qualifications 'for jobs requiring education attainment below *sub-degree* level [original emphasis]'.[53] This prospect was a shocking outcome. Not only would the significant sums spent by post-secondary students and their families on studying for associate degrees turn out to be wasted. Their employment would depend on finding jobs for which not even an associate degree was necessary. This painful situation could have been avoided if Chief Executives and Education Ministers had not retreated from their duty of care for the students in this sector.[54]

**Table 6.1**
Sub-degree and first-degree holders: Supply and demand, 2012–2022

| Year | Supply | | Projected Demand | Surplus/ deficit (−) |
|---|---|---|---|---|
| | 2012 | 2022 | 2022 | 2022 |
| Sub-degree | 186,800 | 251,300 | 238,400 | 12,900 |
| First degree | 714,200 | 914,300 | 965,000 | −50,800 |

Source: Labour and Welfare Bureau, 'Report on Manpower Projection to 2022', 'Table 1: Local Manpower Supply by Education Level in 2012 and 2022', iii; 'Table 7: Projected Manpower Resource Balance by Education Level in 2022', x.

Leung Chun-ying, the third Chief Executive, acknowledged in his 2014 Policy Address the waste and the unfairness that was taking place when so many school leavers were being denied admission to university even though they had passed the necessary examinations. But he had no intention of increasing the number of first-year places to end this situation.[55] Along with his Education Minister, he was waiting for demographics to provide the solution. The falling school population meant that that there would soon be enough places to admit all secondary school leavers to a university degree course who had passed their qualifying public examinations.[56]

For the post-secondary sector, the demographic trends meant that the market would collapse. 'The storm is brewing', a senior education official warned in 2014, and management and staff would find it hard to cope with their shrinking businesses.[57] What practical measures would the government take to avoid chaos and collapse in the sector? The Education Minister chose a strictly advisory role. 'Institutions are reminded to remain prudent in launching new programmes', he told the legislature, 'taking into consideration the availability of similar programmes'.[58]

In the meantime, Leung's interim solution was to make arrangements with mainland universities to accept post-secondary students who had acquired associate degrees or similar qualifications but could not gain a university place in Hong Kong for the extra two years' study which a full degree required. In 2016, Huaqiao University in Fujian province offered a pilot programme to give Hong Kong post-secondary students a chance to obtain a bachelor's degree through two year's further study. To highlight the importance of this particular initiative, Hong Kong's Chief Secretary and future Chief Executive, Carrie Lam Cheng Yuet-ngor, together with officials from the State Council and the Liaison Office, took part in the public launch of the programme.[59] This university is respectable enough but no match for Hong Kong's own universities since it was graded only 125 out of 863 Mainland universities.[60] For Hong Kong to look to a university of this ranking to help rescue its own students was further proof of two decades' mismanagement of education policy by Hong Kong's leaders.

When Carrie Lam took over as Chief Executive in 2017, post-secondary students were at the top of her list of educational priorities. Her announcement of 'a non-means-tested annual subsidy of $30,000' for students in self-financing institutions was well-received.[61] This apparent generosity would do nothing to raise the standards of the post-secondary system, unfortunately, and the quality of sub-degrees and diplomas remained questionable. In other respects, Carrie Lam stuck to her predecessors' policies.[62] The Legislative Council Panel on Education was told that there was no 'genuine need' to provide universities with the funding needed to admit an increased proportion of those students with examination results that qualified them for a first-year course.[63] The 1989 ceiling remained in place.

As with so many challenging issues, Carrie Lam turned to a 'task force' to buy time and, hopefully, to mobilise public support. In this case, the task force would undertake a 'Review of Self-Financing Post-Secondary Education'. Its discussions would take one year and not be completed before the end of 2018. Its terms of reference included 'major issues of concern pertinent to the ecology of the self-financing sector, including the role of the self-financing operation of subvented institutions vis-à-vis self-financing post-secondary institutions'. To parents and students, deliberations on the 'ecology' of educational institutions were likely to

seem remote from the financial burdens and the limited career opportunities that continued to blight the post-secondary sector.[64]

## Conclusion

The makeshift education policies adopted in the first two decades of
the Special Administrative Region seem indefensible on the analysis presented above. For the government, the adoption of the self-financing
principle had been the ideal business strategy for the original shortfall
in university places. For the longer term, demographics could be trusted
to end the mismatch between the long-term limit on university places
and the demand from applicants who had passed the necessary examinations. As the low birth rate reduced the number of potential students,
sub-degree courses would close down in response to the new market situation. The costs for these wasted years of study had been paid in advance
by the students and their parents who had been induced to invest in
qualifications whose credibility would finally evaporate as the post-secondary sector faded away. There were to be no refunds. The introduction of subsidies by Carrie Lam would not compensate the victims of
the past and put right the misguided insistence of Chief Executives that
the market would provide the optimum solutions. Inevitably, the subsidies did not raise the quality of education provided by self-financing
institutions. Nor did they silence public criticism. The lack of first-year
university places remained an on-going complaint.[65]

The students themselves were not to blame for this bleak situation.
Past surveys repeatedly found that their employers regarded them as
performing satisfactorily.[66] But the labour market saw no reason to hire
them at a premium just because they had studied successfully at sub-
degree level. Their futures had been deliberately left at the mercy of
market forces by the first three Chief Executives and their Education
Ministers. There were no indications that Hong Kong's new Chief
Executive and her team were prepared to invest heavily in expanding
those high-quality educational programmes which an economy like
Hong Kong needs, which society fully deserves and whose costs are well
within the affordability of public finances.

## Notes

1.  Xiaogang Wu, 'Hong Kong's Post-80s Generation: Profiles and Predicaments;
    a CPU Commissioned Report', Centre for Applied Social and Economic
    Research, Hong Kong University of Science and Technology (Central Policy
    Unit, May 2010), 35–38.
2.  In retrospect, however, the rise of political anger and the emergence of
    radical activists could have been recognised earlier. See, for example,

Chor-yung Cheung, 'Hong Kong's Systemic Crisis of Governance and the Revolt of the "Post-80s" Youths: The Anti-Express Rail Campaign', in *New Trends of Political Participation in Hong Kong*, ed. Joseph Y. S. Cheng (Hong Kong: City University of Hong Kong Press, 2014).

3. See, for example, the data in Michael E. deGolyer, 'Protests and Post-80's Youth: Sources of Social Instability' (Hong Kong Transition Project, 2010).

4. Inequality of income distribution was measured by the Gini coefficient. UN-Habitat, *State of the World's Cities 2008/2009 Harmonious Cities* (London: Earthscan, 2008), 24.

5. Census and Statistics Department, *2016 Population By-Census Thematic Report: Household Income Distribution in Hong Kong, Hong Kong Special Administrative Region* (Hong Kong: Census and Statistics Department, 2017), 'Table 8.2: Gini Coefficients of Selected Economies (Based on Per Capita/Equivalised Household Income'), 7, 147.

6. Professor Chou Kee-lee, 'HKIEd Study: Disparity in Higher Education Attainment Is Widening between Rich and Poor', Hong Kong Institute of Education (31 January 2013).

7. Lawrence J. Lau et al., 'Yes, Hong Kong CAN!', *Our Hong Kong Foundation* (September 2016), 67–68. The foundation was established by the former Chief Executive, Tung Chee Hwa.

8. The fuller version of Tung's comments shows that he was confused as to what to do when the free market did not provide the solution. 'We need to improve the level of our education. We, in Hong Kong, spend about three per cent of our GDP in education, a figure substantially lower than the United States of America. On the other hand, I'm the first one to recognise throwing money at things doesn't necessarily solve problems. We have to find a better way of educating our youngsters . . . so that they will be more ready five years from now, ten years from now. I'm afraid the way we're grappling with it is on a free market basis.' Tung, Chief Executive, *Government Information Services* (*GIS* hereafter), 12 September 1997.

9. Tung, Chief Executive, *GIS*, 12 November 2003.

10. For the background to this reform programme, see Education and Manpower Bureau, 'LegCo Panel on Education Reforming the Academic Structure of Senior Secondary Education and Higher Education: Actions for Investing in the Future' (CB(2) 90/04-05(01), October 2004).

11. Ibid., 37, 40.

12. After a 5 per cent cut in government funding in the previous three-year period, a further 10 per cent reduction in university budgets had been announced for the current academic year 2004–2005. Tung, Chief Executive, *GIS*, 28 October 2003, 4 December 2004, 6 December 2003.

13. Donald Tsang Yam-kuen, Chief Secretary, *GIS*, 24 October 2001.

14. Donald Tsang, Chief Secretary, *GIS*, 26 June 2002.

15. Donald Tsang, Chief Executive, *Hong Kong Hansard* (*HH* hereafter), 13 October 2010, 22 and 14 October 2010, 188.

16. Donald Tsang, Chief Executive, *HH*, 10 October 2007, 42.

17. C. Y. Leung, 'Manifesto for the Chief Executive Election 2012', 12, 39, 42.

18. Leung Chun-ying, Chief Executive, *HH*, 15 January 2014, 5624–25.

19. Eddie Ng Hak-kim, Secretary for Education, *HH*, 21 January 2015, 4885–86.

20. Eventually, 114 schools were given an exemption from the ban on English medium education.

21. Michael Suen Ming-yeung, Secretary for Education, 'Symposium on Medium of Instruction', 16 March 2008.

22. Material and quotations on the Education Commission are taken from Education Commission, *Learning for Life, Learning through Life: Reform Proposals for the Education System in Hong Kong* (September 2000), 145–46.

23. Education and Manpower Bureau, 'Reforming the Academic Structure for Senior Secondary Education and Higher Education: Actions for Investing in the Future', 40.

24. Education and Manpower Bureau, 'Legislative Council Panel on Education Articulation and Employment Opportunities of Sub-degree Holders' (CB(2)543/06-07(01), December 2006), 1.

25. See Professor Arthur Li Kwok-cheung, Secretary for Education and Manpower, *GIS*, 18 June 2003; Fanny Law Fan Chiu-fun, Permanent Secretary for Education and Manpower, *GIS*, 12 November 2003.

26. Tung, Chief Executive, *GIS*, 6 December 2003.

27. For the financial situation when implementation began, see Education Bureau, 'Item for Finance Committee' (FCR(2007-08)36, November 2007); Michael Suen, Secretary for Education, *GIS*, 23 January 2008.

28. OECD, *Strong Performers and Successful Reformers in Education: Lessons from PISA for Japan* (OECD Publishing, 2012), 168.

29. University Grants Committee, *Higher Education in Hong Kong: A Report by the University Grants Committee*, 'Chapter 8: Expansion since 1989'.

30. The figure was regarded as alarmingly high when first introduced, and a well-respected education expert was so astonished by the initiative that he suspected that it might have hidden political aims. Cheng Kai Ming, 'Educational Policymaking in Hong Kong: The Changing Legitimacy', in *Education and Society in Hong Kong: Toward One Country and Two Systems*, ed. Gerard A. Postiglione (Armonk, NY: M. E. Sharpe, 1991), 113.

31. Eddie Ng, Secretary for Education, *HH*, 14 December 2016, 2429.

32. Legislative Council Secretariat, 'Panel on Education: Background Brief Prepared by the Legislative Council Secretariat . . . Sub-degree education' (CB(2)543/06-07(02), 7 December 2006), 3.

33. Education and Manpower Bureau, 'Legislative Council Panel on Education Articulation and Employment Opportunities of Sub-degree Holders', 2.

34. Michael Suen, Secretary for Education, *HH*, 12 March 2008, 5275.

35. For example, Editorials, *Ming Pao Daily*, 11 August and 31 October 2006; Teddy Ng, 'Aid Plan to Lift Associate Degree', *China Daily*, 11 April 2008.

36. University Grants Committee, 'Aspirations for the Higher Education System in Hong Kong: Report of the University Grants Committee' (LC Paper No. CB(2)602/10-11(01), December 2010), 31, 34, 40.

37. Tim Lui Tim-leung, Committee on Self-Financing Post-Secondary Education Chairman, *GIS*, 26 April 2013.

38. Legislative Council Secretariat, 'Panel on Education Meeting on 13 June 2016 Updated Background Brief on Issues Related to the Governance and Regulation of the Self-Financing Post-Secondary Education Sector' (CB(4)1090/15-16(02, 8 June 2016), 5.

39. Policy 21 Limited, 'Local and International Good Practices in the Governance and Quality Assurance of the Self-Financing Post-Secondary Education Sector' (July 2014), 10.

40. Legislative Council Secretariat, 'Panel on Education Meeting on 13 June 2016 Updated Background Brief on Issues Related to the Governance and Regulation of the Self-Financing Post-Secondary Education Sector', 2.

41. Committee on Self-Financing Post-Secondary Education, *GIS*, 4 October 2017.

42. Eddie Ng, Secretary for Education, *HH*, 19 February 2014, 7220.

43. Legislative Council Secretariat, 'Panel on Education Meeting on 13 June 2016 Updated Background Brief on Issues Related to the Governance and Regulation of the Self-Financing Post-Secondary Education Sector', 5.

44. Eddie Ng, Secretary for Education, *HH*, 14 December 2016, 2435–36.

45. Lawrence J. Lau et al., *Yes, Hong Kong CAN!*, 67–68.

46. Leung Chun-ying, Chief Executive, *HH*, 15 January 2014, 5624–25.

47. Quotations and comments from the foundation's report are from Lawrence J. Lau et al., *Yes, Hong Kong CAN!*, 67–68.

48. By the end of 2016, out of the 15,500 Hong Kong students who had applied for admission to Mainland higher education institutions in the previous five years, only 6,500 had been admitted. Press release, *GIS*, 17 December 2016.

49. For example, *Wen Wei Po* and *Sing Tao Daily*, 27 May 2016; Dara Wang and Honey Tsang, 'Study Reveals Decline in Incomes of Graduates', *China Daily*, 5 August 2016; Hong Kong Council of Social Service, 'A Study of Living Situation of Young Adults in Hong Kong', 10–11.

50. Commission on Strategic Development, 'Young People: Education, Employment and Development Opportunities' (CSD/1/2013, September 2013), 8.

51. Census and Statistics Department, *2016 Population By-Census Thematic Report: Household Income Distribution in Hong Kong, Hong Kong Special Administrative Region* (Hong Kong, 2017), 'Table 2.6: Median Monthly Income from Main Employment of Working Population by Educational Attainment (Highest Level Attended), 2006, 2011 and 2016', 31.

52. Commission on Strategic Development, 'Young People: Education, Employment and Development Opportunities', 8.

53. Labour and Welfare Bureau, 'Report on Manpower Projection to 2022' (Hong Kong SARG, April 2015), 82.

54. The conservatism of the estimates is suggested by the data presented in Labour and Welfare Bureau, 'Report on Manpower Projection to 2022', 'Table 3.31: Projected Manpower Requirements by Economic Sector and Education Level in 2022', 76.

55. Leung Chun-ying, Chief Executive, *HH*, 15 January 2014, 5624–25.

56. Eddie Ng, Secretary for Education, *HH*, 21 January 2015, 4885–86.

57. Cherry Tse Ling Kit-ching, Permanent Secretary for Education, *GIS*, 13 November 2014.

58. Eddie Ng, Secretary for Education, *HH*, 12 November 2014, 1796.

59. Press release, *GIS*, 18 March 2016.

60. 'Top Universities in China by 2016 University Web Ranking'.

61. Kevin Yeung Yun-hung, Secretary for Education, *GIS*, 5 July 2017; Education Bureau, 'Legislative Council Panel on Education Priority Measures to Support Quality Education' (CB(4)1366/16-17(01), July 2017), 'Annex A: Non-Means-Tested Subsidy Scheme for Self-Financing Undergraduate Studies in Hong Kong and the Mainland', 3–4.

62. Although the announcements by Carrie Lam and her Education Minister were publicised as innovative, they faithfully followed existing policies and programmes in the university and post-secondary sectors. This continuity is very plain from comparing them with the account of Leung Chun-ying's term in *Report on the Work of the Fourth-Term Government of the Hong Kong Special Administrative Region June 2017*, 62–63.

63. Education Bureau, 'Annex 1: Panel on Education Follow-Up to the meeting on 10 July 2017 Response to the Four Motions Passed at the Meeting' (LC Paper No. CB(4)1416/16-17(01), 13 July 2017), 5.

64. Press release, *GIS*, 13 November 2017.

65. The continuing ceiling on first-year degree places generated considerable public criticism. See, for example, the coverage in *Ming Pao Daily* and *Sing Tao Daily*, 11 July 2017.

66. Consumer Search Hong Kong Ltd. (commissioned by the Education Bureau), 'Survey on Opinions of Employers on Major Aspects of Performance of Sub-degree Graduates in Year 2013' (2016), 2–45.

# 7
# Lives at risk

Government mismanagement is extensive in Hong Kong and increasing on a scale which neither the public nor the media fully comprehend. Crises occur and scandals in the public services are reported. They are generally regarded as isolated incidents. In reality, they are evidence of the rise of dangerous administrative practices in modern Hong Kong which have worsened during the last two decades. This chapter seeks to illustrate the dimensions of the menace that mismanagement creates with four case studies in which lives have been at risk, directly or indirectly.

The disasters and their causes are only part of this chapter. Equally important is an analysis of the government's response to loss of life and the prevention of future catastrophes. In each case, the dangers to the public have been allowed to continue. The four examples of mismanagement have also been chosen to illustrate how widespread defective administration has become, and thus they range from public health to housing safety and from marine safety to prevention of corruption.

## When public health collapses

Early in 2003, Hong Kong fell victim to an epidemic of atypical pneumonia (SARS) which had broken out on the Mainland the previous year and was to spread to Singapore and other Asian countries. Hong Kong, despite its relatively small population, accounted for 21 per cent of all victims worldwide and almost a third of the global deaths.[1]

This disastrous event was an astonishing reversal of history. In the 1950s, Hong Kong had faced far worse threats as more than a million immigrants poured in from the Mainland, most of them to end up in squatter huts and tenement slums, with only the most primitive sanitary facilities and water supply (as chapter 4 explained in detail). Many of them were destitute, 'near starvation', and suffering from 'a variety of infectious, parasitic and deficiency diseases'. There seemed nothing to prevent large-scale epidemics with very high mortality rates. The health authorities never lost control, however, and the mortality rate from infectious and parasitic diseases dropped from 24 per cent of total deaths to 16 per cent between 1951 and 1961.[2]

On the eve of the 2003 SARS epidemic, a legislator, Cyd Ho Sau-lan, asked the Health Minister how close were contacts with the Mainland, and with Guangdong province in particular. The Minister revealed that in the three previous years, there had been a total of 20 'communications' between Hong Kong and various local administrations in Guangdong. Of these, only two related to the supply of public health data, while another seven were 'to exchange information on general health issues'. How effective were these contacts in 'preventing the spread of diseases', she asked. His reply was carefully worded. Indirectly, he made it plain that the current arrangements were not ideal. He intended, he said, 'to ensure even closer collaboration with the Mainland authorities for timely exchange of information on public health issues'. However, 'for outbreaks of diseases which are of public health importance', he said, 'immediate contacts will be made through the established channels'. This reassurance proved over-optimistic. SARS had already become a serious threat in Guangdong province, which was not supplying the promised information.[3] And SARS had just arrived in Hong Kong.

The epidemic had been imported unwittingly from Guangdong province by a medical professor, Liu Jianlun. A senior colleague travelled to Hong Kong to check Liu's health and then tried to alert the Hong Kong medical authorities to the danger of Liu starting an epidemic. This warning was not treated as urgent partly because of reassurances from provincial officials that the outbreak was under control.[4] It was later to become plain that Hong Kong's public health system, despite a wealth of experience in dealing with epidemics in the past, was badly handicapped by its unfamiliarity with the Mainland's political system.

As SARS was sweeping into Hong Kong, the Mainland 'was preoccupied with [a] change in national leadership at the highest level'. By tradition, this was 'an event of extraordinary importance' during which all government activities should be auspicious, to quote a meticulous study of the epidemic. Thus, the minimal flow of health information that the Guangdong authorities supplied in normal times was disrupted. For the Hong Kong health authorities, this was disastrous because they did not have a complete picture of how the epidemic was developing and the scale of the threat it posed.

To make matters worse, in Hong Kong, maximum publicity for health threats and how the community should act were regarded as key weapons in controlling an epidemic. Mainland officials, however, attacked the extensive press coverage of the spread of SARS in Hong Kong. One prominent Mainland personality denounced the Hong Kong media for 'unbalanced' reporting which could cause public panic, he

said, and damage the economy.[5] Not until the new political leadership
was in place at the national level could an effective system for collaboration on this and other health matters be worked out between Hong
Kong and Guangdong.[6]

SARS and its mishandling also revealed gross shortcomings in the
ministerial system so recently set up by the Chief Executive, Tung Chee
Hwa. In Tung's evidence to the Legislative Council's investigation of
the SARS crisis, he described how 'the Government had made the best
endeavour to handle the SARS outbreak'. He had called for targets to
be set for bringing down the 'the daily reported cases', he said, first to
five and then to zero. His initiative seemed remote from reality: as if
doctors and nurses would be content with anything other than the fastest
possible end to the epidemic. His target-setting was political rhetoric.[7]

Although Tung was described by one senior Hospital Authority staff
member as 'very hands-on' in the handling of the SARS epidemic, the
Chief Executive seemed to have been totally unaware of the leadership
role that he ought to have played. At the start of the outbreak, according to the Hospital Authority's own investigation, there was no 'clear
chain of command, contingency plan or formal mechanism for bringing
together the key decision makers in the HA (Hospital Authority),
DH (Department of Health) and HWFB (Health, Welfare and Food
Branch)'. Warnings from front-line professionals about the mounting
crisis were not followed up with active responses 'at the highest levels'.
'The Government's communications with the community' were misleadingly positive and, as a result, proved 'confusing' to the health
professionals 'who were acutely aware of the escalating situation'. The
government's over-optimistic messages may well have undermined
efforts to develop 'a focused coordinated approach' in tackling the crisis
by HA, MH and HWFB, the official investigation noted.[8]

Particularly revealing was Tung's failure to intervene when the Hospital
Authority's own chief executive was hospitalised with SARS. 'The key
leadership roles', the Hospital Authority investigation reported, 'now
became increasingly confusing'. For a week, the sick official 'continued
to be involved from his hospital bed', and there was no clear transfer of
authority to his deputy.[9] No political skills were needed to realise that an
incapacitated senior manager needs to be replaced without delay. Even
a business executive should understand the importance of making sure
a substitute is quickly appointed and formally authorised to take over.

The Hospital Authority's investigation disclosed how utterly confused
the leadership remained. A new, 'war team' with 20 members was set up
to meet daily. The group proved too large to function as anything more
than a forum for exchanging information. 'The absence of clear leadership' often meant that reaching decisions 'required time-consuming
consensus building'.[10] The lack of coordination and the conflicting

roles of senior officials were aggravated by Tung's failure to provide a proper constitutional framework when he first established his ministerial system to consolidate his control of the civil service and the wider public sector. He had appointed a health minister, to whom the Director of Health was politically accountable. However, this official, and not the Health Minister, was left with the 'primary role' in dealing with infectious diseases and alone possessed the legal powers to carry out this responsibility.

Lam Woon-kwong, Director of the Chief Executive's Office, later admitted that no one had thought of dealing with the legalities involved, and so the Director's statutory powers had not been transferred to the minister. The Director had legal autonomy, which she exercised, and disagreements with the Health Bureau proved unavoidable.[11] Incredibly, even after six years in office, Tung and his appointees did not understand that the work of government, its bureaux, departments and staff was very strictly regulated by laws and regulations. Significantly, such legal restrictions have been among the largest causes of complaint by ministerial appointees over the years and also the misinformed basis of their suspicions that the civil service is basically insubordinate.

Stringency in public spending on health remained a top priority even during SARS. The epidemic created additional and unavoidable costs. Isolation wards and intensive care facilities had to be expanded overnight, and the medical expertise had to be found to bring the epidemic to a halt and to rehabilitate its victims. Tung announced that the government would allocate an extra $200 million to dealing with the crisis.[12] But this sum was not enough to make up for the reduction in total health spending that year which the 2003 budget had imposed as part of Tung's ongoing austerity drive.[13] Furthermore, the hospital sector had already been suffering from severe austerity cuts since the start of the decade. For example, in 2001, the Hospital Authority, for the first time, had to impose charges on the drugs of choice for treatment of breast and other cancers in public hospitals.[14]

The financial strains of combatting SARS aggravated the underfinancing of the hospital services which had already been in urgent need of expansion to cope with the community's normal requirements.[15] During the epidemic, the Hospital Authority stated bluntly that the government's financial cutbacks had increased waiting times and reduced standards of treatment for the general public.[16] In 2005, the Authority's finances had still not recovered. Treatment had to be rationed to 'more urgent conditions', it revealed, and 'quality started to be compromised'.[17] By 2007, because of the failure to solve the financial shortfall, the Hospital Authority was 'limiting or refusing introduction of new technologies and pharmaceuticals, and delaying the replacement of equipment'.[18] In 2008, the plight of patients who could not afford 'self-financed items' was still being dismissed by officials. They claimed that 'the great majority' of alternative but second-choice medication being provided were 'drugs of proven efficacy'.[19] In fact, the patients were getting second-rate treatment. The government was not moved by these public revelations and clung as long as possible to its financial restrictions. For example, interferon, a key drug for such serious illnesses as hepatitis, leukaemia and multiple sclerosis, had been placed on the 'patient pays' list in 2001, where it remained until 2010.[20]

## When ships collide

Shipping creates serious risks for both seamen and passengers, a little-known fact. Data for 1996–2005 showed that seamen's fatalities in Hong Kong waters were 'average': very high by comparison with the United Kingdom, for example, but more than 30 per cent lower than the rates for Denmark and Poland.[21] Overall, an academic study reported, 'the local risk environment of Hong Kong waters compares favourably with international norms'.[22] Potential accidents involving passenger vessels should be a special cause of concern because they cause the greatest casualties. But on the whole, the safety of ferry passengers has been taken very much for granted in Hong Kong.

Soon after the third Chief Executive took office in 2012, the port and its safety standards became an issue of major political importance. A collision occurred between two ferries in which 39 passengers were killed and 92 injured. A thorough public investigation of the tragedy and its causes followed, together with a comprehensive review of the reforms needed within the Marine Department. There were also criminal convictions of senior personnel. Nevertheless, at the end of these proceedings, there was no guarantee that the Department would be able to avoid similar accidents in future. The additional resources needed to meet the required safety standards would not be made available.

The accident had aroused widespread public anger as details emerged of poor navigation by the vessels' masters and also of the Marine Department's failure to enforce safety regulations. Professor Anthony Cheung Bing-leung, the Transport Minister, accepted responsibility for ensuring that this shipping accident was thoroughly investigated. As a result, convincing evidence was uncovered of how the obsession with reducing the headcount and payroll of government departments had undermined the quality of the Marine Department's services. It will be shown later in this section that the Minister exposed the indifference of those in power to the damage done by their tight-fisted policies.[23]

Public indignation over the casualties of the ferry collision compelled the government to quickly set up a Commission of Inquiry. This found that not only had the accident been avoidable but that the casualties had been aggravated by misconduct among Marine Department staff. The Commission focused mainly on who was directly responsible. The two coxswains in command of the vessels were prosecuted. However, of the 17 officials found by the Commission to have contributed to the tragedy, only two were prosecuted, one for deliberate failure to enforce regulations and the other for perjury in seeking to conceal his part in the accident.

This seemed unfair but there was another side to this tragedy which was not fully revealed until 2016 when another report was published with the innocuous title: 'Steering Committee on Systemic Reform of the Marine Department Final Report'.[24] This had been prepared under the chairmanship of the Minister, Professor Cheung. The document showed that the Marine Department had indeed been at fault. However, the frightening truth was that the Department had not been given the human resources needed to carry out its duties and guarantee marine safety in Hong Kong waters.

The Committee's original task had been to recommend reforms to the Marine Department which would prevent future tragedies. In the process, the Committee had to identify the Department's deficiencies which needed to be put right. The evidence it collected turned its report into a convincing denunciation of staff cuts and financial constraints which had been imposed on the civil service as a whole since 2001. For example, the technical standards which the Marine Department set for itself matched best international practice. But operational deficiencies were serious.

- The Local Vessels Safety Section did not have the resources to handle a mounting volume of work. As a result, the Department had not achieved its public 'Performance Pledges' between 2010 and 2012, a failure that should have aroused the attention of the Transport Minister's staff.
- Licensing service staff could not cope with their responsibilities because they 'had been overloaded with duties other than processing licence applications'. The Department had not been given the necessary computer facilities. As a result, professional staff had to carry out 'clerical duties such as printing of certificates', a task which took up 36 per cent of their time apparently.
- The Vessel Traffic Service provided by the Marine Department was of 'world-class standard', according to the Steering Committee. Nevertheless, the regular vetting of staff performance to ensure standards were maintained had been suspended in recent years 'due to manpower shortage'. The immediate priority had become how to keep up with the volume of work. Safety factors seemed less urgent.

Inevitably, laws and regulations went unenforced. Middle-rank officials felt obliged to informally 'suspend' legal and departmental requirements. In any case, the Department's management had no choice: it lacked the manpower to carry out its duties to the full.

In theory, staffing problems might have eased when the civil service recruitment freeze was relaxed in 2007. However, the Steering Committee uncovered a problem unique to the Marine Department. To acquire the technical qualifications and professional experience required for appointment as senior Marine Department personnel took as long as 'about 9.5 years to 12 years'. To make matters worse, the Committee's report commented, the Department's salaries could not match 'the highly competitive remuneration for jobs of comparable professional requirements' offered by the private sector.

The Steering Committee admitted that it could find no better solution to the staffing shortfalls than 'a series of stop-gap measures to address the acute recruitment difficulties and manpower shortage'. Thus, the safety of shipping in Hong Kong waters remained at risk. The long-term solution was clear enough, the Committee's report pointed out: 'Broaden the scope of the Government financial incentives to a higher level of the seafaring professional development'. That initiative would 'need to have the support and collaboration amongst the stakeholders within the Government', it observed. The needed support and resources were not forthcoming.

Even with a chairman of Professor Cheung's political rank, it seemed that there was little confidence within the Steering Committee that its recommendations would win the backing of the third Chief Executive, Leung Chun-ying. He appeared to be no more aware than his predecessors that in Hong Kong, the public services, from the police to the hospitals, already operated at high levels of efficiency. Which meant that standards could not be expected to improve further without additional staff and investment in technology.

In the case of the Marine Department, evidence of the continuing risks was presented in a 2016 report by the Ombudsman. An important tool in ensuring safety at sea is the investigation of reported accidents. Historically, the Marine Department had not had the capacity to review these incidents thoroughly. It was hoped that this problem would be solved by the launch of a new computer system in 2013. The Ombudsman discovered that, in 2016, the Department still had insufficient resources to be able to investigate all reported incidents thoroughly or to ensure that vessel owners complied with the Department's findings. The government's financial policies meant that safety remained at risk unnecessarily.[25] The irony was that the Transport Minister had personally taken charge of drafting the reforms which, the Ombudsman's report complained, had been postponed indefinitely—in breach of the Marine Department's duty.

What makes this situation all the more outrageous is that Hong Kong is among the world's busiest container bases. It is used by about 340 container vessels serving 470 destinations a week. Ships registered in Hong Kong account for nearly 10 per cent of the world's total tonnage.[26] With this volume of business, there should be no difficulty in generating enough fees and charges to finance a Marine Department with enough resources to achieve very high safety standards.

## Building fatalities

In December 1953, a fire made 53,000 squatters homeless overnight but only two people died. Even in that era of unreformed colonialism, the disaster succeeded in forcing a very reluctant administration to begin an immediate and large-scale programme to rehouse squatters.[27] Half a century later, the post-colonial government pointed out that, thanks to the public housing programmes, Hong Kong by the 1990s had 'a housing story that people took pride in' and which had provided safe and affordable homes in the public sector for half the population.[28] But a new crisis was looming in the private sector. Here, government reluctance to take responsibility was to prove intractable.

In January 2010, an entire block of a 55-year-old building complex in a rundown area of Kowloon collapsed, killing four people. This tragedy led to considerable anxiety throughout the community. During the previous two years, the Urban Renewal Authority (URA) had been warning the public that a high proportion of Hong Kong's aging housing stock was no longer safe. The fear now was that other buildings of comparable age and dilapidation could easily suffer a similar catastrophe.

The government faced two challenges. The first was how to launch an immediate safety programme to reassure the people of Hong Kong that there was no need for panic. The second was to ensure that the government took as little blame as possible for the deaths and thus head off demands for more vigorous government intervention to improve building management and maintenance. The minister responsible for rescuing the government from the tragedy's fallout was Carrie Lam Cheng Yuet-ngor, the Development Minister and a future Chief Executive. The two-stage strategy solution she adopted proved successful. The Buildings Department—part of her portfolio—launched an immediate mass safety inspection programme. This was to be followed by an ambitious package of new safety measures. The government also ensured that official investigations into the tragedy would be followed by skilful management of whatever embarrassing information was uncovered.

The first phase got off to a flying start. It was announced that the Buildings Department, with a payroll of less than a thousand civil servants, had mobilised '40 teams of professional and technical staff' to survey 4,000 buildings within the following month and to take 'swift follow-up actions against defects and irregularities'. The Department was also expected to continue with its 'ongoing duties' at the same time, and its normal work pressures were both daunting and increasing, an official report later admitted. That year, complaints from the public of defects and dilapidation requiring investigation rose to 14,111, a 24 per cent increase over 2009. Of this total, 1,000 had been emergency cases.[29]

Nevertheless, the one-month target was declared achieved. No one seemed anxious to question how thorough these 'comprehensive' safety inspections could have been when each team had to examine an average of 25 multi-storey buildings a week. Especially since access to premises had to be arranged with individual owners and tenants, and there was no guarantee of their cooperation. Thus, there was ample room for scepticism about the safety surveys, which was to be reinforced a year later when the Buildings Department announced a new, 'expanded' programme of building inspections for 2011. In fact, its target was not nearly so ambitious, planning to inspect a total of only 500 dilapidated buildings that year.[30] Yet, the year before, the Department had claimed that a 'comprehensive' investigation of 4,000 buildings had been completed in a single month (albeit as an emergency measure).

The Development Bureau had also pledged itself to wider reforms and now launched a series of large-scale campaigns to solve the safety and dilapidation problems in a total of 6,000 buildings. The programme would cover 400,000 unauthorised building works which posed potential hazards and 190,000 existing signboards (which were frequently classified as dangerous in multi-storey Hong Kong). The Buildings Department would be responsible for carrying out the work involved: inspecting premises, identifying owners, issuing statutory warnings and taking legal action against offenders.

To improve its capacity to deal with this daunting increase in its annual workload, this Department was allocated an extra 176 staff, taking the total to 1,142 (together with a promise of additional contract and consultancy personnel). Impressive as this increase looked in percentage terms, the Buildings Department had already been woefully short of the numbers required to enforce maintenance and safety legislation. The shortfalls had been reported in an official investigation conducted by outside experts, whose findings had not been disputed by the Department.[31] An obvious danger was that the focus on external and visible risks like windows and advertising displays would divert inspectors from the far more serious internal hazards caused by structural dilapidation and the deterioration of internal wiring and pipes, which made the buildings themselves unsafe for use as homes. But this risk was not tackled as it should have been.

Efforts by the government to evade liability for the Kowloon tragedy went ahead after an independent inquiry was launched. The collapse had not been an unforeseeable accident, apparently. A Legislative Council paper indicated that the building had been identified as dangerous as early as 2005. But 'no enforcement actions' had been taken by the Buildings Department to apply 'statutory orders' for maintenance and repairs.[32] Nevertheless, as far as the government was concerned, the 2010 collapse and its fatalities would be treated as an exceptional event which did not call for significant changes in official policies or tougher legislation for dealing with building safety.

The government's main line of defence was an insistence 'that, at the end of the day, the responsibility to maintain buildings rests with the owners', to quote Carrie Lam, 'They are bringing risks not only to themselves but also to members of the public'.[33] This appeal to Hong Kong's belief in the sanctity of private property was very effective in reducing political pressures for the additional funding and staff to enforce the laws, limited as they were, designed to keep buildings safe for the million families making their homes in the private sector. Chapter 3 has already explained in detail how market forces proved inadequate in ensuring sound management and maintenance for mass accommodation in multi-storey buildings and that to achieve the standards required, government support and supervision were indispensable.

In the independent inquiry's 2012 report, its experts focused heavily on the availability of staff and their quality. A shortage of manpower made it impossible to respond to the growing number of public complaints about defective buildings, they noted. The lack of minor staff meant that the professionals lost a significant part of every working day because they had to handle routine desk work and answer the phone calls from members of the public making complaints. The experts' recommendations indicated serious worries about declining morale as well as excessive workloads. They called on the Buildings Department to 'promote a corporate culture with an emphasis on providing quality services to the public' and to undertake a review of 'manpower needs in the light of its workload and performance targets'.[34]

When the Legislative Council asked the Buildings Department for its response, its reply offered an excellent example of how refuge in bureaucracy and its protocols provided an escape from public accountability and political danger.

> The Buildings Department agrees with the experts' recommendation and will continue to carry out annual reviews on its manpower needs and, if necessary, request for additional resources with the

help of the Development Bureau pursuant to the established practice for all bureaux and departments.[35]

In plain language, the Department accepted the experts' call for a review of 'manpower needs'. But this exercise would take its place in the usual, annual assessment of staffing levels. If it happened that a shortfall was identified for that year, the Department would refer the matter to minister-level. If it was agreed there to make a formal application for extra staff, the Treasury Branch would process the request in the normal way. This last point was a coded signal that the Buildings Department took it for granted that personnel would not be increased.

More difficult for the government to manage were the findings of the inquest into the deaths. Once again, however, the Department rose to the challenge. In its response to the Coroner's findings, it emphasised that he had found no one guilty of any criminal acts or negligence. He had, however, made two damaging findings, which the Department summarised.

- 'The building should have been declared as dangerous by [the Department] two months before the collapse'.
- The staff had handled the case as 'routine' and had reached an 'incorrect judgment'.

Nevertheless, there were no indications that the Department would put in place measures to prevent any similar 'misjudgements' in the future. As far as it was concerned, the most important message from the Coroner was that the public itself was to blame.

> The findings of the Coroner have revealed once again that to enhance building safety in Hong Kong, vigorous enforcement action [by the Buildings Department] alone is not adequate. We cannot emphasise enough that it is the basic responsibility of owners to upkeep the safety of their buildings and, for this purpose, to carry out regular inspection and timely maintenance and repair of their buildings.[36]

Despite the Kowloon fatalities in January 2010 and the lack of resources subsequently uncovered in the Buildings Department, the Development Minister, Carrie Lam, saw no urgent reason to change either policy or practice. Comprehensive surveillance of building safety and more extensive enforcement of the safety laws were not made a priority feature of the departments under her Bureau. In March 2010, she indicated that it was quite possible that some, if not all, the contract staff who made up half the professional team in the Department might be made redundant in the following year. She did not wait for the inquest and other investigations to report before staff were let go. After all, she had made it plain that the urgent steps taken to identify other dangerous buildings in 2010 had been a temporary measure in the immediate aftermath of the Kowloon disaster.

The Development Minister seemed unworried that her Bureau did not possess the data to estimate the true extent of dangerous breaches of building law and, therefore, the number of staff who would be required to deal with threats to public safety. 'I am afraid that at present, we do not have any more manpower and resources for making any assessments and statistical updates', she confessed. She seemed completely unconcerned about the consequences of her managers having to rely on dubious data when organising inspections and deciding on priorities for remedial measures.[37] But at least she had openly admitted that her bureau and its departments did not have the staff needed to protect the public by enforcing safety legislation.

So, the dangers continued, and the law was defied. Thus, in 2011, the owners' corporation of a 12-storey Kowloon building was directed to comply with fire safety regulations, but completely ignored this order. The case did not get to court until 2014, when the owners' corporation was fined a small penalty, which it ignored. In 2017, the owners' corporation was summoned to court once more and was fined a token amount for a second time.[38] The courts' delays and the small penalties imposed were virtual invitations to house-owners to ignore the threats to life which the government itself had identified. Nevertheless, by the time Carrie Lam took over as Chief Executive that year, public awareness of dangers created by illegal building modifications had increased significantly, a new Development Minister admitted, and efforts were promised to speed up investigations of breaches of the law.

## Complacent about corruption

For Hong Kong, zero tolerance of corruption is among the most important of the community's core values. But not when it comes to homes. Year after year in this century, the annual reports of the Independent Commission against Corruption (ICAC) recorded that the largest number of complaints from the private sector were about building management and maintenance. But the ICAC reports played down the importance of the public's complaints. Its 2000 *Annual Report*, for example, had insisted that 'many of the cases were prompted by misunderstanding or lack of knowledge about building management among members of owners' corporations'.[39] On this analysis, owners should stop complaining and learn to distinguish between honest and dishonest activities by contractors. In 2006, the ICAC was still minimising the importance of corruption in the private buildings sector in much the same terms.[40]

At the same time, the government consistently ignored suggestions that a modern regulatory system was badly needed. In 2006, the
legislature recommended unsuccessfully that property management
should become a licensed profession. A senior legislator commented
subsequently that 'in the absence of a licensing regime, there were no
effective ways to ensure ethical business practices'.[41] The legal barriers
against mismanagement and malpractice were too low to be a deterrent.
It was no surprise, therefore, that corruption got a considerable boost,
or at least so the public believed, from 'Operation Building Bright', an
emergency programme to increase employment opportunities which
was launched in 2009. The then Financial Secretary was worried that
Hong Kong faced an economic downturn and wanted to find a formula
to create 10,000 jobs as fast as possible. He decided to provide cash
grants for a limited period to pay for urgent repairs to 1,000 of the most
dilapidated residential buildings.[42] Since the scheme had been labelled
a 'temporary' measure, there had been little incentive to spend much
time and effort on plugging holes in the programme's integrity. In any
case, the government itself seemed overwhelmed by the challenges
involved in the Operation.

Organising repair and renovation teams for such a large number of
very dilapidated, multi-storey premises created extremely complex financial, administrative and social challenges. Very soon after the launch of
Operation Building Bright, widespread claims surfaced that the government's hasty initiative to improve maintenance standards had, in fact,
created new opportunities for building managements to engage in
corruption and bid-rigging. Within a year, a member of the Executive
Council (and future Housing Minister) was expressing dismay in public
about fraud, misappropriation and corruption in the private housing
sector, which was making individual owners mistrust all government
schemes to improve management and maintenance.[43] To make financial supervision more difficult still, this emergency programme was soon
trebled in size to cover 3,100 buildings aged 30 years or over, with $3.5
billion for cash grants to subsidise repairs. It proved difficult to reach
these targets, and by the conclusion of Operation Building Bright, only
600 buildings had benefitted from the scheme, it was reported in 2015.[44]

The government did little to allay the widespread conviction that corruption was rampant. An official document issued to counter allegations
of fraud and corruption in 2015 contained a series of complacent statements of good intention.[45] But in the same year, a special ICAC anniversary publication openly admitted that corruption had flourished during
Operation Building Bright thanks to its subsidies which had created a
boom in building maintenance works. The handsome profits the programme generated had fostered 'corrupt collusion among owners'
corporation committee members, unscrupulous building consultants,

contractors and other professionals inflating renovation and construction project prices to cover the cost of bribes', this ICAC document
confessed.[46]

At the ministerial level, nevertheless, there was to be no change in the
insistence that malpractice in the private housing sector was too limited
to matter. There was now a new Development Minister, and his officials
responsible for overseeing Operation Building Bright continued to
struggle unsuccessfully to counter widespread complaints about how
the scheme had been mismanaged. The public remained convinced
that the Operation and its compulsory repair programmes had made
owners easy targets for dishonest managers and building contractors.[47]
In response, officials claimed that over the years, measures had been
introduced to help owners protect themselves against corrupt practices.
However, these limited initiatives had only covered the most dilapidated
premises: those over 30 years old and with low market valuations, the
media pointed out.[48]

Finally, in 2015, a renovation subcontractor was gaoled for conspiring
to rig the award of a contract at the Garden Vista Estate. It was alleged
that he had acted in collusion with the chairman of the owners' corporation and two property management company executives. The court was
told that there were another three minor conspirators: an architect, an
engineer and a consultant. None of these parties was charged with any
offences. The plan, it was alleged, was to skim off for themselves 17 per
cent of the $260 million bill that the 840 owners of individual flats in
Garden Vista estate would be charged for the work. The fraud collapsed
when several owners refused to pay what they believed to be grossly
inflated fees. A criminal investigation followed, and the sub-contractor
readily admitted his guilt.[49]

Throughout this scandal, the government remained desperate to
avoid increased involvement in policing management and maintenance.
The Development Minister repeated in the Legislative Council that
maintenance was not the government's business. He refused to set up
an independent body to coordinate the government's 'multi-pronged
approach, covering legislation, enforcement, support assistance to
property owners to prevent bid-rigging'. As a result, the six agencies
most involved in housing matters—the ICAC, police, Home Affairs
Department, Buildings Department, Urban Renewal Authority and the
Hong Kong Housing Society—would be left to cooperate as they saw fit.
The Development Minister tried scaremongering as well, warning flat
owners that if the government did intervene, they would have to pay
a price. An independent regulatory body would create 'administrative
expenses', he said, which would eventually 'very likely be passed on to
building owners, resulting in higher costs of maintenance works'.[50]

A week later, the minister met his match in the Legislative Council. Even the government's closest allies had lost patience. A member of the pro-government Democratic Alliance for the Betterment and Progress of Hong Kong recited a list of the ways in which the government had facilitated corruption and malpractice through its unwillingness to introduce legal and administrative reforms.

- The government had long insisted 'that pure bid-rigging' would only become illegal after a Competition Ordinance came into effect, which it did in late 2015. In addition, an offence would only occur if 'bribery, fraud or criminal elements' were involved.
- The Building Management Ordinance was full of holes. In particular, the building managers had no obligation 'to explain to owners the contents of the repair works'.
- Multiple ownership of buildings and the 'specialized knowledge [needed for] major repair works' required management skills that were well beyond the capacity of the average flat owner.
- The government used the excuse that private property owners should manage their own affairs to avoid giving significant help in solving management problems.
- When government assistance was supposed to be provided, the resources provided were grossly inadequate. Particularly serious was the plight of the Home Affairs Department, which was responsible for direct contacts with owners' corporations that were in difficulty. The Department's staff shortages meant that its Liaison Officers could not cope with the volume of work. 'Inexperienced part-time community organizers' were used as substitutes.
- Administrative complexity and overlapping departmental responsibilities undermined cooperation and coordination in overcoming housing problems. At least 12 government departments and agencies would be involved whenever large-scale repair works took place. This awesome bureaucratic arrangement proved a serious handicap for owners of smaller or older buildings who had to rely on the voluntary endeavours of owners' representatives to organise renovations and regular maintenance.[51]

These charges were not challenged by the two ministers present during the Legislative Council debate which took place on this issue. Indeed, the Development Minister was forced into a begrudging admission of the validity of the complaints, which he had previously dismissed. There were, he conceded, 'possibly problems such as a few property owners colluding with owners' corporations, management companies and maintenance works consultants in order to manipulate building maintenance decisions for seeking advantages, and so on, or even corruption and triad involvement'—as if such situations were only minor threats to the public interest. 'As some property owners lack the knowledge, experience and vigilance in co-ordinating building maintenance works', he went on patronisingly, 'Some black sheep may take advantage of the situation to reap illegal advantages during the maintenance process'. Completely ignored was the fact that, since the start of the century, the ICAC had refused to act on information from the public about these malpractices. As usual, the government was not to be blamed for this inaction. 'Responsibility to maintain and repair private buildings', he emphasised, 'rests with property owners'.[52]

His fellow minister, the Home Affairs Minister, was more straightforward. 'Building maintenance works touch upon many professional areas in which common small property owners may not necessarily be equipped with the relevant knowledge', he acknowledged, 'thus they are vulnerable to be taken advantage of by lawbreakers'.[53] The Home Affairs Department was the link between the government and property owners. This Department was crucial in assisting owners of deteriorating buildings whose finances were too limited to organise themselves to reverse dilapidation. Home Affairs Department staff were also the principal monitors of the ethics as well as the efficiency of the organisations set up to represent owners and to manage their buildings. There were about 120 Liaison Officers performing building management and related duties, making 7,000 visits a year to buildings with no management structures and another 40,000 visits a year to a variety of buildings with some form of residents' representation.[54] On the basis of these statistics, a Liaison Officer's workload was crushing.

Similarly, the Urban Renewal Authority was the government's principal vehicle for the rehabilitation, renovation and replacement of Hong Kong's worst housing conditions. As its work schedule increased, its staffing did not expand to meet the additional workload. The government simply expected the Authority to redeploy personnel to achieve what was, in fact, the impossible. Among other proposals was for the Authority to become responsible not just for the renovation of 3,100 buildings but of '19,000 buildings . . . about 90 per cent of all private residential buildings of age 30 years or above'.[55] It was hard to see how, with its limited human resources, the Authority would be able to ensure that the cash and consultancy services which it provided were not misused for unlawful purposes.

The government seemed to believe that it would be able silence its critics once the Competition Ordinance came into force because responsibility for policing the private housing sector could be assigned to the Competition Commission at the end of 2015.[56] But this new law was unlikely to put an end to the immunity which corrupt practices enjoyed in the property sector. The Commission had even fewer resources than the ICAC for handling criminal investigations of housing estates with hundreds and even thousands of flat owners.

In the last resort, the ICAC housing scandal was not simply the product of the Chief Executives' abiding commitment to leaving market forces to find the best solutions for Hong Kong. Nor was it the result of a genuine belief that the law and the government should not interfere with the management of private assets. Legislation to protect the public prevailed in almost every other sphere of life in Hong Kong. Its markets, from shares to pharmaceuticals, were rigorously supervised. The real reason, in all probability, was that the ICAC's human resources and annual funding could not be stretched to cover the private housing sector.

The ICAC's hands-off approach had been another factor which allowed the private housing sector to fall into disrepair and to become increasingly unhealthy and unsafe. The housing stock continued to deteriorate. The standard of the average family's living accommodation declined. The value of its flats as a marketable asset diminished. This was not how the private sector was supposed to operate. But it was an inevitable result of lawlessness and corruption. It was extraordinary that the people of Hong Kong who had freed themselves from corruption in 1974 must now endure it in their housing.

## Conclusion

This chapter has highlighted another alarming feature of contemporary Hong Kong. Financial stringency came at a price not just in discomfort or inconvenience but in public safety. Across the entire government, challenges increased in this century, and the volume of work grew relentlessly. Departments and other government agencies had no alternative but to find a coping mechanism: duties were 'prioritised' to match the limited staff and other facilities at their disposal. When assessing which laws and regulations to enforce, the senior civil servants involved had to decide which public complaints could not be ignored. The rest had to be shelved.

These officials did not conceal what was happening. Naturally enough, they generally sought to escape liability for what went wrong. But they also provided the information needed to warn the legislature and the general public that their bureau or department lacked the human and financial resources to find solutions for the threats to the public's safety because of financial and staff constraints.

The emergence of perilous conditions in the health, housing and shipping sectors and the ICAC's worrying non-interventionism can be traced back to financial policies adopted by Chief Executives and loyally carried out by their Chief Secretaries, Financial Secretaries and

individual ministers. In almost every area of government, these decisions were dominated by a desire to cut public spending on the theory
that, unlike the private sector, the public service must have considerable surplus capacity and that, in the absence of performance-related
pay systems, its productivity must suffer from lack of motivation. These
dogmas were proved false, at considerable cost to the community.

## Notes

1. Sars Expert Committee, *SARS in Hong Kong: From Experience to Action* (Hong
   Kong: 2003), 5; Dr Yeoh Eng-kiong, Secretary for Health, Welfare and Food
   and Tung Chee Hwa, Chief Executive, *Government Information Services* (*GIS*
   hereafter), 2 October 2003.
2. David R. Phillips, *The Epidemiological Transition in Hong Kong: Changes in
   Health and Disease since the Nineteenth Century* (Hong Kong: Centre of Asian
   Studies, University of Hong Kong, 1988), 18, 30. See also C. Y. Yeung,
   'Health Problems in Chinese Children Are Different', *Hong Kong Journal of
   Paediatrics* 8, no. 2 (2003): 80.
3. Dr Yeoh, Secretary for Health, Welfare and Food, *Hong Kong Hansard* (*HH*
   hereafter), 5 March 2003, 4269–73.
4. Thomas Abraham, *Twenty-First Century Plague: The Story of SARS* (Hong Kong:
   Hong Kong University Press, 2004), 55–58.
5. Long Yongtu, Foreign Trade and Economic Co-operation Ministry Ex-Vice
   Minister, reported in *Hong Kong Economic Journal*, 29 March 2003.
6. Christine Loh, 'The Politics of SARS: The WHO, Hong Kong and Mainland
   China', in *At the Epicentre: Hong Kong and the SARS Outbreak*, ed. Christine
   Loh and Civic Exchange (Hong Kong: Hong Kong University Press, 2004),
   149–56.
7. In evidence to the Legislative Council's investigation, Lam Woon-kwong,
   Director of the Chief Executive's Office, summarised the 'strategic decisions'
   made by the Chief Executive's Steering Committee ('Report of the Select
   Committee to Inquire into the Handling of the Severe Acute Respiratory
   Syndrome Outbreak by the Government and the Hospital Authority, July
   2004', 238). Tung appeared to have no recollection of them in his evidence.
8. 'Report of the Hospital Authority Review Panel on the SARS Outbreak,
   September 2003', 19.
9. Ibid., 20–21, 163.
10. Ibid., 163.
11. 'Report of the Select Committee to Inquire into the Handling of the Severe
    Acute Respiratory Syndrome Outbreak by the Government and the Hospital
    Authority, July 2004', 234.
12. Chief Executive's Office, *GIS*, 25 March 2003.
13. The Financial Secretary, in presenting his 2003 Budget was personally con-
    vinced that spending on social services was unsustainable. Antony Leung
    Kam-chung, Financial Secretary, *HH*, 5 March 2003, 4318–20, 4374.
14. Dr Yeoh, Secretary for Health and Welfare, *HH*, 9 May 2001, 5179.

15. For example, Hospital Authority, *Hospital Authority Annual Plan 2005–06* (Hong Kong: Hospital Authority, 2005), 1–2.

16. Hospital Authority, *Hospital Authority: Annual Plan 2003–2004* (Hong Kong: Hospital Authority, 2003), 34, 35, 53.

17. Hospital Authority, *Hospital Authority Annual Plan 2005–06*, 15.

18. Hospital Authority, *Hospital Authority Annual Plan 2007–08* (Hong Kong: Hospital Authority, 2007), 7.

19. Legislative Council Secretariat, 'Grant for the Samaritan Fund' (CB(2)208/08-09(06), 7 November 2008), 2.

20. See Angora Ngai (Food and Health Bureau) letter to Elyssa Wong (Clerk to Legislative Council Panel on Health Services), 17 May 2012, 'Annex', 8–9.

21. 'Safety and Shipping 1912–2012: From Titanic to Costa Concordia' (Hamburg: Allianz Global Corporate & Specialty, March 2012), 13.

22. Tsz Leung Yip, 'Port Traffic Risks: A Study of Accidents in Hong Kong Waters', *Science Direct*, Transportation Research Part E 44 (2008): 930.

23. It must be recorded that the Secretary for Transport and Housing, Professor Anthony Cheung, was most anxious to minimise the damage done by misguided financial policies in both his policy areas.

24. The quotations and information that follow are from 'Steering Committee on Systemic Reform of the Marine Department Final Report' (April 2016), 22–24, 31, 42, and 45 in particular.

25. Office of the Ombudsman, '主動調查報告, "海事處對海上事故調查報告所作建議的跟進機制"' (14 June 2016), 19.

26. Professor Anthony Cheung, Secretary for Transport and Housing, *GIS*, 4 March 2016.

27. The colonial government's lack of enthusiasm is recorded in HKRS163-1-1578, 'Shek Kip Mei Fire' and HKRS163-1-1677, 'Committees—Shek Kip Mei Fire'.

28. Professor Anthony Cheung, Secretary for Transport and Housing, 'Chairman's Foreword: Long Term Housing Strategy—Providing Adequate Housing for All?', in Long Term Housing Strategy Steering Committee, *Long Term Housing Strategy: Building Consensus, Building Homes* (Consultation Document, September 2013), v, vi.

29. Buildings Department, 'Report on the Findings and Recommendations of the Working Group on Review of Building Safety Enforcement Procedures and Practice' (December 2011), 8.

30. 'BD Responds to Coroner's Verdict', *GIS*, 16 August 2011.

31. Professor Ko Jan-ming, 'An Independent Appraisal of the Buildings Department's "Report on the Findings and Recommendations of the Working Group on Review of Building Safety Enforcement Procedures and Practices"' (11 May 2012), 24–25.

32. Legislative Council Secretariat, 'Paper for the House Committee Meeting on 25 February 2011 Continuation of work of the Subcommittee on Building Safety and Related Issues' (CB(1)1382/10-11), 23 February 2011), 2–3.

33. Carrie Lam Cheng Yuet-ngor, Secretary for Development, *GIS*, 30 January 2010.

34. Ko, 'An Independent Appraisal of the Buildings Department's "Report on the Findings and Recommendations of the Working Group on

Review of Building Safety Enforcement Procedures and Practices"',
24–25; Development Bureau, 'Legislative Council Panel on Development
Subcommittee on Building Safety and Related Issues Buildings Department's
Review of Enforcement Procedures and Practices for Dilapidated Buildings
and Views of Independent Experts', 'Annex C: Independent Expert Review
on the Buildings Department's Enforcement Procedures and Practices in
Relation to Dilapidated Buildings Executive Summary', 6.

35. Ibid., 'Annex D: Buildings Department's Response to the Observations and
    Recommendations of the Independent Experts', 10.

36. Development Bureau, 'Legislative Council Panel on Development
    Subcommittee on Building Safety and Related Issues Buildings Department's
    Initial Response to the Findings of the Coroner's Inquest on the Building
    Collapse Incident at Ma Tau Wai Road' (CB(1)2930/10-11(01), August
    2011), 1–2, 6.

37. Carrie Lam, Secretary for Development, *HH*, 10 March 2010, 5776–80.

38. 'Owners' corporation fined for failing to comply with Fire Safety Compliance
    Orders', *GIS*, 4 October 2017.

39. ICAC Commissioner, *2000 Annual Report by the Commissioner of the Independent
    Commission Against Corruption*, 10.

40. 'Our investigations revealed that the primary cause of many reports was
    ascribed to the lack of transparency in the work of owners' corporations.
    Many reports were minor in nature and were swiftly dealt with by the
    Quick Response Team.' *2006 Annual Report Independent Commission Against
    Corruption*, 12.

41. Legislative Council Secretariat, 'Panel on Home Affairs Minutes of Special
    Meeting Held on Friday, 4 July 2008 . . .' (CB(2)2850/07-08), 22 October
    2008), 10.

42. John Tsang Chun-wah, Financial Secretary, *HH*, 25 February 2009, 4995–97.
    That the priority was about spending money on jobs was confirmed by the
    minister responsible for private sector housing problems. See Carrie Lam,
    Secretary for Development, *GIS*, 26 February 2009.

43. Professor Anthony Cheung, Executive Councillor, 'The To Kwa Wan Tragedy
    Presents an Opportunity to Tackle More Than Just Unsafe Buildings', *South
    China Morning Post*, 9 February 2010.

44. Home Affairs Department, 'Legislative Council Panel on Home Affairs
    Safeguard Measures for Prevention of Corruption and Malpractices in
    Building Repair and Maintenance Works' (CB(2)662/14-15(01), January
    2015), 2. However, the total number of buildings rescued by the Urban
    Renewal Authority during the life of the Programme was 2,000. Legislative
    Council Secretariat, 'Panel on Development . . . Updated Background Brief
    on the Work of the Urban Renewal Authority' (CB(1)1034/15-16(02), 15
    June 2016), 7.

45. Home Affairs Department, 'Legislative Council Panel on Home Affairs
    Safeguard Measures for Prevention of Corruption and Malpractices in
    Building Repair and Maintenance Works' (CB(2)662/14-15(01), January
    2015), 1–2.

46. Independent Commission Against Corruption, *40 Years in the Operations Department Fighting Corruption with the Community (1974–2014)* (Hong Kong: Independent Commission Against Corruption, 2015), 48.

47. Note the Development Minister's claim: '[Legislative Councillor] Mr Lee Cheuk-yan said that the Government's provision of subsidies for building repairs has inflamed bid-rigging. We have not found any bid-rigging case in the projects under Operation Building Bright so far.' Paul Chan Mo-po, Secretary for Development, *HH*, 2 December 2015, 2687. See also Development Bureau, *GIS*, 3 June 2016.

48. Wang Yuke, 'Garden Vista Bid Rigging Case Adjourned', *China Daily*, 26 February 2016.

49. Shadow Li, 'Largest Tender-Rigging Case Goes to Court', *China Daily*, 3 July 2015.

50. Paul Chan, Secretary for Development, *HH*, 25 November 2015, 1972.

51. Christopher Chung Shu-kun, *HH*, 2 December 2015, 2595–97.

52. Paul Chan, Secretary for Development, *HH*, 2 December 2015, 2605–6.

53. Lau Kong-wah, Secretary for Home Affairs, *HH*, 2 December 2015, 2607.

54. 'Written Answer by the Home Affairs Bureau to Mr Cheung Kwok-Che's Supplementary Question to Question 1', *HH*, 25 November 2015, A1.

55. Legislative Council Secretariat, 'Panel on Development . . . Updated Background Brief on the Work of the Urban Renewal Authority' (CB(1)1034/15-16(02), 15 June 2016), 7–8.

56. Home Affairs Department, 'Legislative Council Panel on Home Affairs Safeguard Measures for Prevention of Corruption and Malpractices in Building Repair and Maintenance Works', 3–4.

# 8
# Mismanaging the Mainland

From the very beginning of the People's Republic of China, the survival of Hong Kong and its special status have been underwritten by its success as the nation's international financial centre, for which it has had no rival. There has been no city in China since 1949 which could provide the global banking and currency services, mobilise the investment funds and facilitate the Mainland's entry into the world's currency and financial markets as smoothly and safely as Hong Kong. This role was formalised in the early 1950s and was strengthened with each new phase of the nation's reforms after the introduction of Deng Xiaoping's economic liberalisation policy in 1978. All three of China's premiers in this century have publicly acknowledged the unique contribution which Hong Kong and its financial services have made to the national economy.[1] In 2017, China's President Xi Jinping expressed this indebtedness in touching terms.

> I want to particularly commend Hong Kong people's participation in and significant contribution to China's reform, opening-up and modernization drive. The Central Government and people across the country have never forgotten what you have done.[2]

The crucial feature of this role is that it has been 'offshore', kept carefully separate from the Mainland economy. As a result, in pursuing China's modernisation, the nation had had an advantage available to very few emerging economies. Through Hong Kong, it enjoyed full access to an infrastructure of market regulation, legal and accounting services and communications and logistics facilities of world standard and far in advance of what the Mainland could create for itself.

This gap between Hong Kong and the Mainland in their levels of economic sophistication has rarely been acknowledged by Hong Kong's Chief Executives and their ministers or by its business leaders. On the contrary, they made widespread forecasts from the 1990s that Hong Kong was a wasting asset, which would soon be overtaken by Shanghai. These predictions of doom have continued ever since. The only escape from economic deterioration, Hong Kong's ruling élite insisted, was to integrate with the national economy. This policy was pursued by each of the first three Chief Executives in defiance of the three Premiers' endorsements of Hong Kong's existing business model and of warnings of the serious obstacles that integration would face.

The fourth Chief Executive expressed a similarly uncritical optimism about the Mainland market and integration immediately after taking office in 2017 despite her past experience of the serious difficulties Hong Kong faced on the Mainland.[3] Yet a few weeks earlier, Carrie Lam Cheng Yuet-ngor had been explicitly reminded by Premier Li Keqiang of the importance of Hong Kong's status as 'an international financial, trade and shipping center' while 'promoting a mutually complementary and beneficial relationship between the mainland and Hong Kong'.[4] Integration was not part of the agenda.

The most serious weakness of Chief Executives has been an inability to comprehend the 'political' risk for Hong Kong firms when doing business on the Mainland. State planning agencies continue to exercise extensive control over the economy, and even the lower levels of government can decide which businesses will prosper and which will be wound up in their area. Hong Kong entrepreneurs and investors have long had direct experience of this kind of threat to survival. They had been quick to answer Deng Xiaoping's call in 1978 to play a leading role in China's modernisation, and they transferred Hong Kong's entire manufacturing sector to Guangdong province. As a result, in the 1980s and 1990s, the province was transformed into the nation's major export centre, with a labour force of 10 million workers in Hong Kong–financed factories by 2007.[5] But Mainland policies had changed, and the province had decided that it no longer needed export-driven growth generated by low-technology and labour-intensive consumer products. Measures were taken to make their manufacture unprofitable. By 2010, the work force employed by Hong Kong–financed firms had been halved. The losses suffered by Hong Kong's entrepreneurs and investors will be discussed later in this chapter. The ability of Hong Kong to shrug off a setback on this scale and to continue to expand its role as an international financial services and business centre for China were convincing evidence of Hong Kong's robust flexibility and its survival culture.

This chapter will examine this conflict between economic realities and Hong Kong government policies and will seek to explain the motivation of the policy-makers involved.

## The gap between 'two systems'

The Mainland economy achieved an outstanding growth record from 1978. Nevertheless, four decades later, its business environment remained dauntingly backward by international standards. In a long and detailed critique, Premier Li Keqiang expressed deep dissatisfaction with the rampant weaknesses of the national economy. 'According to the 2015 World Bank Doing Business Report, China ranks 90th out of 189 economies' in terms of ease of doing business, he pointed out. He blamed this alarming situation on the gross inefficiency of government officials and their misguided practices at all levels of the administration, on their extensive insubordination and on their pursuit of personal advantage.[6]

As Table 8.1 illustrates, the Mainland lagged far behind Hong Kong, which also outperformed the United States in several categories.

**Table 8.1**
Business efficiency, 2015 World Bank rankings (1–189)

|                                  | China | Hong Kong | United States |
|----------------------------------|-------|-----------|---------------|
| Overall ease of doing business   | 90    | 3         | 7             |
| Starting a business              | 128   | 8         | 49            |
| Getting credit                   | 71    | 23        | 2             |
| Enforcing contracts              | 35    | 6         | 21            |
| Protecting minority investors    | 132   | 2         | 35            |

Source: World Bank, *Doing Business 2015 Going Beyond Efficiency* (Washington, DC: International Bank for Reconstruction and Development, 2014), 178, 191, 227.

The following year, China had improved to 84th position but was still well behind Hong Kong. Modernising the mainland business environment remained a severe challenge, and the Premier was still struggling in 2017 to boost his national campaign to reduce red tape and overlapping business regulations.[7] Plainly, the current Mainland business environment had little to attract the average Hong Kong firm in the absence of exceptional profit opportunities or extensive state help. In fact, the obstacles in the way of Hong Kong investors and entrepreneurs had increased considerably in this century.

Premier Li's frank analysis of the unattractive business environment on the Mainland was ignored by Hong Kong's government, which continued to declare that such Mainland innovations as its 'Free Trade Zones' and other specially favoured, would-be centres of excellence could carry out the business of an international financial centre. The most successful of these privileged areas was Shenzhen, which is located on Hong Kong's doorstep. It had been launched in 1978 as one of China's four Special Economic Zones which were exempted from normal state controls. It has been an outstanding success. At the same time, it has recently provided yet another example of why Premier Li's critical analysis ought to be taken seriously.

The Central People's Government gave Shenzhen 'a gift' to mark 'its 30th birthday' in 2012 in the form of the 'Qianhai experimental zone' set up 'to spearhead financial liberalization' and 'to speed cooperation between Hong Kong and the mainland'.[8] The volume of business proved disappointing in the initial year, principally because of continuing uncertainty about where and how the funds raised in Qianhai could be used within the Mainland. 'More than 2,600 companies' had been set up within the first year of operations but 'less than six percent' were Hong Kong firms, 'raising doubts over Qianhai's attractiveness to Hong Kong investors', the official news media reported.[9] It was proving extremely difficult for the Mainland authorities to provide the level of liberalisation which Hong Kong firms regarded as the minimum necessary to be able to function efficiently. This uncomfortable reality was publicly noted by Carrie Lam, Chief Secretary and future Chief Executive, but it was beyond Hong Kong's ability to overcome.[10]

By 2016, claims were being made that the project was successful. So it was, but not as a booming financial centre. It seemed to have done best with its 'social service' facilities. Hong Kong was providing some financial expertise and funding, in return for which it was allowed to start a project in Qianhai to care for elderly Hong Kong retirees. In addition, Hong Kong financed the 'Qianhai Shenzhen–Hong Kong Youth Innovation and Entrepreneur Hub', which was a pioneering 'business school' project but obviously not a mainstream financial venture.[11] Even with Qianhai's proximity to Hong Kong and, thus, its easy access to the best of financial and legal expertise, it was proving a slow process for Qianhai to catch up with its neighbour's world class standards—and it would take the national economy as a whole far longer. The lesson for Hong Kong was clear: to flourish, it ought to continue to operate offshore and within the global economy.

## National interest comes first

Tung Chee Hwa took office in 1997 convinced that the people of Hong Kong suffered from acute ignorance of Mainland affairs, which made necessary 'a steep learning process about our Motherland'. In return, he promised, there would be 'a tremendous opportunity to build an even more prosperous society in which to live and work'.[12] The great challenge, Tung insisted, was the way that Hong Kong's economy was, in his view, falling behind the rest of the nation. Hong Kong may have had a useful role for China in the past but not for much longer, he declared in 2001. '[After] the mainland market will be fully opened', he predicted,

'Hong Kong will lose the advantages it used to enjoy because of the closed system that existed on the Mainland in the past'.[13]

Hong Kong had to face the reality, Tung insisted on a later occasion, that other Mainland cities were on the verge of displacing it. 'Hong Kong was for a long time the only city or the only bridge between Mainland China on the one hand and the rest of the world on the other', he said, 'With the onset of the 21st century, Shanghai is a bridge, Beijing, Tianjing [sic], Shenzhen, Guangzhou, every one of them is a bridge'. (None of them has yet matched Hong Kong's global role.) Tung did not go into any detail about why the Mainland's progress must spell ruin for Hong Kong. He contented himself with a pledge of respect: 'In the Mainland, the Central Government have wonderful ideas'.[14]

Tung's remedy was the rapid integration of Hong Kong into the national economy. He believed that, in the past, his plans for Hong Kong's economic future had been thwarted. 'In the immediate aftermath of Hong Kong's return to China', he complained, 'a lagging mindset had persisted among people here'. He complained that there had been resistance from those concerned that 'closer economic ties with the Mainland would undermine our autonomy'.[15] In fact, his head of planning had shown total commitment to Tung's strategy. This official declared in 1998 that 'the long-term development of Hong Kong will become part and parcel of mainland developments, and the reverse is also true'. 'In formulating planning programmes, we would no longer look only at the internal needs of the [Special Administrative Region]', he went on, 'Instead, we would also take into account the development of our neighbouring areas [on the Mainland]'.[16] Furthermore, Tung's suggestion of opposition to seeking business ties with the Mainland was absurd. Hong Kong firms had already established an industrial base in Guangdong province employing millions of workers.

Tung's lobbying of China's leaders led to a pioneering, free-trade pact with the Mainland. The Ministry of Foreign Trade endorsed the proposal publicly in 2001.[17] A formal 'Closer Economic Partnership Arrangement' (CEPA) agreement was published in 2003.[18] CEPA's aims were ambitious: 'To phase out tariffs and non-tariff barriers on trade in goods, phase in liberalization of trade in services and promote trade and investment facilitation' between Hong Kong and the Mainland.[19] There was a specific pledge that Hong Kong companies providing high-quality services would obtain greater access to the mainland market in such sectors as banking, securities, insurance, exhibitions and conventions and advertising.[20]

From the start, however, there were doubts about how large CEPA's benefits to Hong Kong would be. An International Monetary Fund (IMF) report a year after CEPA had been launched predicted that Hong Kong's economic growth would improve only marginally:

- 'A zero tariff policy under CEPA will increase Hong Kong SAR's annual GDP by 0.3 percentage point . . . and increase total employment by about 0.2 percentage point'.
- 'The overall trade balance for Hong Kong SAR will improve by about 0.4 percentage point'.
- There would be some unquantified gains from such improvements as 'more efficient resource allocation' and 'technology innovation and productivity improvements'.

But the IMF cautioned that greater financial integration with the Mainland would leave Hong Kong's economy 'vulnerable to cyclical and structural shocks emanating from the Mainland'.[21]

## Local interests prevail

More ominous was the warning from China's Premier Wen Jiabao that the pact was 'neither a big gift nor a free lunch'.[22] Hong Kong's Chief Executives were to learn the hard way that the formal approval of CEPA by the Central People's Government did not mean that local administrations on the Mainland would promptly comply with Beijing's undertakings and open their markets to Hong Kong firms. For a start, delays of a decade or more in implementing national policies and legislation were a chronic weakness of Mainland governance, which the leadership had battled continuously to eradicate since the 1990s.[23] Furthermore, local protectionism was a major feature of the Mainland economy in spite of efforts by national leaders to create a national market. Quite simply, CEPA could not bring access to a national market, as Tung and his successors expected, because an open, nationwide market did not exist.

As long ago as 1992, President Jiang Zemin had started a campaign to attain this goal but had achieved nothing.[24] In 1997, he again called—but in vain—for a drive to 'remove obstacles to market development, break through regional blockades and sectoral monopolies'. Other national leaders denounced the defiance of Jiang's directive in the harshest terms. 'A cancer in China's domestic market' was how, in 2000, China's most senior trade and industry official, Wang Zhongfu, described the 'administrative monopolies, forced deals, and market blockades' set up by local governments.[25] Jiang himself was still battling against the stubborn protectionism of local governments throughout the country on the eve of his retirement in 2002.[26]

The previous year, Premier Zhu Rongji had included a campaign against local protectionism in the next five-year plan.[27] Nothing changed over the following decade, however. Recalcitrant local officials were not intimidated by denunciations from Chinese Communist Party and state leaders. This defiance of central authority was condemned publicly year after year, to little avail as the following timeline illustrates.

- 2000: Local protectionism was described as all-embracing. 'Blocked goods include everything, ranging from cars to construction materials, fertilizer to instant noodle, and beer . . . Many people call it "vassal separatism" which has been common throughout Chinese history with [local] warlords and princes setting up regimes of their own, and issuing their own orders', lamented the Chinese Communist Party's daily newspaper.[28]

- 2001: Local officials possessed virtually unlimited power, a leading Party official admitted. With local government connections, enterprises could obtain bank loans and deposits under false pretences and refuse to pay migrant workers. The victims would get no relief from the local law-enforcement institutions, which were unable to defy the wishes of the local government. Policies and regulations were subject to arbitrary changes and were neither consistent nor co-ordinated from one district to another. What were 'legitimate activities under one regulation [were] illegal under another'.[29]

- 2004: The Ministry of Commerce launched a coordinated attack on local protectionism, which it denounced for undermining market efficiency and promoting unfair competition. Local officials' misuse of their power meant that 'corruption and money-for-power trades [were] easily generated'.[30]

- 2006: New abuses were coming to light as local officials sought to maintain the highest possible growth rates. In their drive to attract and retain business enterprises, for example, local officials sought ways to cut production costs and were ready to ignore inconvenient legislation and to 'relax their environmental standards or connive with employers to keep workers' wages artificially low'.[31]

- 2008: Insubordination intensified after local governments were encouraged to respond to the 2007–2009 global financial crisis by boosting public expenditure. They were made responsible for 70 per cent of the nation's emergency economic stimulus programme, which they were compelled to finance by any means possible, legal or otherwise. They seized upon this excuse to give local interests priority. This fresh surge in local protectionism undermined efficient production and market reforms, a senior state economist subsequently pointed out.[32]

- 2013: 'The fragmented and distorted market has spawned problems such as higher operation costs and overcapacity in the wider economy, undermining the economies of scale of China's huge market', warned a member of a prestigious think tank, the Development Research Centre of the State Council.[33]

At this point, President Xi Jinping personally intervened to promote reforms but improvement was slow. The Chinese Communist Party announced 'a work plan for the removal of regional blockades' involving 12 ministry-level agencies. Scepticism remained high about its ability to achieve 'a unified market with free flow of capital, labor and goods'.[34] A more high-powered and specialised institution was necessary to carry out this task, it was argued by a leading development specialist. The proper solution was a national authority 'above provincial governments to coordinate efforts and take charge of regional integration'.[35] No such 'overlord' was created, and in 2015, a piecemeal solution was being put together with nine 'pilot cities' selected to demonstrate the benefits of market reforms.[36]

## A statement of intent

Hong Kong's rulers were extremely slow to grasp the reality that on the Mainland, almost all policy announcements were statements of intent rather than decrees for immediate implementation. After the initial launch of CEPA in 2003, Tung Chee Hwa's Trade Minister, Henry Tang Ying-yen, had boasted that 'zero tariff' treatment by the Mainland for imports of Hong Kong products would begin selectively the following year and would become universal within two years. The services sector would be given similarly generous and rapid access to Mainland markets, he said, including 'areas where Hong Kong possesses sharp competitive edges'. A full decade later, implementation of these CEPA commitments would still be incomplete.[37]

Reality started to dawn eventually, and Tung admitted that there would be a considerable time-lag and still more negotiations with Mainland officialdom before CEPA began to generate significant benefits. And even longer delays before all its pledges were implemented. Tung insisted, however, that Hong Kong's future lay in 'China's tremendous potential and . . . in talking and working together with the Central Government on a series of schemes which open up the Mainland market'.[38]

Donald Tsang Yam-kuen, his successor, followed much the same pattern as Tung in dealing with the Mainland. Tsang began by claiming that Hong Kong was ignorant of Mainland affairs. 'Before 1997, our potential was hampered by a lack of direct communication with the Mainland', claimed Donald Tsang in 2005. 'Broadening of contacts took several years', he added, until the adoption of 'such initiatives as CEPA, Pan-Pearl River Delta co-operation and much closer links with Guangdong Province'.[39] Tsang's claim about the lack of direct contacts with the Mainland authorities before 1997 was incorrect, as he should have known. He had been present when a senior civil service colleague had vigorously condemned this fallacy during a debate in the legislature in 1998:

> Many people may have the misconception that prior to the handover, Hong Kong and the Mainland were each doing things in their own way and there was a lack of communication between both places. However, in fact, communication channels between Hong Kong and the Mainland were already established for various fields and issues long before the handover, and there have always been close contacts between both places. Some of these time-tested channels were established back in 1982. The Guangdong-Hong Kong liaison system was put in place that year and this succeeded in enhancing the co-operation between Guangdong and Hong Kong over a number of pragmatic issues.[40]

An important factor in Tsang's obfuscation about the pre-1997 situation was the nervousness that Chief Executives felt about openly criticising Mainland officialdom, even at its lower levels. Blaming the past was a useful way of evading critical discussion of current problems in Mainland relations. And so, from year to year, new CEPA liberalisation measures were discussed, agreed and formally announced. If they had been implemented in full, Hong Kong would have enjoyed large-scale profit opportunities on the Mainland, while helping to drive China's modernisation forward.[41] On the Mainland, however, the delay between the announcement of a new national policy and its full implementation normally ran to at least a decade. For the average Hong Kong firm, that situation made no sense. Only the largest corporations could afford to take such a long-term view of Mainland markets.

A prime victim of serious delays was the services sector, including financial services.

- 2003: CEPA's beneficiaries would include banking, securities and insurance firms, the official media reported.[42]
- 2009: The promise of Mainland access to Hong Kong's banks through CEPA was repeated.[43]
- 2011: Vice Premier Li Keqiang revealed that 2015 was CEPA's deadline for 'a full liberalization of trade in services'.[44]
- 2012: Chief Executive Leung Chun-ying could promise no more than to lobby local governments for 'clearer procedures' and 'better co-operation' in implementing CEPA.[45]
- 2013: There were still only five Hong Kong banks allowed to open sub-branches in Guangdong.[46]
- 2014: Mainland officials admitted that there would continue to be 'bans and restrictions' on CEPA's implementation.[47]
- 2015: Vice Minister of Commerce Wang Shouwen signed a 'new agreement . . . under the framework of CEPA to basically achieve

liberalisation of trade in services between the Mainland and Hong Kong'.[48]

## Mainland frustrations

The reluctance of local governments on the Mainland to honour the terms of CEPA in dealing with Hong Kong firms was a fundamental and persistent problem. In 2014, a business representative in the Legislative Council summed up this decade-long frustration. There is this obstacle: 'the big door has opened but the small door remains shut', he said, 'That is to say, Hong Kong companies are allowed in name to go to the Mainland for job and business opportunities, but in reality, they have no way to carry out such activities.'[49]

The Special Administrative Region authorities tried at every turn to avoid revealing evidence of how unsatisfactory was the implementation of CEPA and how widespread was the obstructionism practised by Mainland officials. In 2009, however, discrimination against Hong Kong firms in Guangdong province was mounting to intolerable levels. Hong Kong's Commerce Minister was emboldened to complain publicly that CEPA's liberalisation measures were being sabotaged because of the obstructionist tactics deployed by Mainland officials, which she listed:

> [Mainland] delay in the promulgation of rules and regulations as well as implementation details; insufficient knowledge of the new measures among local officials on the Mainland; differences in the systems and regulatory regimes governing professional services between the two places; cumbersome and time-consuming application procedures etc.[50]

But on the whole, Hong Kong's frustrations were not for public discussion. For example, in 2011, the prestigious Commission on Strategic Development relegated the business community's catalogue of complaints about mistreatment to a footnote from which specific details of Mainland misconduct were omitted. The Commission tried to disguise how paltry were the benefits derived by Hong Kong businesses with generalisations and scanty data. This selective reporting was particularly conspicuous in the case of the professions, for which the Commission offered only the vaguest of details about the progress being made.

- '*Some* Hong Kong service providers or local doctors . . . have been allowed to set up medical institutions under CEPA'. (emphasis added)
- 'A *number* of Hong Kong law firms have formed associations with Mainland partners'. (emphasis added)

- 'Over 1,000 Hong Kong professionals in the construction and related engineering services sector have obtained Mainland professional qualifications'.[51] (Whether or not they had been allowed to practise on the Mainland was not disclosed.)

By this time, the national leadership itself was becoming impatient with the slow pace at which barriers to Hong Kong businesses operations on the Mainland were being removed. Li Keqiang, then still a deputy premier, had confirmed that 2015 would be the deadline for full 'liberalisation of trade in services'—the most complex sector—as promised by CEPA. Thus, it seemed safe enough for Leung Chun-ying, the third Chief Executive, to begin his term of office in 2012 with an open admission that CEPA had been a disappointment for Hong Kong. 'I hear loud and clear from our business community that the full benefits of CEPA are not being felt', he declared. He blamed Mainland bureaucracy and protectionism and promised serious endeavours to reform CEPA. 'We need clearer procedures. We need better co-operation at the regional level', he said.[52]

A year later, Leung was having no more success in getting a fair deal from Guangdong than his predecessors. He could claim credit for bringing the Central People's Government into the negotiations with the province through the creation of the 'Inter-Ministries Joint Conference'. In practice, however, this body seemed to offer little hope of strengthening his influence on the Mainland. The Conference's agenda was 'to better co-ordinate and resolve problems' in three Guangdong districts designated as special Hong Kong partners.[53] A Hong Kong government statement reported that 'through this new platform, [it was] hoped to convey the views of Hong Kong business sectors to the relevant Mainland authorities effectively'. But the Joint Conference's terms of reference were clear and narrow: deliberations were to deal exclusively with the three designated areas and not even the whole province.[54]

Leung remained trapped, as his predecessors had been, by the superior political status of the Mainland officials with whom he was dealing. As a result, Hong Kong remained, almost always, at the mercy of Guangdong officials even if the highest levels of the nation's economic agencies (including the National Development and Reform Commission, the planning overlord) took part in the negotiations with the province. Despite the 'high regard' and the personal courtesy with which Leung reported that he had been treated by ministers in Beijing when he first took office, Hong Kong's political leverage with Mainland officials at the working level remained limited.[55] The Mainland was not going to leave market forces free to drive business developments despite the market liberalisation which CEPA was supposed to bring.

Li Keqiang's 2015 deadline for full implementation of CEPA came and went, even after he had become Premier. That year, reports on CEPA by the official Mainland media disclosed that 'obstacles still remain' although formal barriers appeared to have been abolished.[56] In 2016, it seemed that the prospects of CEPA ever operating in a genuinely open, competitive and nationwide market had reached their limits. China's Commerce Minister, Gao Hucheng, promised the full implementation of CEPA but by what date was unclear. And now the Mainland's domestic market was no longer the primary target of the latest interpretation of CEPA, he revealed. The goal would be to encourage cooperation between Hong Kong and Mainland firms 'to explore overseas investment and the wider foreign market' and to join the Mainland's four Free Trade Zones in Tianjin, Shanghai, Fujian and Guangdong.[57] This announcement sounded very much like an admission that direct competition from Hong Kong firms remained unacceptable to local governments.

It was now plain that the politics of China's international trade would determine the pace of liberalisation of Hong Kong's access to the Mainland. A leading foreign trade specialist in Beijing warned that progress towards this goal would have 'to be coordinated with the investment negotiations with the United States and the European Union'. In parallel, a senior Ministry of Commerce official involved in managing this final stage of CEPA's implementation disclosed that 'bans and restrictions on [certain] types of foreign investment' would continue after 'full liberalization'. In addition, 'sensitive sectors relating to national security' would need solving.[58]

Carrie Lam began her term as Chief Executive on a very different note to Leung Chun-ying. Unlike him, she did not claim to have special relations with ministers in Beijing.[59] Instead, she recounted her patriotism which had started as a student with her frequent trips to outstanding Mainland universities.[60] Gone, too, were his complaints and criticisms about the Mainland. In their place, the new Chief Executive gave the principal credit for Hong Kong's prosperity to the Mainland authorities. Particularly striking was the gratitude she expressed for CEPA, ignoring the endless delays and difficulties endured by Hong Kong's businesses in seeking to take advantage of the open access to Mainland markets that CEPA was supposed to deliver. Carrie Lam disregarded these disappointments and declared that CEPA 'has been pivotal to Hong Kong's economic development', which was a considerable exaggeration.

She expressed her special thanks for the two latest CEPA agreements in 2017, covering investment and technical cooperation.[61] In the background, however, there were strong hints that implementation would be neither smooth nor swift, and the Mainland side had felt it necessary to provide Hong Kong investors with specific reassurances that efforts would be made to protect them from its usual bureaucratic inefficiency and regional protectionism.[62] The fourth Chief Executive seemed to believe that it would be more profitable to ignore how CEPA's history was studded with similar promises, which had been broken or long delayed, and to be generous instead with her praise for China's Ministry of Commerce. Tung Chee Hwa had taken a similar attitude towards CEPA initially, it was noted earlier, only to be forced to admit later that such optimism had not been justified by the results.[63]

Nevertheless, she could not avoid expressing some awareness of the widespread complaints about the Mainland business environment. But she tried to be as tactful as possible. She confined her criticism to a brief admission that, even in a major new Mainland innovation and technology hub, welcomes were limited and 'Hong Kong residents living and working [there] are still facing barriers' in some areas of life.[64]

## State planning

Experience of constant frustration at the local government level did not deter Donald Tsang, the second Chief Executive, from seeking to join China's five-year plans in order to promote integration with the Mainland economy. This development began in an unexpected way. In March 2006, the first ever proposal to the National People's Congress for Hong Kong to be included in the nation's five-year economic development plan was put forward by Tsang Tak-sing. This Congress deputy was employed by the Hong Kong government but not at the most senior level. However, he was a long-standing and highly respected member of the National People's Congress.

His initiative 'really lifted many a planner's eyebrow', the nation's second highest ranking planning official, Xu Lin, later recounted. The surprise was provoked, he said, 'because pursuant to the Basic Law and the principle of "One Country, Two Systems", Hong Kong's economic and social development plans should be devised by the Special Administrative Region government'. 'For this very reason', he went on, 'the development of Hong Kong had not been given a single chapter in the national plan'. But now it was to receive its first inclusion.[65] Donald Tsang saw this gesture as an invitation for him to lobby for Hong Kong to be more fully incorporated into the next five-year plan. He campaigned hard, apparently, and a special chapter was allocated to Hong Kong (and Macao) in the 12th Five-Year Plan that would begin in 2011.[66]

Once again, Premier Wen recognised the very different nature of Hong Kong's economy. Just as he had warned in 2003 that CEPA might prove less profitable to Hong Kong than was being represented, so he recommended caution about the Special Administrative Region's inclusion in the state's economic plans. This advice was based, he explained, on the Basic Law and the three principles of 'one country, two systems', 'Hong Kong people governing Hong Kong' and 'a high degree of autonomy'. Hong Kong was not supposed to be integrated into the Mainland economy. 'The 12th Five-Year Plan will not be imposed on Hong Kong', he declared, and will 'in no way replace Hong Kong's own development plan'.[67] The Premier's obvious coolness towards Donald Tsang's lobbying did not deter him from describing his victory over defenders of the Basic Law in Beijing as 'a significant breakthrough in Hong Kong's efforts in complementing the National Five-Year Plan'.[68]

What had inspired Hong Kong's second Chief Executive to demonstrate a great deal more enthusiasm than the nation's Premier about state plans as a prescription for Hong Kong's prosperity? An important factor was the difficulty that Hong Kong experienced in getting provinces and the lower levels of government to treat the Special Administrative Region with much respect. The separate Hong Kong chapter in the five-year plan should be viewed, he told a press conference, as 'showing the Central Authorities place great importance on Hong Kong'. Inclusion in the '[plan] document will offer a stable platform for Hong Kong–Mainland co-operation', Tsang forecast, 'and a legitimate foundation for Hong Kong and Mainland authorities to conduct negotiations on policies and measures'—a tactful reminder of how difficult discussions had been in the past.[69]

## State monopoly

There was a specific political problem which Donald Tsang expected to solve through Hong Kong's inclusion in the state plan although the issue was trivial in the extreme in the overall context of the Hong Kong economy and its well-being. The Mainland's food trade was one of a limited number of businesses where a state monopoly had survived from the central planning era before 1978 and the Deng Xiaoping reforms. This relic from the Maoist era was important for Hong Kong as a large proportion of its food supplies were imported from the Mainland. The price and quality of food had a direct impact on Hong Kong's cost of living, and there was no way to silence mounting public complaints provoked by the reluctance of the Mainland's Ministry of Commerce to end the controls it maintained over key food supplies to Hong Kong.

The meat monopoly, in particular, aroused considerable anger during this century. Public protests became too serious for Donald Tsang to ignore. Allegations of price manipulation multiplied, and traders launched a boycott of Mainland suppliers in 2007.[70] Tsang assured the Legislative Council in 2008 that he shared the community's anxieties about abuses which 'the lack of transparency in market operations' could cause. Discussions had been held with the Ministry of Commerce, he revealed, whose officials had failed to concede more than a guarantee of the minimum supply of pigs and a promise that Hong Kong officials would be informed in advance of each day's delivery. In response to these token concessions, Tsang felt obliged 'to express our gratitude to the Ministry of Commerce for their support to us', which was another reminder of the central planning era: the Ministry's policies—rather than market forces—were what counted.[71]

The Ministry's spokesman subsequently seemed to suggest that Hong Kong should be grateful for this state of affairs because the city would go hungry if Mainland grain and meat were not available. The Ministry was ignorant, apparently, of the limited relevance of 'self-sufficiency' to an open economy like Hong Kong. Furthermore, the Ministry asserted that its responsibilities were confined to ensuring physical supplies of key food items without regard to price or quality, an outlook that also belonged to the past era of strict food rationing when state planners were in total control. But the Ministry managed to offer one new concession. Some independent Mainland sources of supply would be approved for shipping meat to Hong Kong, but the long-term issues of price, quality and competitive markets were left unsolved.[72]

At first, public indignation seemed pacified by the attention paid to Hong Kong's complaints by officials both in Beijing and Hong Kong. Indeed, the claim was made that the Ministry's new arrangements would ensure that 'market operations will be more clear, thus making it easier to reduce any price-manipulation activities'.[73] But the conflict between the Mainland's state controls and the free market expectations of Hong Kong did not disappear, and public protests resumed. In 2011, Dr York Chow Yat-ngok, the Food Minister, tried to reassure legislators of the government's commitment to open and competitive food markets. But he was unable to disguise the fact that although 'Hong Kong is a free market, [and] our food comes from all parts of the world', the supply of meat remained firmly under the control of Mainland state agencies.[74]

Donald Tsang believed that Hong Kong's inclusion that year in the next five-year plan would induce the Ministry of Commerce to become more cooperative. In expressing his thanks to the Central People's Government for this 'promotion' for Hong Kong, he singled out the Ministry of Commerce. Its officials had agreed, he said, to 'ensure a stable food supply to Hong Kong to help the city tackle inflationary pressures'.[75] This promise of price stability was not met. According to the government's *Annual Digest of Statistics*, food prices increased at much the same rate for the next two years after 2011 as they had done in the two previous years. Monopoly practices continued as the Ministry of Commerce remained faithful to its state planning legacy. Hong Kong officials tried to conceal how their bargaining power and political standing in Beijing were as limited as ever. But in 2013, they were forced to admit publicly that they had failed yet again to persuade the Ministry of Commerce to relax the restrictions on the Mainland meat suppliers.[76]

Not until 2014 did a Legislative Council Panel induce the government to specify the obstacles it faced in negotiating with Mainland counterparts. Officials revealed that they had been informed that the Mainland faced an acute meat shortage as demand had risen in response to rising incomes and living standards. The Mainland's meat industry was expected to take several years to improve supplies sufficiently to meet total demand. The National Development and Reform Commission had drawn up a 'State Development Plan for Beef and Mutton Production' covering the period 2013 to 2020 whose goal was to 'encourage the development of beef and mutton production industries' through 'enhanced policy support and market regulation'—which meant further delays in allowing Hong Kong free access to Mainland suppliers. In the meantime, there was an acute meat shortage on the Mainland, which had to take priority when allocating available supplies. All that the Ministry of Commerce could do in response to Hong Kong complaints about market manipulation was to request state-owned agencies 'to ensure a stable supply' for Hong Kong and 'to maintain the quality'.[77]

The third Chief Executive, Leung Chun-ying, was no more successful than his predecessor in resolving this problem. When he first assumed office, he had taken special pride in his access to national leaders and decision-makers, boasting of his personal 'strong G2G [government-to-government] contacts' at all levels of both central and local administration.[78] Nevertheless, his ministerial team was forced to confess that it could do no more than 'continue to monitor the supply of live pigs and maintain dialogue with the trade and relevant Mainland authorities'.[79]

## Hong Kong's plans begin

Inclusion in the state plan meant that Hong Kong had to identify sectors and industries whose development would be open to government direction. This innovation proved a dismal failure. The totally different nature of the Hong Kong economy had been ignored.[80] The government had no power to direct entrepreneurs or investors to follow the state's business plan or to accept its priorities. Indeed, the Basic Law specifically laid down that capitalism and the free market should reign in Hong Kong, and not socialism. In theory, Hong Kong could provide financial incentives in the form of subsidies or tax concessions for industries which the national five-year plan had identified as priorities for Hong Kong to develop. In low-tax Hong Kong, however, the scope for such financial leverage was very limited. The Chief Executive and his ministers could try persuasion, pointing to the goodwill that cooperation with the national plan might bring when doing business on the

Mainland. On the other hand, the Hong Kong business community knew from decades of experience how little goodwill was likely to be extended to them by local governments.

Nevertheless, Donald Tsang began direct cooperation with China's planning system. In 2008, the National Development and Reform Commission published its blueprint for the development of Guangdong's Pearl River Delta for the next decade. This document included prospective growth sectors for Hong Kong. In 2009, Donald Tsang's administration responded by identifying six development industries: 'testing and certification; medical services; innovation and technology; cultural and creative industries; environmental industry; and educational services'. Surprisingly, these six were also described as potential replacements for Hong Kong's financial services as the source of future prosperity.[81] This lack of confidence in the long-term prospects of the financial sector was astonishing. Premier Wen earlier that same year had emphasised how Hong Kong was 'irreplaceable' as China's international financial centre.[82] Furthermore, Article 109 of the Basic Law specifically required 'the Government of the Hong Kong Special Administrative Region [to] provide an appropriate economic and legal environment for the maintenance of the status of Hong Kong as an international financial centre'.

From a business point of view, it was alarming that there had been no prior government research and there was no hard statistical or other evidence to justify the selection of these six as 'priority' industries and future drivers of high-speed growth.[83] According to the government's own calculations (not completed until two years later), the six were generating in total only 8 per cent of GDP and 11 per cent of employment.[84] These figures exaggerated their true potential as key 'growth' industries, however, and the commercial attractions of these sectors were doubtful. In the case of the medical, educational and related 'industries', the bulk of their services were not supplied 'commercially' but provided by the public sector. The government financed the Hospital Authority, many of the schools and universities and provided subsidised care for elderly people and non-profit-making kindergartens.

Public reaction was hostile. Hong Kong's 'planners' had ignored the existing pressure on social services which had been struggling since 2000 to maintain an adequate supply of good quality services in the face of government funding cuts. Almost at once, the 'plan' for medical services, which was supposed to be a key item in the high-growth sector, began to unravel. The aim had been to exploit medical tourism from the Mainland, which it did all too successfully. Fee-paying Mainland patients swamped local maternity wards at the expense of Hong Kong mothers. The government was forced to retreat and had to impose severe restrictions on the entry to Hong Kong of pregnant Mainlanders.[85]

Ambitions to create an international education hub faced a similar obstacle because Hong Kong's existing supply of education services fell short of local demand. Fees in the private sector were already alarmingly high, while universities had not been allowed to increase their annual intake of undergraduates since the previous century. There were also serious complaints about the quality of self-financed post-secondary education in Hong Kong. (These problems are discussed in Chapter 6.) An attempt to 'import' substantial numbers of students to Hong Kong could only succeed at the expense of the already limited facilities available for its own students, which was politically not acceptable.

The third Chief Executive, Leung Chun-ying, quickly retreated from his predecessor's controversial style of state planning.[86] But planning itself was not totally rejected, and the less unpopular segments of Tsang's programme were repackaged and relaunched.[87] Leung was careful to abandon all suggestion that Hong Kong could no longer depend on financial and other services which had generated prosperity over so many decades and on which the Mainland itself was dependent. He had no choice, of course. China's launch of the RMB as a global currency had been highly successful because Hong Kong had the regulatory and market institutions that globalisation required, and it also had the financial capacity. 'No other province or city in our country can play the role that we do, or draw on the breadth of experience that we have in dealing with the rest of the world', Leung stated early in his term of office, 'That's a unique attribute of Hong Kong and therefore our unique strength and advantage in the country'.[88]

Although Leung's views on the Mainland limitations were more realistic than those of his predecessors, he remained convinced that future prosperity depended on becoming part and parcel of the Mainland economy. He successfully lobbied the state planners handling Hong Kong to allow it to become 'more involved in implementing and formulating the . . . National Five-Year Plan'. He presented no forecast of the concrete benefits that the people of Hong Kong could expect as a result. Instead of an estimate of faster GDP growth, for example, he offered the vague promise that the larger planning role would 'help meet the aspirations of Hong Kong and make the most of our city's advantages in our country's development'.[89]

Leung argued that Hong Kong had been handicapped in the past because under colonialism, laisser-faire had reigned. It would have done better if there had been active government intervention in directing economic development, which was the formula that had made Singapore, among other Asian states, so successful, he argued. This was not a propitious choice of models. Singapore's experiences of government-led business relations with the Mainland had been very unhappy. In 1994, Singapore had pioneered a massive government-to-government deal, the China-Singapore Suzhou Industrial Park Development Group. The US$30 billion project proved a financial disaster with an annual loss of around US$25 million. But this poor performance had occurred not through Singapore's incompetence but because of deliberate Mainland decisions. Singapore Prime Minister, Lee Kuan Yew, later observed that 'when doing business in China, signing a contract marks not the end, but the start, of negotiations'. The solution to the Suzhou disaster? Agreement in 1999 that 'a Chinese consortium [would become] the largest share holder and play the major role in administration and management'. Efficiency and profitability improved dramatically thereafter but at the expense of the original Singapore investors.[90]

Nevertheless, Leung's ambition was for the laisser-faire and 'positive non-interventionism' so proudly adopted by Hong Kong in the past, to be modified by a 'new idea'. The government would be 'appropriately active in promoting Hong Kong's economy'. Integration now meant more than expanding business activities located on the Mainland. It would also include accepting an active role in the Chinese economy's ambitious overseas programmes.[91] Thus, Mainland policies and China's national development programmes were to dictate Hong Kong's economic future rather than the free market forces that had reigned supreme in the past.

Patriotic as this ambition sounded, the nation's leaders had long held a very different view of Hong Kong's role as a major contributor to the national economy. In the context of state planning, Premier Wen had declared in 2009 that 'the status of an international financial centre [like Hong Kong] is established not by a government decision but through market competition'. He listed the criteria which had enabled Hong Kong to flourish: 'a long history of financial management, extensive channels of financial operation, a full-fledged legal system and a rich pool of financial expertise'.[92] He made no mention of state planning. As China struggled to build a modern financial sector, Wen's successor, Premier Li, had drawn attention to specific examples of Hong Kong's new contributions to building links with world financial markets. 'The roll-out of the Shenzhen-HK Stock Connect after the one between Shanghai and Hong Kong marks another concrete step for China's capital market in becoming more law-based, market-oriented and global', he stated.[93] In both cases, the role of the state was being reduced, and Mainland dependence on Hong Kong was becoming clearer.

For President Xi Jinping, Hong Kong's role remained unique. In 2017, he referred to it as 'the legendary city' which would surely enjoy 'a new chapter of development and prosperity'. In an extraordinary testimonial, he summed up the astonishing range of its involvement in the nation's pursuit of modernisation.

> Hong Kong is an important international financial, shipping and trade center, a major conduit connecting the mainland and international markets and a two-way service platform for China both to attract foreign investment and enter the international market. Hong Kong is by far the mainland's biggest source of external direct investment and non-local financing platform and it has grown into the mainland's largest non-local investment destination and the biggest offshore RMB business center in the world.[94]

He saw no Mainland rivals apparently. His only concern, it seemed, was the danger of complacency, and he reminded Hong Kong about the 'enormous challenges posed by profound changes in the global economic environment'.[95]

## The rise and fall of the Hong Kong model

Hong Kong entrepreneurs and investors needed no coaching from Chief Executives about the Mainland, either in terms of business opportunities or serving the nation. Deng Xiaoping's endorsement of plans for Guangdong province to achieve a faster rate of modernisation than the rest of the nation had been based on its proximity to Hong Kong. 'The resources [of Chinese living in Hong Kong] are relatively abundant', the Chinese Communist Party's provincial chief had explained in 1979, 'They possess many favourable conditions for accelerating economic development'.[96] Similarly, a senior Beijing official during a visit in 1979 to promote investment opportunities on the Mainland made a point of citing Hong Kong as a model, thanks to its 'rapid progress in industry and commerce in the last 20 years'.[97]

Shortly afterwards, Guangdong officials began an energetic drive to woo investors, soliciting frank and open comment from Hong Kong businessmen on how to overcome obstacles to speeding up expansion of cross-border business. From 1979, the province was allowed considerable freedom to manage its own finances and other resources. Lower levels of the administration were no longer forced to comply with the normal planning and other restrictions still in force at that time. Instead, they were given ample scope to act as entrepreneurs. The province also had two Special Economic Zones, Shenzhen and Zhuhai, which enjoyed even greater freedom from state controls and could connect up with Hong Kong.

Guangdong's early retreat from a command economy allowed the 'Hong Kong model' to flourish. It generated half the province's export growth in the 1980s and made it possible for Guangdong to overtake Shanghai as the Mainland's biggest exporter. Quite simply, Shanghai enterprises relied very heavily on the domestic market. They were subject to much tighter state control and were less able to respond to changing demand on global markets. As a result, they had not enjoyed the same opportunities to develop a high-growth, competitive culture as Guangdong.[98]

The province's strategy of partnership with Hong Kong made good sense. Hong Kong could supply the province instantaneously with every kind of service from financial, technical and professional to spare parts and maintenance. As a result, by the 1990s, the province had developed an industrial sector 'that mirrored Hong Kong in the 1970s'.[99] Nevertheless, relocation to the Mainland was not simply a change of address for Hong Kong firms. Its manufacturers faced a completely new business environment which, unlike Hong Kong, was still overseen by the government and where political connections were essential for success despite the high degree of economic liberalisation enjoyed by Guangdong.[100] Furthermore, many of the business operations of Hong Kong firms were technically unlawful at that time because capitalist activities, including rights to obtain factory sites, import equipment and raw materials and to export the products, had not been legally clarified.

But it was worth the political and legal risks. In 1985, it was estimated that, on average, Guangdong workers were paid only 7 per cent of their Hong Kong counterparts' earnings.[101] This difference in the costs of production made it possible to provide the incentives to convince Mainland officials of the developmental and personal dividends to be reaped from the 'open door' policies. Hong Kong businessmen pioneered arrangements, often informal or downright unlawful, to overcome both the infrastructural obstacles and the bureaucratic barriers which hindered Hong Kong and overseas capitalists from manufacturing and marketing profitably from a Guangdong base. Hong Kong became 'a catalyst in China's economic reforms and trade liberalization'.[102]

The province did not remain easy money. According to a Federation of Hong Kong Industries report in 1993, only 11 per cent of firms surveyed described their Mainland plants as 'very profitable', while 33 per cent reported them to be only 'potentially profitable' or downright 'not profitable'.[103] Nevertheless, Hong Kong funds and factories continued to flood into Guangdong. In 1998, a government report estimated that there were more than five million workers employed by 'Hong Kong-based manufacturing firms' in Guangdong.[104] By 2007, this labour force was over 10 million. Hong Kong industrialists' investments there now totalled US$200 billion. This partnership with the province had enabled Guangdong's GDP to grow at an annual rate 3.5 percentage points higher than the national average. Its total GDP overtook Singapore in 1998 and Taiwan in 2007. By then, Guangdong had the largest economy of any province and was generating well over 10 per cent of the national GDP.[105]

The Hong Kong model had been highly successful in mobilising the funds needed for Guangdong's modernisation. But, the model came under increasing attack for manufacturing goods 'at the very end of the relevant product cycle'. Despite the fact that they were manufactured to the appropriate technological standards and marketed under famous brand names, they were attacked as 'sunset industries'.[106] The business reality was that Hong Kong entrepreneurs had never had anything to gain from investing in high-tech industries and original designs, and they preferred their businesses to be driven by their export opportunities and their industrial expertise.[107]

Guangdong's leaders took a different view of the province's needs. Hong Kong-style capitalist success was not enough. By the end of the last century, they had decided that the manufacturing complex created by Hong Kong would not be needed to achieve the province's next economic targets. Evidence started to accumulate that long-term prospects for Hong Kong firms manufacturing on the Mainland were deteriorating sharply. A Chinese Manufacturers Association's survey in 2000 reported that 'at least 80 per cent' of those surveyed had serious complaints. They were dismayed by 'the unsound legal system' and unhappy about the 'onerous' additional financial charges imposed on them. But what worried them most were 'the new initiatives by the Mainland Government to tighten up its supervision over foreign-funded enterprises' (including Hong Kong firms). The business community realised that Mainland officials no longer regarded Hong Kong investors and entrepreneurs as essential for maintaining high-speed growth. On the contrary, Hong Kong was being criticised as technologically backward and a hindrance to the nation's efforts to join the ranks of the world's advanced economies.[108]

By 2002, the provincial authorities had made it clear to the Hong Kong business community that Guangdong's welcome to offshore manufacturing subsidiaries was gone for good and that there was no future for 'low-wage, low-tech industry'.[109] In place of the free-wheeling, profit-driven factories of the previous century, Hong Kong's investors and entrepreneurs would soon be subject to increasing restrictions, including new laws on minimum wages and environmental protection. Guangdong felt very confident in adopting this stand reportedly because that year saw its GDP overtake that of Hong Kong. This city could now be relegated to a subordinate category.

At first, Hong Kong's industrialists had been experienced enough to be able to adjust to this painful change in policy, and they managed to maintain their growth momentum. But from 2006–2007, national policy reinforced the drive against labour-intensive, low-cost manufacturing for export markets—the so-called 'processing trade' in which Hong Kong specialised. This had allowed Hong Kong and foreign firms to import raw materials and other inputs and to re-export the finished products as if operating offshore. These concessions ended. Tax rebates were abolished, and import and export bans were imposed on a range of commodities in order to limit the scope of processing trade manufacturing.[110] In theory, there had been an escape route from the discrimination against the processing trade. A Hong Kong firm could convert its status to 'foreign-invested enterprise'. In practice, Mainland bureaucratic inefficiency prevented most of them from making this change. As a government advisory body in Hong Kong reported in 2007, most companies were willing to comply with the new policy for the processing trade. However, it lamented, 'at present, the Mainland does not have a set of clear and standard approval procedures and protocol of transformation' enabling these firms to change their status.[111]

A severe downturn for Hong Kong firms in Guangdong was under way. As the squeeze on Hong Kong's Guangdong factories intensified, Donald Tsang found himself powerless to intervene. It did not help that the province had a new First Party Secretary, Wang Yang, who far outranked a Hong Kong Chief Executive. To make matters worse for Tsang, Beijing had delegated to the province much of the responsibility for negotiating new CEPA deals,[112] and Wang himself had been given a more direct role in state planning for the future economic development of Hong Kong.[113]

At first, Tsang tried to be diplomatic. But it was no longer possible for him to pretend that the provincial authorities had no part in the disaster that had overtaken Hong Kong investors and entrepreneurs in Guangdong. The situation had become so serious that in the middle of the 2007–2009 global financial crisis, he felt compelled to state: 'Most of [Hong Kong's] problems are not here, they're right there in Guangdong Pearl River Delta'.[114] A month later, he was openly begging provincial leaders to allow smaller Hong Kong firms to survive by upgrading or relocating elsewhere. He also pleaded for concessions for them over taxes and a new labour law.[115] Without success.

The impact of the Mainland restrictions was severe, a 2008 Hong Kong Trade Development Council research report stated. Guangdong profits had been badly hit, with 'one-third' of Hong Kong firms preparing to close down or reduce production.[116] A 2013 government report estimated that the average profit margin for the processing trade had almost halved, falling from 18 per cent five years earlier to 10 per cent.[117] By 2015, the labour force employed in Hong Kong enterprises had fallen to 'about 4.5 million to 5 million workers', half the 2007 figure.[118] Firms and factories were going out of business not because of market failure or defective management but because of the changing development strategy of the central and provincial governments.[119]

There is a general tendency to claim that Hong Kong businesses have only themselves to blame for the tougher line taken by the Mainland authorities towards the Hong Kong manufacturing model based on labour-intensive, low technology, low-value products for export. Quite rightly, the nation's leaders in this century would no longer tolerate sweated labour or factories which grossly polluted the environment. Hong Kong manufacturers had made themselves vulnerable because, for years, they had been convinced that they could disregard laws to protect the welfare of their employees and, later on, to prevent pollution, just as many Mainland firms continued to do. By 2007, few Hong Kong firms possessed the level of political connections to obtain immunity once these laws became well-publicised national priorities.

The downgrading of the Hong Kong model has also been attributed to the global financial crisis and China's emergency measures to avoid recession from 2008. These events have been highlighted as triggering the reassessment of the role of international trade as a driving force for the nation's modernisation. However, a careful academic study discovered no market factors—loss of competitiveness, for example, or decline in market demand—which would have justified the closure of Hong Kong firms.[120] Nor was there any evidence to demonstrate that positive economic gains were obtained from closing an entire segment of the provincial economy by state decree regardless of firms' performance when judged by such market criteria as profits, productivity or export earnings. Quite simply, the state had made a long-term decision to introduce 'more policies . . . designed to facilitate the development of domestic enterprises rather than to attract foreign investors as before'.[121]

## End-of-term report

Despite all the setbacks and disappointments that Chief Executives and their ministers encountered on the Mainland, they remained reluctant to admit how little had been achieved. How could they do otherwise when official Mainland descriptions of Hong Kong's advantages there promised unlimited opportunities? 'With an enormous market, abundant opportunities and strong growth driven by economic restructuring and upgrades, the motherland welcomes Hong Kong aboard the high-speed train of development and will continue to offer solid backing for its prosperity', the Chinese Communist Party's daily paper declared in 2017.[122]

However, the openness which remains a major feature of governance in Hong Kong meant that the disappointing realities of the relationship could not be concealed. Thus, as Leung Chun-ying was preparing to leave office in 2017, an official report was published entitled 'Progress Made by the Current-Term Government on Mainland Co-operation

2012–2017'. Its tactful wording did not disguise how little tangible profit for Hong Kong was generated by the achievements claimed for his term of office in this document.

In the leading section, 'Open up new development opportunities', Hong Kong's gains from incorporation into the national five-year plans were described in glowing generalisations, but there was a marked absence of concrete targets and the benefits to be expected. Next came a description of the network of Hong Kong government offices set up on the Mainland. Business promotion came at the very end of the list of their duties, with a vague generalisation about their role: 'to enhance support for career and business development of Hong Kong people and enterprises on the Mainland'. No details were provided of the actual business they generated. There then followed some optimistic reporting on CEPA, which was presented as if this Agreement had first come into force in 2014 and was to be fully implemented nationwide from 2016. There was an absence of statistical information about CEPA's value to Hong Kong.

The next section of this official report was labelled: 'Facilitate mutual access in financial markets'. It provided a statistic on the volume of trading conducted by funds authorised for sale to retail investors in Mainland centres as well as in Hong Kong. Otherwise, there were only generalisations, and there were no data in the reporting on other measures to liberalise the Mainland financial and currency environment. There also seemed a desperation to find newsworthy developments to pad out this section. So, the next item in the list of measures to improve access to financial markets was the 'Scheme for Cross-Border Study Tour for Post-Secondary Financial Talents', from which 'over 260 students' had benefitted between 2012 and 2017. This was hardly an impressive result. How and when these study courses would contribute to business development was left to the reader's imagination.

When it came to recording Mainland enthusiasm for establishing business operations in Hong Kong, there were some impressive data. Nevertheless, this section left the impression that the government's role in attracting Mainland firms was limited. Hardly surprising, perhaps, because Hong Kong's attractions as an advanced and open economy and a major player on global markets needed no advertising on the Mainland. There had never been a shortage of large Mainland corporations anxious to establish a presence in Hong Kong.

Overall, this official report on progress between 2012 and 2017 left the impression that Mainland business still fell embarrassingly short of what Chief Executives had been promising since 1997.[123]

## Conclusion

In managing Hong Kong's business relationship with the Mainland, there was an obvious comparison to be made with foreign trade negotiations. In lauding a pioneering model for inter-provincial economic integration in 2005, the official Mainland media had described this proposal as 'like an international free trade pact' designed to 'limit protectionism and bring down artificial barriers for commercial transactions and labour mobility' within the Mainland.[124] (No such happy result was achieved.) Wrongly, Tung Chee Hwa had believed that Hong Kong could reach such a goal through 'talking and working' with the Central Government on schemes to open up the Mainland.[125] The trouble was that most of the negotiations had to be with local governments that had too much to lose—in the short run at least—from opening up to Hong Kong.

The efforts made to find ways of incorporating Hong Kong into the five-year plans were also doomed to failure as long as Hong Kong remained a capitalist economy. It was bizarre that Premier Wen should make this point and be ignored. It was equally strange that his observation that the Basic Law did not envisage Hong Kong's participation in state planning was not taken seriously. Attempts to use the five-year plans to integrate Hong Kong into the Mainland economy were ineffectual and distracted attention from Hong Kong's most important function: to provide China with a centre of excellence for the provision of services—financial services especially—to meet the needs of the nation's economic modernisation.

Perhaps the most significant finding of this chapter is how serious have been the economic costs of China's uncompleted reforms. Until the Mainland achieves the goal set by President Jiang Zemin in 1992 and establishes a truly open and competitive market embracing the entire nation, Hong Kong's ability to achieve the sort of integration urged by its Chief Executives will remain restricted. And until the long delays in the implementation of national policies are reduced, the Mainland opportunities for Hong Kong entrepreneurs and investors will remain limited. Finally, until the Mainland overcomes the sources of its business backwardness so roundly denounced by Premier Li in 2015, the nation's modernisation will continue to be seriously hampered, and only a very limited partnership with Hong Kong will be possible.

## Notes

1. 'Central Government to Fully Back HK's Development: Premier Zhu', *Renmin Ribao* (*RR* hereafter), 19 November 2002; 'Hong Kong's Traditional Advantages as Int'l Financial Center Unchanged: Premier Wen', *New China*

*News Agency* (*NCNA* hereafter), 14 March 2011; 'Chinese Vice Premier Li Delivers Keynote Speech at Forum in Hong Kong', *NCNA*, 17 August 2011. Li Keqiang was appointed Premier in 2013.

2.  'Full Text of Speech by President Xi Jinping at Welcome Dinner in HK', *NCNA*, 1 July 2017.

3.  Carrie Lam Cheng Yuet-ngor, Chief Executive, *Government Information Services* (*GIS* hereafter), 11 July 2017.

4.  Premier Li Keqiang, 'Premier Li Grants Appointment Certificate to Incoming HKSAR Chief Executive', *NCNA*, 11 April 2017.

5.  These factories were located in the Pearl River Delta. Frederick Ma Si-hang, Secretary for Commerce and Economic Development, *Hong Kong Hansard* (*HH* hereafter), 28 November 2007, 2219.

6.  'Full Text of Chinese Premier's Teleconference Address on Streamlining Administration Procedures, Cutting Red Tape', *NCNA*, 22 May 2015.

7.  'Premier Li Urges More Efforts to Integrate Business Licenses', *NCNA*, 29 May 2017.

8.  Zhang Xiaoqiang, National Development and Reform Commission Deputy Director, reported in 'China Unveils Policies for Pilot Zone to Cement Mainland-HK Ties', *NCNA*, 29 June 2012.

9.  'Focus: Offshore Yuan Loans in Qianhai to Grow Tenfold by 2015', *NCNA*, 18 December 2013.

10. Carrie Lam, Chief Secretary, *GIS*, 21 February 2013.

11. Constitutional and Mainland Affairs Bureau, 'Legislative Council Panel on Commerce and Industry Hong Kong/Shenzhen Co-operation Meeting' (CB(1)750/15-16(01), April 2016), 4–6.

12. Tung Chee Hwa, Chief Executive, *GIS*, 31 July 1997.

13. Tung, Chief Executive, *GIS*, 10 May 2001.

14. Tung, Chief Executive, *GIS*, 12 November 2003.

15. Tung, Chief Executive, *GIS*, 9 January 2003.

16. Bowen Leung Po-Wing, Secretary for Planning, Environment and Lands, *HH* (Provisional), 8 April 1998, 384, 395–96.

17. 'Wu Yi Calls for Strengthened Trade with HK, Macao, Taiwan', *RR*, 23 December 1999; 'China Considering to Set Up Special Trade Area: Long Yongtu', *RR*, 29 October 2001.

18. It was now misleadingly presented as part of the Mainland's programme to rescue Hong Kong from the economic fallout after an epidemic of atypical pneumonia (SARS) that year.

19. 'Wen: CEPA is Special Arrangement under "One Country, Two Systems" Principle', *RR*, 30 June 2003.

20. 'Economic Integration Advances through Pact: Analysis', *RR*, 30 June 2003.

21. International Monetary Fund, 'People's Republic of China—Hong Kong Special Administrative Region: Selected Issues', *IMF Country Report* No. 05/62 (February 2005), 6–7.

22. Press release, *GIS*, 30 June 2003.

23. For an overview of this phenomenon, see Leo F. Goodstadt, 'The Local Government Crisis 2007–2014: When China's Financial Management Faltered', *HKIMR Working Paper* No. 27/2014, October 2014.

24. In 1992, Jiang Zemin was General Secretary of the Chinese Communist Party. He was appointed President in addition in March the following year.

25. 'Breaking Barriers: China's "Nationalization" Drive', *RR*, 1 July 2000.

26. President Jiang Zemin, 'Accelerating the Reform, the Opening to the Outside World and the Drive for Modernization, so as to Achieve Greater Successes in Building "Socialism With Chinese Characteristics"', Report at the 14th National Congress of the Party (12 October 1992); 'Hold High the Great Banner of Deng Xiaoping Theory for an All-Round Advancement of the Cause of Building "Socialism With Chinese Characteristics Into the 21st Century"', Report Delivered at the 15th National Congress of the Communist Party of China (12 September 1997); 'Build a Well-Off Society in an All-Round Way and Create a New Situation in Building Socialism with Chinese Characteristics', Report at 16th National Congress of the Chinese Communist Party (8 November 2002).

27. Premier Zhu Rongji, 'Report on the Outline of the Tenth Five-Year Plan for National Economic and Social Development (2001–2005)', *NCNA*, 5 March 2001.

28. 'Breaking Barriers: China's "Nationalization" Drive', *RR*, 1 July 2000.

29. Zhou Tianyon, Chinese Communist Party Central Party School Research Office, 'Build up Credible Government', *China Daily* (*CD* hereafter), 21 November 2002.

30. 'Unifying the Market', *CD*, 1 July 2004.

31. 'Readjust Tax System', *CD*, 9 June 2006.

32. Feng Fei, State Council Development Research Centre Industrial Economic Research Head, quoted in *NCNA*, 14 April 2013.

33. 'Xinhua Insight: Further Reforms Needed to Build Unified Market, Improve Efficiency', *NCNA*, 27 October 2013.

34. 'China Moves to Clear Blockades for Unified Market', *NCNA*, 10 December 2013.

35. Wen Kui, Capital University of Economics and Business, described as 'the leading researcher and consultant on integrated development in Beijing' quoted in Li Yang, 'Provinces vie for Beijing's Industrial Castoffs', *CD*, 8 April 2014.

36. 'China to Improve Domestic Trade Circulation', *NCNA*, 26 August 2015.

37. Henry Tang Ying-yen, Secretary for Commerce, Industry and Technology, *GIS*, 3 July 2003.

38. Tung, Chief Executive, *GIS*, 4 December 2004.

39. Donald Tsang Yam-kuen, Chief Executive, *GIS*, 24 August 2005.

40. Bowen Leung Po-wing, Secretary for Planning, Environment and Lands, *HH* (Provisional), 8 April 1998, 383.

41. A good example of the impressive but difficult to implement agreements promising Hong Kong wide-ranging additional access to Mainland markets was 'New Agreement Signed under Framework of CEPA to Basically Achieve Liberalisation of Trade in Services between the Mainland and Hong Kong', *GIS*, 27 November 2015.

42. 'Economic Integration Advances through Pact: Analysis', *RR*, 30 June 2003.

43. Hong Kong Monetary Authority, *GIS*, 9 October 2009.

44. Vice Premier Li Keqiang reported in 'Li Announces Measures to Boost HK's Growth', *CD*, 17 August 2011.
45. Leung Chun-ying, Chief Executive, *GIS*, 29 November 2012.
46. Leung, Chief Executive, *GIS*, 17 July 2013.
47. Zhuang Rui, Beijing University of International Business and Economics Deputy Dean and Sun Tong, Ministry of Commerce Deputy Director-General, reported in Li Jiabao, 'Agreement with HK Likely to Try Out "Negative List"', *CD*, 24 January 2014.
48. Press release, *GIS*, 27 November 2015.
49. Christopher Cheung Wah-fung, *HH*, 12 February 2014, 6331.
50. Rita Lau Ng Wai-lan, Secretary for Commerce and Economic Development, *HH*, 18 November 2009, 1869.
51. Commission on Strategic Development, 'Hong Kong SAR's Work Direction in Complementing the National Twelfth Five-Year Plan' (CSD/2/2011, May 2011), 18.
52. Leung, Chief Executive, *GIS*, 29 November 2012.
53. The three were Qianhai, Nansha, and Hengqin. Commission on Strategic Development, 'Hong Kong SAR's Work Direction in Complementing the National Twelfth Five-Year Plan', 20, note 6.
54. Constitutional and Mainland Affairs Bureau, 'Legislative Council Panel on Commerce and Industry Co-operation between Hong Kong and the Mainland—Hong Kong/Guangdong Co-operation and National 13th Five-Year Plans' (CB(1)1258/13-14(01), April 2014), 4.
55. Leung, Chief Executive, *GIS*, 22 March 2013.
56. Zhou Mo, 'Tagging the Hong Kong Brand across the Border', *CD*, 20 May 2015.
57. 'Chinese Commerce Ministry Supports HK Economic Development', *NCNA*, 24 February 2016.
58. Sun Tong, Commerce Ministry Deputy Director-General and Zhuang Rui, University of International Business and Economics Deputy Dean, 'Agreement with HK Likely to Try Out "Negative List"', *CD*, 24 January 2014.
59. Leung, Chief Executive, *GIS*, 22 March 2013.
60. Carrie Lam, Chief Executive, *GIS*, 1 October 2017.
61. Carrie Lam, Chief Executive, *GIS*, 8 August 2017.
62. The continuing causes for investor anxiety were illustrated by the need for the Mainland to provide specific promises of the most basic standards of fair and proper treatment: 'The Mainland will endeavour to establish uniform standards and procedures in examining and approving investment applications, stipulate a reasonable timeframe for examining investment applications and making decisions, keep the costs of the investors in the application process to the lowest on a best endeavour basis, etc.' Trade and Industry Department, 'The Mainland and Hong Kong Closer Economic Partnership Arrangement: Investment Agreement and Agreement on Economic and Technical Cooperation' (28 June 2017), 4.
63. See note 37.
64. Carrie Lam, Chief Executive, *GIS*, 9 October 2017.

65. Xu Lin, National Development and Reform Commission's Development Planning Department Deputy Director-General, reported in Joseph Li, 'HK to "Gain from Mainland Development"', *CD*, 29 March 2006.

66. For background, see Leo F. Goodstadt, 'Hong Kong: Market or "Command" Economy?', *Hong Kong Economic Journal Monthly*, No. 414 (September 2011).

67. '12th Five-Year Plan Not to Replace HK's Own Development Plan', *NCNA*, 14 March 2011.

68. Donald Tsang, Chief Executive, *GIS*, 16 March 2011.

69. Donald Tsang, Chief Executive, *GIS*, 7 March 2011.

70. On the beef and pork boycotts in 2007, note the editorial comment in *Hong Kong Economic Journal*, 8 August 2007. Hong Kong's resentment was well reported in China's official media, e.g., *CD*: Teddy Ng and Peggy Chan, 'Hong Kong Traders Call Off Bidding Boycott', 6 December 2007; Peggy Chan, 'Fewer Pigs Mean Higher HK Pork Prices', 9 January 2008.

71. Donald Tsang, Chief Executive, *HH*, 17 January 2008, 3930–31.

72. Wang Xinpei, Ministry of Commerce spokesperson, 'Mainland Assures HK, Macao of Grain Supplies', *NCNA*, 25 January 2008. The minimal expansion in supply sources was noted in Legislative Council Secretariat, 'Background Brief Supply of Live Cattle in Hong Kong', Panel on Food Safety and Environmental Hygiene (CB (2)1676/13-14, 4 June 2014), p. 1, footnote.

73. It was Chief Executive, Donald Tsang, who made this favourable interpretation possible. Joseph Li, 'Mainland to Send 4K Pigs Daily', *CD*, 18 January 2008.

74. Dr York Chow Yat-ngok, Secretary for Food and Health, *HH*, 16 February 2011, 5627–37.

75. Donald Tsang, Chief Executive, 'National Plan Highlights HK's Role: CE', *GIS*, 7 March 2011 and 'National Plan Elaborates HK Position', *GIS*, 16 March 2011.

76. Legislative Council Secretariat, 'Background Brief Supply of Live Cattle in Hong Kong', Panel on Food Safety and Environmental Hygiene (CB(2)1511/12), 4 July 2013), 3.

77. Food and Health Bureau, 'Supply of Live Cattle in Hong Kong Legislative Council Panel on Food Safety and Environmental Hygiene' (CB(2)1676/13-14(03), June 2014), 4–5.

78. See, for example, Leung, Chief Executive, *GIS*, 22 March 2013.

79. Food and Health Bureau spokesperson, GIS, 4 January 2013.

80. For a summary of the complications confronting the Hong Kong authorities in seeking to join the Mainland's state planning, see, Goodstadt, *Hong Kong Economic Journal Monthly*.

81. Donald Tsang, Chief Executive, *GIS*, 2 November 2009; Henry Tang Ying-yen, Chief Secretary, *GIS*, 4 November 2009.

82. 'Wen: Economy Shows Positive Changes', *NCNA*, 11 April 2009.

83. Donald Tsang, Chief Executive, *GIS*, 3 April 2009 and John Tsang Chun-wah, Financial Secretary, *HH*, 22 April 2009, 6377–78; 10 June 2009, 8797; and 29 October 2009, 727.

84. Census and Statistics Department, *Hong Kong Monthly Digest of Statistics March 2012*, 'The Situation of the Six Industries in Hong Kong in 2010', FB8–9.

85. 'Medical Services Dumped as Pillar Industry, Says Minister Ko Wing-man', *South China Morning Post*, 5 September 2012.

86. This was made plain by Julia Leung Fung-yee, Secretary for Financial Services and the Treasury, *HH*, 31 October 2012, 1067–69.

87. Leung, Chief Executive, *HH*, 17 January 2013, 4983; John Tsang, Financial Secretary, *GIS*, 18 March 2013; Gregory So Kam-leung, Secretary for Commerce and Economic Development, *HH*, 18 December 2013, 4739–40.

88. Leung, Chief Executive, *GIS*, 6 December 2012.

89. Leung, Chief Executive, *GIS*, 12 June 2013.

90. 'Board Meeting of Suzhou Industrial Park', *RR*, 15 September 1999; Lee Su Shyan, 'Profit Tide Turns for S'pore Companies in China', *Straits Times*, 21 November 2003; 'Lessons Learnt in the Suzhou School', *Straits Times*, 29 May 2004.

91. Yan Hao, 'Interview: HK to Play Super-Connector for China's "Belt and Road": Chief Executive', *NCNA*, 9 August 2015; Kahon Chan, 'Leung Affirms Need for Proper Intervention', *CD*, 25 August 2015. For a good summary of the underlying Mainland concerns, see Leung, Chief Executive, *GIS*, 23 June 2014 and 8 June 2015.

92. Premier Wen Jiabao, quoted in 'Premier: Chinese Economy Shows Signs of Positive Changes', *NCNA*, 12 April 2009.

93. Premier Li Keqiang reported in 'Shenzhen, HK Prepare for Stock Connect Program', *NCNA*, 16 August 2016.

94. 'Full Text of Speech by President Xi Jinping at Welcome Dinner in HK', *NCNA*, 1 July 2017.

95. It was significant that, in a speech the following day, President Xi also listed Hong Kong's considerable economic achievements. 'Full Text: Xi's Speech at Meeting Marking HK's 20th Return Anniversary, Inaugural Ceremony of 5th-Term HKSAR Gov't', *NCNA*, 1 July 2017.

96. Xi Zhingxun, Provincial First Party Secretary, 'Address to the Guangdong Conference on Increasing Production and Practicing Economy in Industrial and Communications Work', *Nanfang Ribao*, 12 August 1979.

97. Liu Nianzhi, All-China Federation of Industry and Commerce Vice Chairman, *NCNA*, 30 November 1979.

98. Nicholas R. Lardy, 'Chinese Foreign Trade', in *The Chinese Economy under Deng Xiaoping*, ed. Robert F. Ash and Y. Y. Kueh (Oxford: Clarendon Press, 1996), 238.

99. These comments reflect the findings of a study of Shenzhen which are, in fact, applicable to the Pearl River Delta as a whole. Weiping Wu, 'Proximity and Complementarity in Hong Kong–Shenzhen Industrialization', *Asian Survey* 37, no. 8 (August 1997): 776, 777, 781.

100. A detailed case study of the importance of these political skills to the business of a Hong Kong firm in Guangdong Province can be found in Leslie Yip Sai-Ching and G. P. Walters, 'Wah Hoi Industrial Company', *Entrepreneurship: Theory and Practice* 22, no. 3 (1998): 87–99.

101. Victor F. S. Sit, 'Hong Kong's '"Transferred" Industrialization and Industrial Geography', *Asian Survey* 38, no. 9 (September 1998): 896.

102. Yun-wing Sung, *Explaining China's Export Drive: The Only Success Among Command Economies* (Hong Kong: Hong Kong Institute of Asia-Pacific Studies, Chinese University of Hong Kong, 1991), 16–22, 26.
103. Federation of Hong Kong Industries, *Investment in China: 1993 Survey of Members of the Federation of Hong Kong Industries* (Hong Kong: Federation of Hong Kong Industries, 1993), 26–27.
104. Chief Executive's Commission on Innovation and Technology, *First Report* (September 1998), para 2.8.
105. 'South China Boom Province Pays Tribute to Opening-Up Policy', *NCNA*, 15 December 2008; 'PRD Region Blueprint Unveiled' and 'Economic Hubs Face Tough Times amid Crisis', *CD*, 9 January 2009.
106. Y. Y. Kueh, 'Foreign Investment and Economic Change in China', in *The Chinese Economy under Deng Xiaoping*, ed. Robert F. Ash and Y. Y. Kueh (Oxford: Clarendon Press, 1996), 181, 189.
107. This business model is impressively described in the context of the electronics industry in Tony Fu-lai Yu, 'Hong Kong's Entrepreneurship: Behaviours and Determinants', *Entrepreneurship & Regional Development* 12, no. 3 (2000): 182, 184–85.
108. HKTDC Research, 'Economists' Pick', '2000 Survey on CMA Members' Investment in Mainland China' (1 December 2000).
109. 'Vision for Hong Kong' Study Group, *To Be the Services Metropolis of the Pearl River Delta: A Blueprint for Hong Kong* (Hong Kong: Hong Kong General Chamber of Commerce and Hong Kong Coalition of Service Industries, 2002), 18, 23.
110. HKTDC Research Department, *Implications of Mainland Processing Trade Policy on Hong Kong: Research Report (June 2007)* (Hong Kong: Greater Pearl River Delta Business Council, 2007), 7, 60.
111. The Greater Pearl River Delta Business Council, '2012/13 Term Report' (Constitutional and Mainland Affairs Bureau, 2013), 8, 63.
112. 'Further Liberalisation under CEPA', *GIS*, 29 July 2008.
113. 'Three-Way Economic Zone under Discussion', *CD*, 4 March 2008.
114. Press release, *GIS*, 17 October 2008.
115. Press release, *GIS*, 12 November 2008.
116. HKTDC Research, 'Economists' Pick', 5 September 2008.
117. The Greater Pearl River Delta Business Council, '2012/13 Term Report', 18.
118. Federation of Hong Kong Industries, 'Made in PRD Study: Made in PRD Study—"Hong Kong Industry: The Way Forward"' (Hong Kong, 2015), 3.
119. Naubahar Sharif and Can Huang, 'Innovation Strategy, Firm Survival and Relocation: The Case of Hong Kong–Owned Manufacturing in Guangdong Province, China', *Research Policy* 41, issue 1 (February 2012): 70.
120. Ibid.
121. The case against Hong Kong manufacturers is usefully summarised in Haifeng Felix Liao and Roger C. K. Chan, 'Industrial Relocation of Hong Kong Manufacturing Firms: Towards an Expanding Industrial Space beyond the Pearl River Delta', *GeoJournal* 76, issue 6 (December 2011): 628, 630.

122. Commentator, 'Hong Kong Needs Continued Success of "One Country, Two Systems"', *RR*, 29 June 2017.
123. Constitutional and Mainland Affairs Bureau, 'Progress Made by the Current-Term Government on Mainland Co-operation 2012–2017', 10–12, 15–17, 19.
124. 'A Co-Operative Move', *CD*, 7 August 2006.
125. Tung, Chief Executive, *GIS*, 4 December 2004.

# Conclusion

The rule of law is supposed to reign unchallenged in Hong Kong. It is accepted by China's leaders as crucial for continued economic success and regarded by the people of Hong Kong as essential for the survival of their core values. It makes possible open, accountable and honest administration and a government which does not tolerate corruption and privilege. This book shows that survival is under threat in Hong Kong because disregard for the law has become a recurring feature of Hong Kong's mismanagement.

In the case of the Basic Law—the blueprint for both survival and well-being—enforcement has been selective. Chief Executives and their ministers regarded the Law's Articles on conservative budgetary policies as their primary obligation. This attitude created the excuse for passive policies in which only a minimum effort would be made to tackle a range of serious threats to Hong Kong's well-being. The victims, it has been repeatedly shown, have come from all strata of society, not just the poor and vulnerable. Furthermore, it made no difference whether or not the steps needed to rectify mismanagement were straightforward and the costs manageable. Increased public spending in general would be resisted. In addition, those in power preferred to postpone remedial action, which compounded the damage done and led to cumulative financial and other costs to the community.

As this book shows, middle-class homeowners had to watch the value of their property erode because the government did not enforce existing laws or enact the additional legislation needed to prevent further dilapidation of private housing into slums. Then, there were the parents fortunate enough to have sufficient funding to see that their teenagers got a post-secondary education and what they believed to be the next best thing to a degree after they had been refused admission to university because of the government's ceiling on first-year places. Parents and students eventually had to accept that this investment may well turn out to be wasted. By 2010, the qualifications acquired were already proving of limited value in the market place. There were other, more serious victims of mismanagement. Particularly distressing were the lives that were lost as a direct consequence of the failure to provide sufficient manpower and funding to enforce the law. A separate chapter was devoted to case studies of the causes of these tragedies.

## Basic Law Ltd

Failure to fully implement the Basic Law was a key component of this unholy equation. It is plain that its drafters expected the future rulers of Hong Kong to be committed to improvements and innovations to raise the quality of life for its people and to provide an environment that would continue to match world standards, thus ensuring prosperity for its open, competitive and capitalist economy and a stable society. If the Special Administrative Region government had faithfully followed the Basic Law, there would have been no crisis over dilapidation of private sector homes, an inadequate housing supply or the limitations of the education system. The decline in the quality of administration would have been avoided. The painful costs of misinformed and mismanaged attempts to integrate Hong Kong into the Mainland economy and its five-year plans would not have occurred.

The Basic Law did not endorse the passive policies and the postponement of reforms which became such marked features of Hong Kong during the last two decades. Nor did the Basic Law anticipate that Hong Kong's first three Chief Executives would prove so unsuccessful that by the time they left office they would have forfeited their credibility with the general public, while their flawed policies had left all sectors of society except the affluent significantly worse off.

This sorry saga had begun with the 1997–1998 Asian financial crisis at the start of the Tung Chee Hwa era when a search for ways to save money seemed the rational solution. Since Hong Kong did not collapse under the economic disruption and social distress which these austerity measures created and neither did the civil service, there seemed no reason to halt Tung's policies of cutting government spending and staffing. It became a distressing feature of modern Hong Kong that almost all public debate relating to government responsibilities and performance quickly turned into financial discussions. These were usually one-sided, with a majority opposed to government intervention. The damage that followed this sort of approach, especially the decline in the quality of public administration, was dismissed all too often with assertions that the best solution was to leave matters to the private sector and market forces. Serious threats to the quality of life of Hong Kong people seemed to matter very little.

## Homes in peril

The most extensive area of mismanagement which the book uncovered was housing. Hong Kong has an extraordinary record of success. Its people have created a sophisticated, post-industrial city whose economic performance is awesome even by comparison with Asia's other 'miracle' economies. Its financial services sector has long been the largest single source of China's financing, both for hard currency earnings before 1978 and for foreign direct investment (FDI) and the creation of a global RMB in the reform decades that followed.[1] Its work force has always been highly efficient, pragmatic and astonishingly flexible. As a result, Hong Kong continued to thrive even after the entire manufacturing sector—the original foundation of its prosperity—was relocated to the Mainland in the 1980s and 1990s. The place of factories in the economy was taken over by financial and other services which operated at standards only matched by the international financial centres of New York and London. So outstanding has Hong Kong's performance been that, in the national interest, China's leaders have shown a firm commitment to the economic survival of this unique asset. These achievements make it difficult to understand why its people are not assured of safe and comfortable homes.

That so many homes were at risk in the private sector is a serious indictment of those in power for the last two decades. This major challenge to the quality of life cannot be dismissed as a poverty or welfare issue. The public's access to safe, comfortable and affordable homes is a basic right of the people of Hong Kong. Their homes are being destroyed on a scale that cannot be halted without government intervention. For decades, the owners were unaware of the limited life of concrete buildings and their relatively rapid deterioration unless they are properly maintained. Homes were built that were not designed to outlive their owners. The people of Hong Kong live in multi-storey buildings, taller and more densely occupied than in most other cities, which turns their management into a daunting challenge for the families who make their homes in them. The destruction of the housing stock in the private sector through dilapidation that has already taken place cannot be reversed without considerable state funding, principally because it has been allowed to continue unchecked for so long. The government has an added obligation to provide effective solutions because this crisis can be linked directly to the flawed decision to dismantle a housing strategy that had come close to ending all Hong Kong's problems by 2002 and which had won international acclaim.

For the last two decades, the government has played down the seriousness of the situation and denied its responsibility for finding a solution. Can the public expect the introduction of a radical change in policy now? Will the fourth Chief Executive and her team of ministers convince the public and the politicians to cooperate with the radical reform measures required after 20 years of obfuscation and who will form the ministerial team capable of managing the new housing programmes? It is hard to be optimistic. There is no longer any prestige in accepting high office because of the poor performance of the ministerial system since it was set up in 2002.

There are other obstacles which the book has identified: in particular, the lack of building sites, of qualified personnel and of basic office technology. Unless these shortfalls are put right, the supply of the new homes that Hong Kong people require will remain far below demand in both the private and public sectors. The vicious circle will continue of families in need of rehousing because of the dilapidation of the homes they worked so hard to buy being unable to find new homes in the public sector. Their only option will be the modern equivalent of squatter huts. This slum accommodation is being created within existing buildings, adding to their deterioration and their dangers. The problems to be overcome in rectifying this situation are daunting. But the challenge should be less difficult than the first resettlement housing programme in 1956 when there was no blueprint for building public housing on a mass scale and Hong Kong had only the restricted finances of a 'third world' economy. What is missing in contemporary Hong Kong is government acceptance of a duty to ensure an adequate supply of decent homes.

## Failed government

It is important to emphasise that the grim situation in the housing sector is not an isolated example of failed government. On the contrary, the following section will show, there are other, very similar examples of the destruction of family assets and serious threats to the individual's quality of life.

### *Employees' wealth destroyed*

A close parallel with the government's responsibility for the destruction of private homeowners' wealth is provided by the Mandatory Provident Fund (MPF). Combined opposition from the business community and the colonial administration had blocked proposals for the creation of a compulsory retirement protection scheme on five occasions between 1967 and 1995.[2] When the MPF was launched in 2000, its immediate limitation was that the average retirees would not accumulate enough savings from this contributory scheme to fully support their life in retirement before 2030–2040. In the meantime, the retirement needs of a large part of the labour force would still have to be covered by the social security system.

There were other flaws. The government had created a structure for this retirement protection scheme which permitted handsome profits for the financial institutions running it and which provided inbuilt bonuses for employers. However, the fees imposed on members were excessive, as the Treasury Minister himself admitted.[3] As a result, the savings being accumulated to ensure a safe and comfortable retirement were lower than they could and should have been. As with dilapidation of housing, the full costs caused by this bias in favour of fund managers and employers would only become fully visible to the MPF's members years later.

For the average employee there were other, more immediate defects. The MPF was designed to be as employer-friendly as possible. As a result, the cost of long service gratuities and severance payments to which an employee would have a legal right could be deducted from the MPF entitlements. Employers fought stubbornly to retain this advantage, which Chief Executives did little to resist. The second Chief Executive, Donald Tsang Yam-kuen, expressed a passing interest in MPF reforms. His successor, Leung Chun-ying, achieved some minor changes to address the concerns over 'high fees and difficulty in making [investment] choices in some Mandatory Provident Fund schemes'.[4] His final Policy Address seemed to adopt a more generous attitude towards employees. He promised 'to progressively abolish the "offsetting" of severance payments or long service payments with MPF contributions'. By this late stage, these promises commanded no respect even from pro-government legislators. 'We do not want you to just talk the talk and think that words spoken are actions taken', Leung was told in the Legislative Council in 2017 in a discussion of this issue.[5]

Because of the MPF's deficiencies, there were increasing calls for a conventional state pension system. The government led the opposition to any form of pension principally on the ground of doubts 'whether such a model is sustainable in the long term in view of the ageing population, lower fertility rate and increasing life expectancy'. To convince the public that a pension would bring ruin, it mobilised academic expertise.[6] The government also had recourse to a cruder strategy in the form of scaremongering. The Welfare Minister claimed that the government's opposition reflected fears that both employers and the workforce would have to finance any improvements through their contributions, which would amount to 'a form of taxation'.[7] It was hard to see why compulsory contributions to a pension fund should be regarded as a tax while compulsory contributions to the MPF scheme were not.

### *Insurance cover rejected*

A very similar problem arose with health insurance, which was an obvious way to relieve any excessive burden on the health budget. Chief Executives and Health Ministers were extremely reluctant to introduce such a scheme, and they adopted the usual postponement strategy. Public consultations began in 1999 and were repeated in 2005, 2008, 2012, and 2014.[8] The report of this last survey of the community's attitudes towards insuring themselves against costly medical care was published in 2017, with a commitment to launch a voluntary scheme which had still to be designed.[9] The truth was that ministers wanted to prevent the expansion of the government's financial responsibilities, as the Health Minister frankly explained in 2012: 'Public subsidies might aggravate moral hazards in using private health insurance and private healthcare services, hence contributing to medical inflation'.[10]

What made this situation inexcusable was that over 40 per cent of the workforce already had some form of health cover by 2010, either as part of their employment package or through a personal insurance policy. By 2015, the proportion was close to half.[11] Health insurance was already a well-developed and well-accepted practice, providing the basic infrastructure on which the government could build a universal system. There was also a financial absurdity: the less comprehensive the health insurance enjoyed by the average family, the larger the bills to be paid for hospital and related services out of taxation.

When the government finally accepted the case for launching a health insurance scheme in 2017, the official report left unsolved the amount of financial support the government should provide for the scheme, either directly or through tax concessions and other incentives.[12] Similarly, the report was in favour of implementation through 'nonlegislative means' in order to reduce 'the unintended impact of a brand new regulatory regime' on the insurance industry. In plain language, this decision seemed to mean that a government-sponsored health insurance scheme should avoid improving the accountability of insurance companies and providing effective protection for members of the public buying health cover. In 2018, two decades of consultations and delayed decisions ended. The government at last announced a 'Voluntary Health Insurance Scheme' and promised tax concessions to its members.

There were important differences between the housing and health crises. It was impossible for the government to ignore the health needs of the community to the same degree as it had disregarded the decay of private housing. Treatment of the seriously ill could not be postponed indefinitely, unlike housing maintenance. In addition, the health professionals involved felt a duty of care to their patients, which limited the extent to which the government could cut the standards of treatment.

*Maintenance of the elderly*

A further example of mismanagement which threatened a large segment of the population regardless of social class was the demographic crisis, as the ageing population left the workforce in increasing numbers. A high proportion of the retirees had only limited means of support. This situation was a development which the Hospital Authority could not ignore. It launched a limited programme in 2004 to provide early health checks for the elderly. These 'first-time assessments' proved highly successful in cutting the costs of medical care for the aged. By identifying as early as possible threats to their health, research showed that they could be given 'targeted, proactive and community-based preventive care' which was both cost-effective and helped to maintain their quality of life.

The parallel with the housing sector is, unfortunately, all too obvious. Human beings also need maintenance. If neglected, their health problems become increasingly difficult—and expensive—to treat. The total number screened each year by the Hospital Authority began at around 40,000, a mere five per cent of the elderly population. This figure was to remain unchanged for the next decade, although the population aged 65 and above increased by 26 per cent to over a million individuals. The additional staff needed to expand the programme were not available, the Director of Audit reported in 2014.[13] The failure to fund this programme on an adequate scale was not just inhumane. It was also not good financial management. The costs to the public health services of providing medical care for elderly people were increased by the failure to carry out the most basic 'maintenance'—to screen as many of them as early as possible.

## The best chance of survival

As the decades roll by and 2047 and the expiry of the Basic Law gets ever closer, the current expectation is that fears about political risk will worsen. In many contexts, Hong Kong is portrayed by the leadership, both local and national, as a supplicant, a fragile entity which relies on the Mainland's assistance to survive. Among the arguments put forward by the Central People's Government in 2014 to convince the people of Hong Kong to trust it and respect its decision not to proceed with electoral reforms was the Mainland's generosity. It set out what it expected to be a convincing example.

> Since the early 1960s, . . . the central government and the relevant local governments on the mainland have made great efforts to ensure the supply of foodstuff, agricultural and sideline products, water, electricity, natural gas, etc., to the HKSAR'. . . By the end of 2013, some 95 percent of live pigs, 100 percent of live cattle, 33

percent of live chicken, 100 percent of freshwater fish, 90 percent of vegetables and 70 percent or more of flour on the Hong Kong market had been supplied by the mainland.[14]

This assumption that the people of Hong Kong must be impressed by such 'generosity' reflects a Mainland reality. There, food supplies are still subject to central planning because of national shortages (as chapter 8 explained). In Hong Kong's case, both the public and the food trade believe that the prices charged for Mainland supplies are excessive because there is a state cartel. Food imports are regarded by Hong Kong not as economic aid or social assistance but as just another commodity which ought to be subject to full market competition. There is thus no cause for gratitude.

Nevertheless, the chapter on the Mainland demonstrated that, fortunately, misconceptions about how Hong Kong should be treated have been counter-balanced in the past by realism at the highest levels of the nation's leadership about Hong Kong's value and the impossibility of any Mainland city replacing it. In 2000, a national leader had summed up what the nation owed Hong Kong for pioneering and underwriting China's emergence as a global economy.

> Over half of [Mainland] China's exports and imports have either gone through or come from Hong Kong [since 1978], and so it is with the capital influx. Without Hong Kong, the Chinese mainland could not have accessed the global markets and sent its commodities to every corner of the world as smoothly as it has for the past 20 years.[15]

This debt was soon to be forgotten by local Mainland officials, as chapter 8 explained, and Hong Kong investors and entrepreneurs were to find themselves unwelcome in Guangdong province. The Hong Kong model which had transformed the impoverished province into the nation's leading growth centre was denigrated as if it had obstructed the province's emergence as an advanced industrial centre.

This 'ingratitude' for Hong Kong's enthusiastic response to Deng Xiaoping's call for assistance in making a success of his 'open door' policy provided a useful reminder of the realpolitik of the Mainland's political leaders. Hong Kong had earned its 'high degree of autonomy' through its irreplaceable contribution to the national economy's initial takeoff. Its best hope of retaining this status for the future is to continue to rank high among the world's most advanced economies and to excel as a financial centre above all—which is a task assigned to Hong Kong by the Basic Law. The question is whether it can continue to play such a role. So far, the Mainland has found no substitute, no matter how much state support has been given to its 'Free Trade Zones' and other specially favoured, would-be centres of excellence.

Shanghai tried but failed to catch up with Hong Kong. It began planning a Free Trade Zone in 2003, and in 2009 it was authorised to launch an 'international trading board' to enable 'foreign firms to sell RMB-denominated shares in China', which would lay the foundations for an international financial centre. The launch was said to be imminent. In 2012, this project was abandoned because of 'very, very complicated' factors including 'legal, systematic, technical and social matters'.[16] It was revived in 2013 as 'a testing ground for financial reform' which was planned to achieve international standards including a free currency market, adequate market supervision and a respectable legal environment.[17] None of which was in place.[18] Once it became operational three years later, it was welcomed, not feared, by Hong Kong as a source of new business which would assist in 'reinforcing Hong Kong's role in connecting the financial markets in the Mainland and the rest of the world'.[19] Shanghai was still no sort of rival.

Thus, when it comes to political risk, a crucial issue for Hong Kong families, this book offers some reassurance. Throughout Hong Kong's history since the Chinese Communist Party came to power, its people have maintained their right to a 'separate system' through an economic performance which has contributed in a unique way to national development. There is no reason to believe that Hong Kong will cease to be able to play that role. There has been nervousness, of course, about how much longer the political freedom enjoyed by this unique city will be allowed to last. In the past, it is worth recalling, the nation's leaders tolerated much more serious 'non-conformity' in Hong Kong: colonialism itself, the use of its port by United States naval forces and the activities of the Guomindong. Current non-conformity is at a somewhat lower level of 'offensiveness'.

## Open and accountable

It is still possible in Hong Kong to have confidence in the general integrity of those in the public service, this book shows. There is a general awareness that the primary cause of mismanagement has been the misguided policy decisions which one Chief Executive after another has made. Their defects have been identified, leading to a loss of personal prestige and more serious penalties. As a result, politicians, pressure groups, professional bodies, academics and the media have remained critical but not disillusioned about open and accountable government.

Furthermore, insistence by the community on the transparency of the political system has prevented Hong Kong from being engulfed by the corruption and other malpractices that flourished before 1974 and the creation of the Independent Commission Against Corruption (ICAC). There is little indication of a systemic breakdown of the public administration's ethical or professional performance at the operational level. The resilience and adaptability of those working in the government have been invaluable in Hong Kong's struggle for survival. It would be unrealistic, however, to believe that the understaffed, underfunded and undervalued civil service which this book has described can maintain this quality of performance indefinitely.

The community cannot be expected to tolerate indefinitely and without mounting discontent the failure to protect its families' homes, to ensure quality education for the next generation and to create programmes to cope with such emerging challenges as an ageing population. At that point, the political environment alters. The electorate increasingly feels that the only way to compel those in power to take Hong Kong's survival seriously—including its quality of life—is to vote for candidates at elections whose protests will make mismanagement a priority political issue. That scenario has begun to get closer, creating a very new kind of threat to Hong Kong's long-term survival.

## Notes

1.  On Hong Kong's financial importance to the Mainland, see Leo F. Goodstadt, 'Fiscal Freedom and the Making of Hong Kong's Capitalist Society', in *Negotiating Autonomy in Greater China: Hong Kong and Its Sovereign Before and After 1997*, ed. Ray Yep (Copenhagen: NIAS Press, 2013).
2.  Unless otherwise specified, information on the background to the MPF in the discussion which follows is taken from Michael Yu et al., 'Retirement Protection System in Selected Places' (Research Division, Legislative Council Secretariat) (RP01/11-12, updated 7 May 2012), 71, 80, 92 in particular.
3.  Even ministers can find it hard to defend MPF providers. For example, 'MPF fees and charges have come down to 1.74 per cent, representing a 17 per cent reduction [since 2008]. Clearly, to the general public this is too little and too slow.' Professor Chan Ka-keung, Secretary for Financial Services and the Treasury, *Government Information Services* (*GIS* hereafter), 14 December 2012.
4.  'Improving Livelihood Building for the Future Report on the Work of the Current-Term Government in Its Fourth Year' (2007).
5.  *Hong Kong Hansard* (*HH* hereafter), Leung Chun-ying, Chief Executive, 18 January 2017, 3135, and Ho Kai-ming, 19 January 2017, 3241–42.
6.  Dr Wong Man Kit, 'Problems of PAYG Pension Scheme and Pension Reform: A Note on Overseas Experience and International Guidelines', Economic Analysis and Business Facilitation Unit (November 2015), 31–32. It is made clear that Dr Wong's research was both professional and independent.
7.  Matthew Cheung Kin-chung, Secretary for Labour and Welfare, *GIS*, 23 October 2014.
8.  Harvard Team, *Improving Hong Kong's Health Care System: Why and For Whom?* (Hong Kong: Government Printer, 1999); Food and Health Bureau, Health and Medical Development Advisory Committee, *Building a Healthy Tomorrow:*

*Discussion Paper on the Future Service Delivery Model for our Healthcare System* (Hong Kong: Health, Welfare and Food Bureau, 2005); Food and Health Bureau, *Your Health Your Life Healthcare Reform Consultation Document* (Hong Kong: SAR Government, 2008); Dr York Chow Yat-ngok, Secretary for Food and Health, *GIS*, 11 July 2011.

9.  Food and Welfare Bureau, *Voluntary Health Insurance Scheme Consultation Report* (January 2017).

10. Dr Ko Wing-man, Secretary for Food and Health, *HH*, 31 October 2012, 1107–9.

11. Census and Statistics Department, 'Provision of Medical Benefits by Employers/Companies and Coverage of Medical Insurance Purchased by Individuals', *Thematic Household Survey Report No. 45* (Hong Kong: Census and Statistics Department, October 2010), 129; 'Provision of Medical Benefits by Employers/Companies and Coverage of Medical Insurance Purchased by Individuals', *Thematic Household Survey Report No. 58* (Hong Kong: Census and Statistics Department, October 2015), 8.

12. For details, see Food and Health Bureau, *Voluntary Health Insurance Scheme Consultation Report*, 'Chapter Seven: Conclusion and Way Forward'.

13. Audit Commission, *Report No. 63*, 'Chapter 2: Department of Health Hospital Authority Provision of Health Services for the Elderly' (Hong Kong, 2014), 'Figure 2: Number of Health Assessments Provided by EHCs vis-à-vis the Growth in Elderly Population (2004 to 2013)', 11 and 10, 14–15.

14. State Council Information Office, 'Full Text: The Practice of the "One Country, Two Systems" Policy in the Hong Kong Special Administrative Region', *New China News Agency (NCNA hereafter)*, 10 June 2014.

15. Li Ruihuan, Politburo member and Chinese People's Political Consultative Conference Chairman, quoted in 'Li Ruihuan on HK's Role', *China Daily*, 7 November 2000.

16. Han Zheng, Shanghai Mayor quoted in 'Not Now for Int'l Board: Shanghai Mayor', *NCNA*, 6 March 2012.

17. 'Chinese Domestic Banks Can Conduct Offshore Business', *NCNA*, 28 September 2013.

18. See 'Rules for Shanghai FTZ Expected Next Quarter: Report', *NCNA*, 11 November 2013; 'China Adjusts Measures in Shanghai FTZ', *NCNA*, 6 January 2014; Wei Tian, 'Panel to Push Financial Reform in FTZ', *China Daily*, 4 January 2014.

19. Chan, Secretary for Financial Services and the Treasury, *HH*, 14 December 2016, 2471.

# Bibliography

## Official Chinese statements

'Build a Well-Off Society in an All-Round Way and Create a New Situation in Building Socialism with Chinese Characteristics'. Report at the 16th National Congress of the Chinese Communist Party, 8 November 2002. http://news.xinhuanet.com/english/2002-11/18/content_633685.htm.

'Hold High the Great Banner of Deng Xiaoping Theory for an All-round Advancement of the Cause of Building "Socialism with Chinese Characteristics into the 21st Century"'. Report Delivered at the 15th National Congress of the Communist Party of China on 12 September 1997. http://www.bjreview.com/document/txt/2011-03/25/content_363499_7.htm.

Jiang Zemin. 'Accelerating the Reform, the Opening to the Outside World and the Drive for Modernization, so as to Achieve Greater Successes in Building "Socialism with Chinese Characteristics"'. Report at the 14th National Congress of the Party, 12 October 1992. http://www.bjreview.com.cn/document/txt/2011-03/29/content_363504_13.htm.

Li Keqiang. 'Full Text of Chinese Premier's Teleconference Address on Streamlining Administration Procedures, Cutting Red Tape'. *New China News Agency*, 22 May 2015. http://news.xinhuanet.com/english/china/2015-05/22/c_134261597.htm.

National People's Congress Standing Committee. 'Full Text of NPC Decision on Universal Suffrage for HK Chief Executive Selection'. *New China News Agency*, 31 August 2014. http://www.china.org.cn/china/2014-08/31/content_33390388.htm.

State Council Information Office. 'Full Text: The Practice of the "One Country, Two Systems" Policy in the Hong Kong Special Administrative Region'. *New China News Agency*, 10 June 2014. http://www.china.org.cn/government/whitepaper/node_7207387.htm.

## Public Records Office Hong Kong

HKRS156-3-95 'Squatters on Land Not Required for Development'
HKRS163-1-1578 'Shek Kip Mei Fire'
HKRS163-1-1677 'Committees—Shek Kip Mei Fire'

HKRS163-3-64 'Squatter Clearance and Resettlement 1. General Questions of
. . . 2. Programmes of . . .'
HKRS163-3-219 'Working Party on Squatters, Resettlement and Government
Low-Cost Housing'
HKRS163-3-264 'Coordination of Social Service Policies'
HKRS163-9-217 '(A) Meeting of Senior Commonwealth Finance Officials
1970. Sterling Area Balance of Payments—Developments and Prospects to
Mid-1971 (B) Overseas Sterling Area Countries Statistics'
HKRS163-9-486, 'Social Security—Implications of Change in HK Status-Quo . . .'
HKRS229-1-807 'Financial Aid (Including Loans) Received from the United
Kingdom and Other Governments Record of . . .'
HKRS394-20-8 'Resettlement Policy Committee'
HKRS890-2-31 'Correspondence with the Governor and Notes of Discussion
with H. E.'

## Hong Kong official documents and publications

*Hong Kong Annual Departmental Report by the Registrar General 1959–60.* Hong
Kong: Government Printer, n.d.
'Improving Livelihood Building for the Future Report on the Work of the
Current-term Government in its Fourth Year' (2017). http://www.ceo.gov.
hk/report-yearfour/eng/files/Year4.pdf.
'Operation Building Bright' (2009). http://www.bd.gov.hk/english/docu-
ments/OBB/OBB_e.pdf.
*Report by the Inter-Departmental Working Party to Consider Certain Aspects of Social
Security.* Hong Kong: Government Printer, 1967.
*Report of the Commission of Enquiry on the New Airport.* Hong Kong: Government
Information Services, 1999.
'Report of the Hospital Authority Review Panel on the SARS Outbreak,
September 2003'. http://www.ha.org.hk/sars/ps/report/reviewpanel_e.
pdf.
'Report of Investigation Task Force on Statistical Data Quality Assurance'
(March 2013). http://www.gov.hk/en/residents/government/policy/gov-
ernment_reports/reports/docs/DQA.pdf.
*Report of the Legislative Council Select Committee to Inquire into the Circumstances
Leading to the Problems Surrounding the Commencement of the Operation of the New
Hong Kong International Airport at Chek Lap Kok since 6 July 1998 and Related
Issues.* Hong Kong, January 1999.
'Report of the Select Committee to Inquire into the Handling of the Severe
Acute Respiratory Syndrome outbreak by the Government and the Hospital
Authority, July 2004'. http://www.legco.gov.hk/yr03-04/english/sc/sc_
sars/reports/sars_rpt.htm.
*Report on the Work of the Fourth-Term Government of the Hong Kong Special
Administrative Region June 2017.* http://www.ceo.gov.hk/archive/2017/
report-yearfive/eng/index.html.
*Review of the Institutional Framework for Public Housing: The Report June 2002.* Hong
Kong: SAR Government, 2002.

'Steering Committee on Systemic Reform of the Marine Department Final Report' (April 2016). http://www.mardep.gov.hk/en/publication/pdf/steeringcom.pdf.

Audit Commission. *Report 39*, 'Chapter 5: Special Finance Scheme for Small and Medium Enterprises' (Hong Kong, 15 October 2002). http://www.aud.gov.hk/pdf_e/e39ch05.pdf.

Audit Commission. *Report No. 47*, 'Chapter 4: Four Small and Medium Enterprise Funding Schemes' (Hong Kong, 23 October 2006). http://www.aud.gov.hk/pdf_e/e47ch04.pdf.

Audit Commission. *Report No. 58*, 'Chapter 7: Lands Department: Unlawful Occupation of Government Land' (Hong Kong, 28 March 2012). http://www.aud.gov.hk/pdf_e/e58ch07.pdf.

Audit Commission. *Report No. 63*, 'Chapter 2: Department of Health Hospital Authority Provision of Health Services for the Elderly' (Hong Kong, 2014). http://www.aud.gov.hk/pdf_e/e63ch02.pdf.

Audit Commission. *Report No. 64*, 'Chapter 1: Buildings Department's Actions on Unauthorised Building Works' (Hong Kong, 2015). http://www.aud.gov.hk/pdf_e/e64ch01.pdf.

Buildings Department. 'Report on the Findings and Recommendations of the Working Group on Review of Building Safety Enforcement Procedures and Practice' (December 2011). http://www.bd.gov.hk/english/documents/reports/ReviewBuildingSafety_201206.pdf.

Census and Statistics Department, *2011 Population Census. Thematic Report Household Income Distribution in Hong Kong*. Hong Kong: Census and Statistics Department, 2012.

Census and Statistics Department. *2016 Population By-Census Thematic Report: Household Income Distribution in Hong Kong, Hong Kong Special Administrative Region*. Hong Kong Census and Statistics Department: 2017.

Census and Statistics Department. *Hong Kong 1976 By-Census Main Report Volume 1: Analysis*. Hong Kong: Government Printer, 1979.

Census and Statistics Department. *Hong Kong 2011 Census Main Report: Volume 1*. Hong Kong: SAR Government, 2012.

Census and Statistics Department. *Hong Kong Population and Housing Census 1971 Main Report*. Hong Kong: Government Printer, n.d.

Census and Statistics Department. 'Provision of Medical Benefits by Employers/Companies and Coverage of Medical Insurance Purchased by Individuals', *Thematic Household Survey Report No. 45*. Hong Kong: Census and Statistics Department, October 2010.

Census and Statistics Department. 'Provision of Medical Benefits by Employers/Companies and Coverage of Medical Insurance Purchased by Individuals', *Thematic Household Survey Report No. 58*. Hong Kong: Census and Statistics Department, October 2015.

Chan Mo-po, Paul, Secretary for Development. 'The Development Potential of New Territories North', 13 October 2013. http://www.devb.gov.hk/en/home/my_blog/index_id_37.html.

Cheng, Ivy. 'Impacts of the Lump Sum Grant Subvention System on the Subvented Welfare Sector: Information Note', Legislative Council

Secretariat (IN14/07-08, 8 May 2008). http://www.legco.gov.hk/yr07-08/english/sec/library/0708in14-e.pdf.

Chief Executive's Commission on Innovation and Technology. *First Report* (September1998).http://www.itc.gov.hk/en/doc/First_report_98_%28eng%29.pdf.

Civil Engineering and Development Department. 'Legislative Council Panel on Development North East New Territories New Development Areas Planning and Engineering Study' (CB(1)203/12-13(01), November 2012). http://www.legco.gov.hk/yr12-13/english/panels/dev/papers/dev1030cb1-203-1-e.pdf.

Civil Service Bureau. 'Legislative Council Panel on Public Service General Overview of the Civil Service Strength, Retirement and Resignation' (CB(1)1817/07-08(01), June 2008). http://www.legco.gov.hk/yr07-08/english/panels/ps/papers/ps0616cb1-1817-1-e.pdf.

Commerce and Economic Development Bureau. *Item for Finance Committee,* HEAD 152 Subhead 700, 'New item "SME Financing Guarantee Scheme—Special Concessionary Measures"' (FCR(2012-13)12, April 2012).

Commission on Strategic Development. *Bringing the Vision to Life: Hong Kong's Long-Term Development Needs and Goals.* Hong Kong: Central Policy Unit, 2000.

Commission on Strategic Development. 'Hong Kong SAR's Work Direction in Complementing the National Twelfth Five-Year Plan' (CSD/2/2011, May 2011). http://www.cpu.gov.hk/doc/en/commission_strategic_development/csd_2_2011.pdf.

Commission on Strategic Development. 'Summary of the Views Expressed at the Fifth Meeting of the Executive Committee of the Commission on Strategic Development Held on 10 August 2006' (Secretariat, September 2006). http://www.cpu.gov.hk/doc/en/commission_strategic_development/csd_ec_summary_5.pdf.

Commission on Strategic Development. 'Young People—Education, Employment and Development Opportunities' (CSD/1/2013, September 2013). http://www.cpu.gov.hk/doc/en/commission_strategic_development/csd_1_2013e_without_Annex_F.pdf.

Constitutional and Mainland Affairs Bureau. 'Legislative Council Panel on Commerce and Industry Co-operation between Hong Kong and the Mainland—Hong Kong/Guangdong Co-operation and National 13th Five-Year Plans' (CB(1)1258/13-14(01), April 2014). http://www.cmab.gov.hk/upload/LegCoPaper/cicb1-1258-1-e.pdf.

Constitutional and Mainland Affairs Bureau. 'Legislative Council Panel on Commerce and Industry Hong Kong/Shenzhen Co-operation Meeting' (CB(1)750/15-16(01), April 2016). http://www.legco.gov.hk/yr15-16/english/panels/ci/papers/cicb1-750-1-e.pdf.

Constitutional and Mainland Affairs Bureau. 'Progress Made by the Current-Term Government on Mainland Co-operation 2012–2017'. http://www.cmab.gov.hk/doc/en/documents/publications_and_press_releases/Booklet_on_Mainland_Co-operation.pdf.

Development Bureau. 'Legislative Council Panel on Development Enforcement against Unauthorised Building Works in New Territories Exempted Houses'

(CB(1)2530/10-11(05), June 2011). http://www.legco.gov.hk/yr10-11/english/panels/dev/papers/dev0628cb1-2530-5-e.pdf.

Development Bureau. 'Legislative Council Panel on Development Subcommittee on Building Safety and Related Issues: Buildings Department's Initial Response to the Findings of the Coroner's Inquest on the Building Collapse Incident at Ma Tau Wai Road' (CB(1)2930/10-11(01), August 2011). http://www.legco.gov.hk/yr10-11/english/panels/dev/dev_bs/papers/dev_bs0826cb1-2930-1-e.pdf.

Development Bureau. 'Legislative Council Panel on Development Subcommittee on Building Safety and Related Issues: Buildings Department's Review of Enforcement Procedures and Practices for Dilapidated Buildings and Views of Independent Experts'. http://www.devb.gov.hk/filemanager/en/content_31/Subcom_Paper_Eng_Final_Full.pdf.

Development Bureau. 'Legislative Council Panel on Development Subcommittee on Building Safety and Related Issues: Consolidation of Financial Assistance Schemes for Building Maintenance and Repair' (CB(1)2087/10-11(02), May 2011). http://www.legco.gov.hk/yr10-11/english/panels/dev/dev_bs/papers/dev_bs0511cb1-2087-2-e.pdf.

Development Bureau. 'Legislative Council Panel on Development Subcommittee on Building Safety and Related Issues: Measures to Enhance Building Safety in Hong Kong', Annex: 'Legislative Council Brief Measures to Enhance Building Safety in Hong Kong (File Ref: DEVB(PL-CR) 12/2010)', (CB(1)681/10-11(01), December 2010). http://www.legco.gov.hk/yr10-11/english/panels/dev/dev_bs/papers/dev_bs0113cb1-681-1-e.pdf.

Development Bureau. 'Legislative Council Panel on Development Subcommittee on Building Safety and Related Issues: Measures to Enhance Building Safety in Hong Kong (File Ref: DEVB(PL-CR) 12/2010)' (Development Bureau, CB(1)681/10-11(01), December 2010). http://www.legco.gov.hk/yr10-11/english/panels/dev/dev_bs/papers/dev_bs0113cb1-681-1-e.pdf.

Development Bureau, 'Task Force on Land Supply Demand for Land' (Paper No. 02/2017, 1 September 2017). http://www.devb.gov.hk/filemanager/en/content_1054/Paper_02_2017.pdf.

Development Bureau, 'Task Force on Land Supply Land Supply Initiatives' (Paper No. 03/2017, 6 September 2017). https://www.devb.gov.hk/filemanager/en/content_1054/Paper_03_2017.pdf.

Development Bureau, 'Task Force on Land Supply Work Plan of the Task Force' (Paper No. 04/2017, 6 October 2017). http://www.devb.gov.hk/filemanager/en/content_1054/Paper_04_2017.pdf.

Economic Analysis Division. *First Quarter Economic Report 2012* (May 2012). http://www.hkeconomy.gov.hk/en/pdf/er_12q1.pdf.

Economic Analysis Division. 'Hong Kong Poverty Situation Report 2012' (September 2013). http://www.povertyrelief.gov.hk/pdf/2012_Poverty_Situation_Eng.pdf.

Economic Analysis Division. 'Hong Kong Poverty Situation Report 2015' (October 2015). http://www.povertyrelief.gov.hk/pdf/poverty_report_2015_e.pdf.

Chief Executive's Commission on Innovation and Technology. *First Report* (September 1998). http://www.itc.gov.hk/en/doc/First_report_98_%28eng%29.pdf.

Education and Manpower Bureau. 'Legislative Council Panel on Education Articulation and Employment Opportunities of Sub-degree Holders' (CB(2)543/06-07(01), December 2006). http://www.legco.gov.hk/yr06-07/english/panels/ed/papers/ed1211cb2-543-1-e.pdf.

Education and Manpower Bureau. 'LegCo Panel on Education Reforming the Academic Structure of Senior Secondary Education and Higher Education—Actions for Investing in the Future' (CB(2) 90/04-05(01), October 2004). http://www.legco.gov.hk/yr04-05/english/panels/ed/papers/edcb2-1304-1e[1].pdf.

Education and Manpower Bureau. *Reforming the Academic Structure for Secondary Education and Higher Education—Actions for Investing in the Future.* Hong Kong: Education and Manpower Bureau, 2004.

Education Bureau. 'Annex 1: Panel on Education Follow-Up to the Meeting on 10 July 2017 Response to the Four Motions Passed at the Meeting' (LC Paper No. CB(4)1416/16-17(01), 13 July 2017). http://www.legco.gov.hk/yr16-17/english/panels/ed/papers/ed20170710cb4-1416-1-e.pdf.

Education Bureau. 'Legislative Council Panel on Education Priority Measures to Support Quality Education' (CB(4)1366/16-17(01), July 2017). http://www.legco.gov.hk/yr16-17/english/panels/ed/papers/ed20170710cb4-1366-1-e.pdf.

Education Commission. *Learning for Life, Learning through Life: Reform Proposals for the Education System in Hong Kong* (September 2000). http://www.e-c.edu.hk/eng/reform/index_e.html.

Efficiency Unit. 'Serving the Community by Using the Private Sector—Policy and Practice', 2nd ed. (January 2007). http://www.eu.gov.hk/en/reference/publications/PolicyPractice2007.pdf.

Financial Bureau. 'Report on the Profits Tax Review' (1998). http://www.budget.gov.hk/1998/english/green/report.htm.

Financial Services and the Treasury Branch, 'Public Consultation on Tax Reform Final Report' (June 2007). http://www.taxreform.gov.hk/eng/pdf/final-report.pdf.

Food and Health Bureau, Health and Medical Development Advisory Committee. *Building a Healthy Tomorrow: Discussion Paper on the Future Service Delivery Model for Our Healthcare System.* Hong Kong: Health, Welfare and Food Bureau, 2005.

Food and Health Bureau. 'Supply of Live Cattle in Hong Kong Legislative Council Panel on Food Safety and Environmental Hygiene' (No. CB(2)1676/13-14(03), June 2014). http://www.legco.gov.hk/yr13-14/english/panels/fseh/papers/fe0610cb2-1676-3-e.pdf.

Food and Health Bureau. *Voluntary Health Insurance Scheme Consultation Report.* http://www.vhis.gov.hk/doc/en/full_consultation_report/VHIS_full_report.pdf1.

Food and Health Bureau. *Your Health Your Life Healthcare Reform Consultation Document.* Hong Kong: SAR Government, 2008.

Home Affairs Department. *A Guide on Building Management Ordinance (Cap. 344),* 8th ed. (January 2016). http://www.buildingmgt.gov.hk/file_manager/en/documents/bmo_guide/a_guide_on_building_management_ordinance_cap344_en.pdf.

Home Affairs Department. 'Legislative Council Panel on Home Affairs Regulation of the Property Management Industry' (CB(2)457/13-14(06), December 2013). http://www.legco.gov.hk/yr13-14/english/panels/ha/papers/ha1213cb2-457-6-e.pdf.

Home Affairs Department. 'Legislative Council Panel on Home Affairs Review of the Building Management Ordinance (Cap. 344)' (CB(2)238/14-15(03), November 2014). http://www.legco.gov.hk/yr15-16/english/panels/ha/papers/ha20160517cb2-1502-4-e.pdf.

Home Affairs Department. 'Legislative Council Panel on Home Affairs Review of the Building Management Ordinance (Cap. 344)' (CB(2)1502/15-16(03), May 2016). http://www.legco.gov.hk/yr15-16/english/panels/ha/papers/ha20160517cb2-1502-3-e.pdf.

Home Affairs Department. 'Legislative Council Panel on Home Affairs Safeguard Measures for Prevention of Corruption and Malpractices in Building Repair and Maintenance Works' (CB(2)662/14-15(01), January 2015). http://www.legco.gov.hk/yr14-15/english/panels/ha/papers/ha20150124cb2-662-1-e.pdf.

Hospital Authority. *Hospital Authority Annual Plan 2003–2004*. Hong Kong: Hospital Authority, 2003.

Hospital Authority. *Hospital Authority Annual Plan 2005–06*. Hong Kong: Hospital Authority, 2005.

Hospital Authority. *Hospital Authority Annual Plan 2007–08*. Hong Kong: Hospital Authority, 2007.

Hospital Authority. *Hospital Authority Annual Plan 2013–14: Keeping Healthcare in Sync*. Hong Kong: Hospital Authority, 2013.

Housing Bureau. 'LegCo Panel on Housing Minutes of Meeting . . . 17 October 2000' (CB(1) 121/00-01, 4 November 2000). http://www.legco.gov.hk/yr00-01/english/panels/hg/minutes/hg171000.pdf.

Hui Siu-wai, Director of Buildings. 'Examination of Estimates of Expenditure 2016–17 Reply Serial No.DEVB(PL)283'. http://www.bd.gov.hk/english/documents/SFCQ2016/PL283.pdf.

ICAC Commissioner. *2000 Annual Report by the Commissioner of the Independent Commission Against Corruption.* http://www.icac.org.hk/filemanager/tc/Content_1238/2000.pdf.

ICAC Commissioner. *2006 Annual Report Independent Commission Against Corruption.* http://www.icac.org.hk/filemanager/tc/Content_1238/2006.pdf.

Independent Commission Against Corruption. *40 Years in the Operations Department Fighting Corruption with the Community (1974–2014)*. Hong Kong: Independent Commission Against Corruption, 2015. http://www.icac.org.hk/filemanager/en/Content_1239/ops2014.pdf.

Labour and Welfare Bureau. 'Legislative Council Panel on Welfare Services: Long-Term Social Welfare Planning' (LC Paper No. CB(2)2279/10-11(03), July 2011). http://www.legco.gov.hk/yr10-11/english/panels/ws/papers/ws0711cb2-2279-3-e.pdf.

Labour and Welfare Bureau. 'Report on Manpower Projection to 2022' (Hong Kong SARG, April 2015). http://www.lwb.gov.hk/report/mp2022_en.pdf.

Legal Service Division. 'Subcommittee on Poverty Alleviation: Paper on the Constitutionality of the One-Year Continuous Residence Requirement for the Comprehensive Social Security Assistance Scheme' (LC Paper No. LS18/09-10, 26 November 2009). http://www.legco.gov.hk/yr08-09/english/panels/ws/ws_pa/papers/ws_pa0515ls-18-e.pdf.

Legislative Council Secretariat. 'Background Brief Supply of Live Cattle in Hong Kong', Panel on Food Safety and Environmental Hygiene (CB(2)1511/12, 4 July 2013). http://www.legco.gov.hk/yr12-13/english/panels/fseh/papers/fe0709cb2-1511-1-e.pdf.

Legislative Council Secretariat. 'Background Brief Supply of Live Cattle in Hong Kong', Panel on Food Safety and Environmental Hygiene (CB(2)1676/13-14, 4 June 2014). http://www.legco.gov.hk/yr13-14/english/panels/fseh/papers/fe0610cb2-1676-4-e.pdf.

Legislative Council Secretariat. 'Grant for the Samaritan Fund' (CB(2)208/08-09(06), 7 November 2008). http://www.legco.gov.hk/yr08-09/english/panels/hs/papers/hs1110cb2-208-6-e.pdf.

Legislative Council Secretariat. 'Panel on Development Minutes of Meeting Held on Tuesday, 26 January 2010 . . .' (CB(1)1508/09-10, 8 April 2010). http://www.legco.gov.hk/yr09-10/english/panels/dev/minutes/dev20100126.pdf.

Legislative Council Secretariat. 'Panel on Development Subcommittee on Building Safety and Related Issues . . . Updated Background Brief on Unauthorized Building Works in New Territories Exempted Houses' (CB(1)524/11-12(02), 7 December 2011). http://www.legco.gov.hk/yr11-12/english/panels/dev/dev_bs/papers/dev_bs1208cb1-524-2-e.pdf.

Legislative Council Secretariat. 'Panel on Development: Updated Background Brief on the Work of the Urban Renewal Authority' (CB(1)1034/15-16(02), 15 June 2016). http://www.legco.gov.hk/yr15-16/english/panels/dev/papers/dev20160621cb1-1034-2-e.pdf.

Legislative Council Secretariat. 'Panel on Education: Background Brief Prepared by the Legislative Council Secretariat . . . Sub-degree education' (CB(2)543/06-07(02), 7 December 2006). http://www.legco.gov.hk/yr06-07/english/panels/ed/papers/ed1211cb2-543-2-e.pdf.

Legislative Council Secretariat. 'Panel on Education Meeting on 13 June 2016 Updated Background Brief on Issues Related to the Governance and Regulation of the Self-Financing Post-Secondary Education Sector' (CB(4)1090/15-16(02), 8 June 2016). http://www.legco.gov.hk/yr15-16/english/panels/ed/papers/ed20160613cb4-1090-2-e.pdf.

Legislative Council Secretariat. 'Panel on Education Subcommittee on Integrated Education Report September 2014' (CB(4)1087/13-14(01). http://www.legco.gov.hk/yr13-14/english/panels/ed/ed_ie/reports/ed_iecb4-1087-1-e.pdf.

Legislative Council Secretariat. 'Panel on Home Affairs Background Brief . . . 2013 Proposed Regulatory Framework for the Property Management Industry' (CB(2)457/13-14(07), 6 December 2013). http://www.legco.gov.hk/yr13-14/english/panels/ha/papers/ha1213cb2-457-7-e.pdf.

Legislative Council Secretariat. 'Panel on Home Affairs Background Brief Prepared . . . for the Meeting on 17 November 2014 Review of the Building

Management Ordinance' (CB(2)238/14-15(04), 13 November 2014). http://www.legco.gov.hk/yr14-15/english/panels/ha/papers/ha20141117 cb2-238-4-e.pdf.

Legislative Council Secretariat. 'Panel on Home Affairs Minutes of Meeting Held on Tuesday, 17 May 2016 . . .' (CB(2)2016/15-16, 1 September 2016). http://www.legco.gov.hk/yr15-16/english/panels/ha/minutes/ha2016 0517.pdf.

Legislative Council Secretariat. 'Panel on Home Affairs Minutes of Special Meeting Held on Friday, 4 July 2008 . . .' (CB(2)2850/07-08, 22 October 2008). http://www.legco.gov.hk/yr07-08/english/panels/ha/minutes/ha 080704.pdf.

Legislative Council Secretariat. 'Panel on Housing Report of the Subcommittee on the Long Term Housing Strategy' (CB(1)1705/13-14, 2 July 2014). http://www.legco.gov.hk/yr13-14/english/panels/hg/papers/hg0707cb1-1705-e.pdf.

Legislative Council Secretariat. 'Panel on Public Service Meeting . . . Updated Background Brief on the Overview of the Civil Service Establishment, Strength, Retirement, Resignation and Age Profile' (CB(4)963/14-15(11), 15 May 2015). http://www.legco.gov.hk/yr14-15/english/panels/ps/papers/ps20150518cb4-963-11-e.pdf.

Legislative Council Secretariat. 'Paper for the House Committee Meeting on 25 February 2011 Continuation of Work of the Subcommittee on Building Safety and Related Issues' (CB(1)1382/10-11, 23 February 2011). http://www.legco.gov.hk/yr10-11/english/panels/dev/dev_bs/reports/dev_bscb1-1382-e.pdf.

Legislative Council Secretariat. 'Provision of Residential Care Places for Persons with Disabilities' (CB(2)1149/09-10(02), 23 March 2010). http://www.legco.gov.hk/yr09-10/english/panels/ws/ws_rccs/papers/ws_rccs0329cb2-.

Legislative Council Secretariat. 'Report of the Bills Committee on Property Management Services Bill' (CB(2)765/15-16, 28 January 2016). http://www.legco.gov.hk/yr13-14/english/bc/bc57/reports/bc570203cb2-765-e.pdf.

Legislative Council Secretariat, 'Report of the Panel on Public Service for submission to the Legislative Council' (CB(4)1294 /16-17, 23 June 2017) http://www.legco.gov.hk/yr16-17/english/panels/ps/reports/ps20170705cb4-1294-e.pdf.

Long Term Housing Strategy Steering Committee. *Long Term Housing Strategy: Building Consensus, Building Homes* (Consultation Document, September 2013). http://www.thb.gov.hk/eng/policy/housing/policy/lths/lthb_con-sultation_doc_201309.pdf.

Lump Sum Grant Independent Review Committee. 'Review Report on the Lump Sum Grant Subvention System December 2008'. http://www.swd.gov.hk/doc/ngo/(5)-Report%20eng.pdf.

Market Research Division. 'Survey of the Financing Situation of Small and Medium-Sized Enterprises', *Hong Kong Monetary Authority Quarterly Report*, October 2000.

Miller, Tony, Director of Housing. 'Becoming Stakeholders of Hong Kong: Home Ownership', Speech to the Hong Kong Institute of Real Estate

Administration (19 February 1997). http://www.housingauthority.gov.hk/en/about-us/news-centre/speeches/1435.html.

Office of The Ombudsman. 'Direct Investigation: Enforcement against Unauthorised Building Works in New Territories Exempted Houses', *Issue No. 1 of Reporting Year 2011/12* (19 April 2011). http://www.ombudsman.hk/ombudsnews/ombe_1_1112.pdf.

Office of The Ombudsman. 'Direct Investigation into Method of Calculation of Waiting Time for Public Rental Housing and Release of Information', *Issue No. 3 of Reporting Year 2015/16* (10 December 2015). http://ofomb.ombudsman.hk/abc/files/OmbudNews_E-10_12_2015.pdf.

Office of The Ombudsman. 'Direct Investigation Report: Enforcement against Unauthorised Building Works in New Territories Exempted Houses, March 2011' (Ref. OMB/DI/203, 31 March 2011) http://ofomb.ombudsman. hk/abc/files/DI203.pdf.

Office of The Ombudsman. 'Direct Investigation Report: Lands Department's System of Regularisation of Illegal Occupation of Government Land and Breach of Lease Conditions', *Issue No. 2 of Reporting Year 2016/17* (13 September 2016). http://ofomb.ombudsman.hk/abc/files/OmbudsNews_E-13_9_2016.pdf.

Office of The Ombudsman. 'Direct Investigation Report: "Special Procedures" of Buildings Department for Handling UBW Cases Involving Celebrities' (Ref. OMB/DI/316, January 2014). http://ofomb.ombudsman.hk/abc/files/DI316_full_E-2014_1_23_0.pdf.

Office of The Ombudsman. 'Investigation Report: The Enforcement Action on Unauthorised Building Works in New Territories Exempted Houses' (August 2004). http://ofomb.ombudsman.hk/abc/files/8-2004-1.pdf.

Office of The Ombudsman. '主動調查報告，海事處對海上事故調查報告所作建議的跟進機制', (14 June 2016). http://ofomb.ombudsman.hk/abc/files/DI334_full_TC-14_6_2016.pdf.

Price Statistics Branch. *2014/15 Household Expenditure Survey and the Rebasing of the Consumer Price Indices.* Hong Kong: Census and Statistics Department, 2016.

Research Office. 'The 2017–2018 Budget March 2017', Research Brief, Issue No. 3 (2016–17). Hong Kong: Legislative Council Secretariat, 2017. http://www.legco.gov.hk/research-publications/english/ 1 61 7rb03-the-2017-2}18-budget-20170329-e.pdf.

Sars Expert Committee. *SARS in Hong Kong: From Experience to Action.* Hong Kong, 2003. http://www.sars-expertcom.gov.hk/english/reports/reports/reports_fullrpt.html.

Social Surveys Section. *Thematic Household Survey Report—Report No. 60—Housing Conditions of Sub-Divided Units in Hong Kong.* Census and Statistics Department, March 2016.

Social Welfare Department. *The Five-Year Plan for Social Welfare Development in Hong Kong: Review 1998.* http://www.swd.gov.hk/doc/pubctn_ch/e5yrplan.pdf.

The Greater Pearl River Delta Business Council. '2012/13 Term Report' (Constitutional and Mainland Affairs Bureau, 2013). http://www.cmab.gov.hk/tc/images/issues/ar2012-2013/m_2012-13termreport.pdf.

Trade and Industry Department. 'The Mainland and Hong Kong Closer Economic Partnership Arrangement: Investment Agreement and Agreement on Economic and Technical Cooperation' (28 June 2017). http://www.tid.gov.hk/english/cepa/legaltext/files/Info_Note_2017.pdf.

Transport and Housing Bureau. 'Long Term Housing Strategy Annual Progress Report 2015' (December 2015). http://www.thb.gov.hk/eng/policy/housing/policy/lths/LTHS_Annual_Progress_Report_2015.pdf.

Transport and Housing Bureau. *Long Term Housing Strategy, December 2014.* http://www.thb.gov.hk/eng/policy/housing/policy/lths/LTHS201412.pdf.

Transport and Housing Bureau. 'Ove Arup & Partners Hong Kong Ltd, "Planning and Engineering Study for the Public Housing Development and Yuen Long Industrial Estate Extension at Wang Chau"' (REP-025-01/Final/May 2014). http://www.thb.gov.hk/eng/popup/wangchau_report_details.htm.

Transport and Housing Bureau. 'Report on Public Consultation on Subsidising Home Ownership' (October 2010). http://www.thb.gov.hk/eng/policy/housing/policy/consultation/con_report1005.pdf.

Treasury Branch Financial Services and the Treasury Bureau. 'Report of the Working Group on Long-Term Fiscal Planning (Phase 2)'. http://www.fstb.gov.hk/tb/en/report-of-the-working-group-on-longterm-fiscal-planning-phase2.htm.

University Grants Committee. 'Aspirations for the Higher Education System in Hong Kong: Report of the University Grants Committee' (LC Paper No. CB(2)602/10-11(01), December 2010). http://www.legco.gov.hk/yr10-11/english/panels/ed/papers/edcb2-602-1-e.pdf.

Urban Renewal Authority. *Annual Report 2010–2011.* http://www.ura.org.hk/media/578181/ura_annual_report_2010-2011_english_edition_low_resolution.pdf.

Urban Renewal Authority. *Annual Report 2012–2013.* http://www.ura.org.hk/en/download-centre/publications/annual-report/ura-annual-report/2012-2013.aspx.

Urban Renewal Authority, Steering Committee on Review of the Urban Renewal Strategy. 'Report on the Building Conditions Survey' (SC Paper No. 18/2009, 30 June 2009). http://www.ursreview.gov.hk/eng/doc/SC%20paper%2018-2009%20Progress%20Report%20on%20%20Building%20Conditions%20ENG.pdf.

Urban Renewal Authority, Steering Committee on Review of the Urban Renewal Strategy. 'Study on Building Maintenance' (SC Paper No. 19/2009, July 2009). http://www.ursreview.gov.hk/eng/doc/SC%20paper%2019-%20Study%20on%20Building%20Maintenance%20ENG.pdf.

Wong, Diana, Research Office, Legislative Council Secretariat. 'Information Note: Subdivided Flats in Hong Kong' (IN22/12-13, 28 May 2013). http://www.legco.gov.hk/yr12-13/english/sec/library/1213in22-e.pdf.

Wu, Jackie, Legislative Council Secretariat. 'Information Note: Tenancy Control in Selected Places' (IN18/13-14, 2 July 2014). http://www.legco.gov.hk/research-publications/english/1314in18-tenancy-control-in-selected-places-20140702-e.pdf.

Yu, Michael et al. 'Retirement Protection System in Selected Places' (Research Division, Legislative Council Secretariat) (RP01/11-12, updated 7 May 2012). http://www.legco.gov.hk/yr11-12/english/sec/library/1112rp01-e. pdf.

## Government-sponsored research publications

Chiu, Ernest, Wing-tak et al. *Elderly Commission's Study on Residential Care Services for the Elderly Final Report*. Hong Kong: University of Hong Kong, December 2009. http://www.elderlycommission.gov.hk/en/download/library/Residential %20Care%20Services%20-%20Final%20Report(eng).pdf.

Consumer Council. *How Competitive Is the Private Residential Property Market?* Hong Kong: Consumer Council, 1996.

Consumer Search Hong Kong Ltd. (commissioned by the Education Bureau). 'Survey on Opinions of Employers on Major Aspects of Performance of Sub-degree Graduates in Year 2013' (2016). http://www.cspe.edu.hk/GetFile. aspx?databaseimageid=12598-0.

Harvard Team. *Improving Hong Kong's Health Care System: Why and For Whom?* Hong Kong: Government Printer, 1999. http://www.fhb.gov.hk/en/press_ and_publications/consultation/HCS.HTM

HKTDC Research Department. *Implications of Mainland Processing Trade Policy on Hong Kong: Research Report (June 2007)*. Hong Kong: Greater Pearl River Delta Business Council, 2007. http://www.cmab.gov.hk/doc/ProcessingTrade June_eng.pdf.

HKTDC Research. 'Economists' Pick', '2000 Survey on CMA Members' Investment in Mainland China' (1 December 2000). http://economists-pick-research.hktdc.com/business-news/article/Economic-Forum/2000-Survey-on-CMA-Members-Investment-in-Mainland-China-Executive-Summary/ef/ en/1/1X000000/1X00PMFR.htm.

HKTDC Research. 'Economists' Pick', 5 September 2008. www.hktdc.com/busi-ness-news/article/Economic-Forum/Beyond-Cheap-Labour-Building-a-Competitive-Edge-through-Adding-Value/ef/en/1/1X000000/1X0041HG. htm.

Ko, Jan-ming. 'An Independent Appraisal of the Buildings Department's "Report on the Findings and Recommendations of the Working Group on Review of Building Safety Enforcement Procedures and Practices"' (11 May 2012). http://www.devb.gov.hk/filemanager/en/content_31/Report_Prof_Ko_ Full.pdf.

Li, Si Ming. 'Land and Housing Policies in Post-Handover Hong Kong: Political Economy and Urban Space' (Final Report, 31 March 2015). http://www. cpu.gov.hk/en/public_policy_research/pdf/2013_A2_001_13A_Final_ Report_Prof_Li.pdf.

Policy 21 Limited. 'Local and International Good Practices in the Governance and Quality Assurance of the Self-financing Post-Secondary Education Sector' (July 2014). http://www.cspe.edu.hk/GetFile.aspx?databaseimage id=4157-0.

Public Policy Research Institute, Polytechnic University. 'A Focus Group Study on Subsidising Home Ownership' (Central Policy Unit, September, 2010). http://www.cpu.gov.hk/doc/en/research_reports/Subsidising%20 Home%20Ownership_e.pdf.

Visiting Panel. *A Perspective on Education in Hong Kong November 1982*. Hong Kong: Government Printer, 1983.

Wong, Man Kit. 'Problems of PAYG Pension Scheme and Pension Reform—A Note on Overseas Experience and International Guidelines', Economic Analysis and Business Facilitation Unit (November 2015). http://www.hke-conomy.gov.hk/en/pdf/PAYG.pdf.

Wu, Xiaogang. 'Hong Kong's Post-80s Generation: Profiles and Predicaments; a CPU Commissioned Report', Centre for Applied Social and Economic Research, Hong Kong University of Science and Technology (Central Policy Unit, May 2010). http://www.cpu.gov.hk/english/documents/new/press/ HK%27s%20Post%2080s%20Generation%20-%20Profiles%20and%20 Predicaments.pdf.

## International agencies

Dodsworth, John, and Dubravko Mihaljek. *Hong Kong, China. Growth, Structural Change, and Economic Stability During the Transition*. Washington, DC: International Monetary Fund, 1997.

International Monetary Fund. 'People's Republic of China—Hong Kong Special Administrative Region: Selected Issues', *IMF Country Report No. 05/62* (February 2005). http://www.imf.org/external/pubs/ft/scr/2005/cr0562. pdf.

Jansen, Cornelis J. A., and Mark Cherniavsky. 'Current Economic Situation and Prospects of Hong Kong'. Asia Department IBRD, 9 May 1967, mimeo.

UN-HABITAT. *The State of the World's Cities Report 2006/2007: 30 Years of Shaping the Habitat Agenda*. London: Earthscan, 2006. https://unhabitat.org/books/ state-of-the-worlds-cities-20062007/.

UN-Habitat. *State of the World's Cities 2008/2009: Harmonious Cities*. London: Earthscan, 2008. https://unhabitat.org/books/state-of-the-worlds-cities-20082009-harmonious-cities-2/.

UN-HABITAT and ESCAP. *The State of Asian and Pacific Cities 2015 Urban Transformations Shifting from Quantity to Quality* (2015). http://unhabitat. org/books/the-state-of-asian-and-pacific-cities-2015/.

OECD. *Strong Performers and Successful Reformers in Education: Lessons from PISA for Japan*. OECD Publishing, 2012. http://dx.doi.org/10.1787/ 9789264118539-en.

World Bank. *Doing Business 2015 Going Beyond Efficiency*. Washington, DC: International Bank for Reconstruction and Development, 2014.

## Books and journals

Abraham, Thomas. *Twenty-First Century Plague: The Story of SARS*. Hong Kong: Hong Kong University Press, 2004.

Barnett, K. M. A., Census Commissioner, 'Introduction'. In *Hong Kong Urban Rents and Housing*, by W. F. Maunder. Hong Kong: Hong Kong University Press, 1969.

Bristow, Roger. *Hong Kong's New Towns: A Selective Review*. Hong Kong: Oxford University Press, 1989.

Castells, M. et al. *The Shek Kip Mei Syndrome: Economic Development and Public Housing in Hong Kong and Singapore*. London: Pion Limited, 1990.

Chao, Kang. 'Industrialization and Urban Housing in Communist China'. *Journal of Asian Studies* 25, no. 3 (May 1966): 381–96.

Chau, Kenneth L., and Chack-kie Wong. 'The Social Welfare Reform: A Way to Reduce Public Burden'. In *The First Tung Chee-hwa Administration: The First Five Years of the Hong Kong Special Administrative Region*, edited by Lau Siu-kai. Hong Kong: Chinese University Press, 2002.

Cheng, Kai Ming. 'Educational Policymaking in Hong Kong: The Changing Legitimacy'. In *Education and Society in Hong Kong: Toward One Country and Two Systems*, edited by Gerard A. Postiglione. Armonk, NY: M. E. Sharpe, Inc., 1991.

Cheung, Anthony B. L. 'Civil Service Reform in Post-1997 Hong Kong: Political Challenges, Managerial Responses?' *International Journal of Public Administration* 24, no. 9 (2001): 929–50.

Cheung, Chor-yung. 'Hong Kong's Systemic Crisis of Governance and the Revolt of the "Post-80s" Youths: The Anti-Express Rail Campaign'. In *New Trends of Political Participation in Hong Kong*, edited by Joseph Y. S. Cheng. Hong Kong: City University of Hong Kong Press, 2014.

Chiu, Fred Y. L. 'Politics and the Body Social in Colonial Hong Kong'. In *Formations of Colonial Modernity in East Asia*, edited by Tani E. Barlow. Durham, NC: Duke University Press, 1997.

Chou, Kee-lee. 'HKIEd Study: Disparity in Higher Education Attainment Is Widening between Rich and Poor'. Hong Kong Institute of Education (31 January 2013). http://www.ied.edu.hk/media/news.php?id=20130131.

Chow, Nelson. 'Social Welfare and the Challenges of a New Era'. In *Hong Kong Economy and Society: Challenges in the New Era*, edited by Wong Siu-lun and Toyojiro Maruya. Hong Kong: Centre of Asian Studies, University of Hong Kong, 1998.

DeGolyer, Michael E. 'How the Stunning Outbreak of Disease Led to a Stunning Outbreak of Dissent'. In *At the Epicentre: Hong Kong and the SARS Outbreak*, edited by Christine Loh and Civic Exchange. Hong Kong: Hong Kong University Press, 2004.

DeGolyer, Michael E. 'Protests and Post-80's Youth: Sources of Social Instability'. (Hong Kong Transition Project, 2010). http://hktp.org/list/protest_and_post_80s_youths.pdf.

Federation of Hong Kong Industries. *Investment in China: 1993 Survey of Members of the Federation of Hong Kong Industries*. Hong Kong: Federation of Hong Kong Industries, 1993.

Federation of Hong Kong Industries. 'Made in PRD Study: Made in PRD Study—"Hong Kong Industry: The Way Forward"' (Hong Kong, 2015). https://www.industryhk.org/upload/news/attachment/14df7bb52ef8d9c4dfc69781acdfa73f.pdfP.

Goodhart, Charles, and Lu Dai. *Intervention to Save Hong Kong: Counter-Speculation in Financial Markets.* Oxford: Oxford University Press, 2003.

Goodstadt, Leo F. 'China and the Selection of Hong Kong's Post-Colonial Elite'. *China Quarterly* 163 (September 2000): 721–41.

Goodstadt, Leo F. 'Fiscal Freedom and the Making of Hong Kong's Capitalist Society'. In *Negotiating Autonomy in Greater China: Hong Kong and its Sovereign Before and After 1997,* edited by Ray Yep. Copenhagen: NIAS Press, 2013.

Goodstadt, Leo F. 'Painful Transitions: The Impact of Economic Growth and Government Policies on Hong Kong's "Chinese" Banks, 1945–70'. *HKIMR Working Paper* No. 16/2006, November 2006.

Goodstadt, Leo F. 'The Local Government Crisis 2007–2014: When China's Financial Management Faltered'. *HKIMR Working Paper* No. 27/2014, October 2014.

Goodstadt, Leo F. *Profits, Politics and Panics: Hong Kong's Banks and the Making of a Miracle Economy, 1935–1985.* Hong Kong: Hong Kong University Press, 2007.

Goodstadt, Leo F. *Poverty in the Midst of Affluence: How Hong Kong Mismanaged Its Prosperity.* 2nd ed. Hong Kong: Hong Kong University Press, 2015.

Hong Kong Council of Social Service. 'A Study of Living Situation of Young Adults in Hong Kong'. http://www.hkcss.org.hk/uploadfileMgnt/0_2016722103523.pdf.

Hong Kong Council of Social Service. 'Response to SWAC's 2nd Stage Consultation Exercise on Long Term Social Welfare Planning in Hong Kong'. http://webcontent.hkcss.org.hk/ltwp/download/HKCSS_LTSW_Planning_2nd_consult%20final.pdf.

Huang, Yasheng. *Capitalism with Chinese Characteristics: Entrepreneurship and the State.* New York: Cambridge University Press, 2008.

Kong, Karen. 'Adjudicating Social Welfare Rights in Hong Kong'. *I•CON* 10, no. 2 (2012): 588–99.

Kueh, Y. Y. 'Foreign Investment and Economic Change in China'. In *The Chinese Economy under Deng Xiaoping,* edited by Robert F. Ash and Y. Y. Kueh. Oxford: Clarendon Press, 1996.

La Grange, Adrienne. 'Housing (1997–2007)'. In *The Hong Kong Special Administrative Region in Its First Decade,* edited by Joseph Y. S. Cheng. Hong Kong: City University of Hong Kong Press, 2007.

Lam, Carrie. 'We Connect: Connecting for Consensus and a Better Future: Manifesto of Carrie Lam Chief Executive Election 2017'. (Campaign Office of Carrie Lam, February 2017). http://www.carrielam2017.hk/media/my/2017/01/Manifesto_e_v2.pdf.

Lam, Jermain T. M. 'Enhanced Productivity Program in Hong Kong: A Critical Appraisal'. *Public Performance & Management Review* 27, no. 1 (September 2003): 53–70.

Lardy, Nicholas R. 'Chinese Foreign Trade'. In *The Chinese Economy under Deng Xiaoping,* edited by Robert F. Ash and Y. Y. Kueh. Oxford: Clarendon Press, 1996.

Lau, Siu-kai. 'Government and Political Change in the Hong Kong Special Administrative Region'. In *Hong Kong the Super Paradox: Life after Return to China,* edited by James C. Hsiung. London: Macmillan, 2000.

Lau, Lawrence J. et al. 'Yes, Hong Kong CAN!', *Our Hong Kong Foundation* (September 2016). http://ourhkfoundation.org.hk/sites/default/files/media/pdf/Yes_Hong_Kong_CAN_eng.pdf.

Lee, Eliza W. Y. 'The Politics of Welfare Developmentalism in Hong Kong', *Social Policy and Development Programme Paper No. 21* (ISSN 1020-8208, August 2005), United Nations Research Institute for Social Development, 1–18.

Leung, Chun-ying. 'The Transition and Unexpected Changes'. In *Hong Kong's Transition: A Decade after the Deal*, edited by Wang Gungwu and Wong Siu-lun. Hong Kong: Oxford University Press, 1995.

Leung, C. Y. 'Manifesto for the Chief Executive Election 2012: One Heart, One Vision'. http://www.ceo.gov.hk.

Li, Pang-kwong. 'The Executive'. In *Contemporary Hong Kong Politics: Governance in the Post-1997 Era*, edited by Lam Wai-man, Percy Luen-tim Lui and Ian Holliday. Hong Kong: Hong Kong University Press, 2007.

Liao, Haifeng Felix, and Roger C. K. Chan. 'Industrial Relocation of Hong Kong Manufacturing Firms: Towards an Expanding Industrial Space beyond the Pearl River Delta'. *GeoJournal* 76, issue 6 (December 2011): 623–39. doi:10.1007/s10708-009-9316-3.

Littlewood, Michael, *Taxation without Representation: The History of Hong Kong's Troublingly Successful Tax System*. Hong Kong: Hong Kong University, 2010.

Loh, Christine. 'The Politics of SARS: The WHO, Hong Kong and Mainland China'. In *At the Epicentre: Hong Kong and the SARS Outbreak*, edited by Christine Loh and Civic Exchange. Hong Kong: Hong Kong University Press, 2004.

Lui, Hon-Kwong. *Income Inequality and Economic Development*. Hong Kong: City University of Hong Kong Press, 1997.

Ngan, Raymond M. H., and Mark K. Y. Li. 'The Dilemma and Crisis for Public Welfare Payments in Hong Kong'. In *The July 1 Protest Rally: Interpreting a Historic Event*, edited by Joseph Y. S. Cheng. Hong Kong: City University of Hong Kong Press, 2005.

Nissim, Roger. *Land Administration and Practice in Hong Kong*. Hong Kong: Hong Kong University Press, 1998.

Nissim, Roger. 'A Fresh Look at Housing, Planning and Land Policy'. In *Hong Kong's Budget: Challenges and Solutions for the Longer Term*, edited by Tony Latter. Hong Kong: Civic Exchange, 2009. http://www.civic-exchange.org/eng/upload/files/200902_budget.pdf.

Palan, Ronen. 'Trying to Have Your Cake and Eating It: How and Why the State System Has Created Offshore'. *International Studies Quarterly* 42 (1998): 625–43.

Phillips, David R. *The Epidemiological Transition in Hong Kong: Changes in Health and Disease since the Nineteenth Century*. Hong Kong: Centre of Asian Studies, University of Hong Kong, 1988.

Reardon, Lawrence C. *The Reluctant Dragon: Crisis Cycles in Chinese Economic Policy*. Hong Kong: Hong Kong University Press, 2002.

Redding, Gordon. 'Culture and Business in Hong Kong'. In *Dynamic Hong Kong: Business & Culture*, edited by Wang Gangwu and Wong Siu Lun. Hong Kong: Centre of Asian Studies, University of Hong Kong, 1997.

'Safety and Shipping 1912–2012: From Titanic to Costa Concordia'. Hamburg: Allianz Global Corporate & Specialty, March 2012. http://www.agcs.allianz. com/assets/PDFs/Reports/AGCS_safety_and_shipping_report.pdf.

Sharif, Naubahar, and Can Huang. 'Innovation Strategy, Firm Survival and Relocation: The Case of Hong Kong-Owned Manufacturing in Guangdong Province, China'. *Research Policy* 41, issue 1 (February 2012): 69–78. doi:10.1016/j.respol.2011.06.003.

Sit, Victor F. S. 'Hong Kong's "Transferred" Industrialization and Industrial Geography'. *Asian Survey* 38, no. 9 (September 1998): 880–904.

So, Alvin Y. 'Hong Kong's Problematic Democratic Transition: Power Dependency or Business Hegemony?' *Journal of Asian Studies* 59, no. 2 (May 2000): 359–81.

Sung, Yun-win. *Explaining China's Export Drive: The Only Success Among Command Economies.* Hong Kong: Hong Kong Institute of Asia-Pacific Studies, Chinese University of Hong Kong, 1991.

Task Force of Social Welfare Planning. 'Planning Mechanism and Protocol of Social Welfare Policy (Discussion Paper)' (Hong Kong Council of Social Service, 12 July 2000). http://www.hkcss.org.hk/er/SvcPlan.doc.

Tobin, Damian. 'Renminbi Internationalisation: Precedents and Implications'. *Journal of Chinese Economic and Business Studies* 11, no. 2 (May 2013): 2–23. doi:10.1080/14765284.2013.789677.

'Top Universities in China by 2016 University Web Ranking'. http://www.4icu. org/cn/.

University Grants Committee. *Higher Education in Hong Kong: A Report by the University Grants Committee.* http://www.ugc.edu.hk/HERVW/CHAPTER8. html

'Vision for Hong Kong' Study Group. *To Be the Services Metropolis of the Pearl River Delta: A Blueprint for Hong Kong.* Hong Kong: Hong Kong General Chamber of Commerce and Hong Kong Coalition of Service Industries, 2002.

Wong, Timothy Ka-ying, and Shirley Po-san Wan. 'The Implementation of the Accountability System for Principal Officials: Efficacy and Impact'. In *The July 1 Protest Rally: Interpreting a Historic Event,* edited by Joseph Y. S. Cheung. Hong Kong: City University of Hong Kong Press, 2005.

Wong, Wilson. 'From a British-style Administrative State to a Chinese-style Political State: Civil Service Reforms in Hong Kong after the Transfer of Sovereignty'. *The Brookings Institution* (June 2003). https://www.brookings. edu/fp/cnaps/papers/wong2003.pdf.

Wong, Y. C. Richard. 'Hong Kong Healthcare and Finance Reform', *HKCER Letters* 56 (May–July 1999). http://www.hkcer.hku.hk/Letters/v56/health-care.htm.

Wong, Yiu-chung. 'Absorption into a Leninist Polity: A Study of the Interpretations by the National People's Congress of the Basic Law in Post-Handover Hong Kong'. In *Trends of Political Participation in Hong Kong,* edited by Joseph Y. S. Cheng. Hong Kong: City University of Hong Kong Press, 2014.

Wu, Weiping. 'Proximity and Complementarity in Hong Kong-Shenzhen Industrialization'. *Asian Survey* 37, no. 8 (August 1997): 771–93.

Xiao Weiyun. *One Country, Two Systems: An Account of the Drafting of the Hong Kong Basic Law.* Beijing: Peking University Press, 2001.

Yash, Ghai. *Hong Kong's New Constitutional Order: The Resumption of Chinese Sovereignty and the Basic Law.* 2nd ed. Hong Kong: Hong Kong University Press, 1999.

Yep, Ray. '"One Country, Two Systems" and Special Administrative Regions: The Case of Hong Kong'. In *China's Local Administration: Traditions and Changes in the Sub-National Hierarchy,* edited by Jae Ho Chung and Tao-chiu Lam. Abingdon, UK: Routledge, 2009.

Yeung, C. Y. 'Health Problems in Chinese Children Are Different'. *Hong Kong Journal of Paediatrics* 8, no. 2 (2003): 70–86.

Yeung, Henry Wai-chung. *Transnational Corporations and Business Networks: Hong Kong Firms in the Asian Region.* London: Routledge, 1998.

Yip, Leslie Sai-Ching, and G. P. Walters. 'Wah Hoi Industrial Company'. *Entrepreneurship: Theory and Practice* 22, no. 3 (1998): 87–99.

Yip, Tsz Leung. 'Port Traffic Risks: A Study of Accidents in Hong Kong Waters'. *Science Direct,* Transportation Research Part E 44 (2008). http://nych2o. wikispaces.com/file/view/Port%20traffic%20risks-HK%20accidents%20 study.pdf.

Yu, Tony Fu-lai. 'Hong Kong's Entrepreneurship: Behaviours and Determinants'. *Entrepreneurship & Regional Development* 12, no. 3 (2000): 179–94.

Yu, Tony Fu-lai. *The East Asian Miracle: Economic Growth and Public Policy.* New York: Oxford University Press, 1993.

# Index